TECHNICIANS OF THE SACRED

Also by Jerome Rothenberg

NEW YOUNG GERMAN POETS (1959)

WHITE SUN BLACK SUN (1960)

THE SEVEN HELLS OF THE JIGOKU ZOSHI (1962)

SIGHTINGS I–IX (1964)

AMERICAN PLAYING VERSION OF HOCHHUTH'S "THE DEPUTY" (1965)

THE GORKY POEMS (1966)

RITUAL: A BOOK OF PRIMITIVE RITES & EVENTS (1966)

BETWEEN: POEMS 1960–1963 (1967)

THE FLIGHT OF QUETZALCOATL (1967)

CONVERSATIONS (1968)

POEMS 1964–1967 (1968)

GOMRINGER BY ROTHENBERG (1968)

POLAND/1931 (1969)

NARRATIVES & REALTHEATER PIECES (1969)

Technicians of the Sacred

A RANGE OF POETRIES
from AFRICA, AMERICA
ASIA & OCEANIA

edited with commentaries by

JEROME ROTHENBERG

Anchor Books
Doubleday & Company, Inc., Garden City, New York

Grateful acknowledgment is made to the following for permission to reprint material copyrighted or controlled by them:

George Allen & Unwin, Ltd., *Oceania,* and Raymond Firth, for "Twelve Kuru Songs" from *Tikopia Ritual and Belief* by Raymond Firth. Reprinted by permission.

George Allen & Unwin, Ltd., for excerpts from *Specimens of Bushman Folklore* by Bleek and Lloyd; for excerpts from *Coral Gardens and Their Magic* by Malinowski; and for excerpts from *The Nine Songs* and *Chinese Poems* by Waley. Reprinted by permission of the publisher.

Amber House Press, for Clayton Eshleman's translation of "Alberto Rojas Jimenez Viene Volando" by Pablo Neruda, in *Residence On Earth* (1962). Reprinted by permission of the publisher.

The American Anthropological Association and Helen Codere, for excerpts from *The Amiable Side of Kwakiutl Life* by Helen Codere, from *American Anthropologist,* Volume 58, April, 1956. Reprinted by permission of the publisher and the author.

W. G. Archer, for "The Witch" and "The Illegitimate Child in Santal Society," from *Man in India.* Reprinted by permission of the author.

J. J. Augustin, Inc., for excerpts from *Flight of the Chiefs* by Buell H. Quain. Reprinted by permission of the publisher.

Ulli Beier, for excerpts from *Yoruba Poetry* by Ulli Beier and Bakare Gbadamosi and *Black Orpheus.* Reprinted by permission of the author.

Ronald M. Berndt, for excerpts from *Kunapipi* by Ronald M. Berndt. Reprinted by permission of the author.

Bernice P. Bishop Museum Press, for excerpts from *Kapingamarangi* (Bulletin 228) by Kenneth P. Emory; and for excerpts from *Tuamatoan Religion* (Bulletin 103) by J. Frank Stimson. Reprinted by permission of Bernice P. Bishop Museum, Honolulu, Hawaii.

The Bollingen Foundation and Editions Payot, for excerpts from *Shamanism: Archaic Techniques of Ecstasy* by Mircea Eliade, translated from the French by Willard R. Trask. Reprinted by permission of the publishers.

The Bollingen Foundation, for excerpts from *Egyptian Religious Texts and Representations,* translated by Alexandre Piankoff and edited by N. Rambova; excerpts from *The Road of Life and Death* by Paul Radin; and for excerpts from *Navaho Religion* by Gladys A. Reichard. Reprinted by permission of the publisher.

The Bollingen Foundation and Routledge & Kegan Paul, Ltd., for excerpts from *The I Ching,* translated from Chinese into German by Richard Wilhelm and rendered into English by Cary F. Baynes. Reprinted by permission of the publishers.

The British Academy, for excerpts from *A Comparative Study of the Literature of Egypt, Palestine, and Mesopotamia* by T. E. Peet. Reprinted by permission of the publisher.

Cambridge University Press, for the adaptation of "Peacemaking Event" from *The Andamen Islanders* by A. R. Radcliffe-Brown. Used by permission of the publisher.

Cambridge University Press and T. G. H. Strehlow, for excerpts from *Aranda Traditions* by T. G. H. Strehlow, published by Melbourne University Press. Reprinted by permission of Cambridge University Press and the author.

City Lights Books, for excerpts from *Carnival/Late at Night* by Kenneth Patchen. Copyright © 1942, 1943, 1945, 1946, 1962, 1964, 1966 by Kenneth Patchen. Reprinted by permission of the publisher.

The Clarendon Press, for excerpts from *Ch'u Tz'u* by David Hawkes (1959); and from *Ashanti* by R. S. Rattray. Reprinted by permission of the publisher.

Jess Collins, for excerpt from *O!* by Jess Collins. Reprinted by permission of the author.

Doubleday & Company, Inc. and William Heinemann Ltd., for excerpts from *In the Shadow of the Bush* by T. A. Talbot (1912). Reprinted by permission of the publishers.

Doubleday & Company, Inc. and Theodore H. Gaster, for an adaptation of an excerpt from *Thespis* by Theodore H. Gaster. Reprinted by permission of the publisher and author.

Robert Duncan, for excerpts from *Passages 22–27 of the War*, Oyez. Reprinted by permission of Robert Duncan.

E. P. Dutton & Company and Routledge & Kegan Paul, Ltd., for excerpts from *Argonauts of the Western Pacific* by Bronislaw Malinowski. Dutton Paperback Edition (1961). Reprinted by permission of the publishers.

E. P. Dutton & Company, Inc. and Routledge & Kegan Paul, Ltd., for an adaptation from *Sorcerers of Dobu* by R. F. Fortune. Copyright 1932 by E. P. Dutton & Company, Inc. Renewal © 1960 by R. F. Fortune. Dutton Paperback Edition. Reprinted by permission of the publishers.

E. P. Dutton & Company, Inc., for excerpts from *The Last of the Seris* by Dane and Mary Roberts Coolidge. Copyright 1939 by Dane and Mary Roberts Coolidge. Renewal © 1967 by Coit Coolidge and Mrs. Calvin Gaines Coolidge. Reprinted by permission of the publisher.

George Economou, for adaptions of "Hyena," "Cattle," and "The Train." Reprinted by permission of the author.

Editions Seghers, for excerpts from *Chants Haoussa* by Roger Rosfelder. Copyright 1952 by Editions Seghers. Reprinted by permission of the publisher.

Editorial Joaquin Mortiz and David Ossman, for "Dance Scene: The Death of Tlacahuepan" translated by David Ossman, from *La Literatura de Los Aztecas,* by Angel M. Garibay K. Reprinted by permission of Editorial Joaquin Mortiz, the Instituto Indigenista Interamericano, and the translator.

Mrs. Lila Elwin, for "Three Love-Charms from Chhattisgarh" from *Man in India.* Reprinted by permission of Mrs. Lila Elwin.

Estate of Knud Rasmussen, for excerpts from *Intellectual History of Copper Eskimos* and *Intellectual Culture of Iglulik Eskimos* by Knud Rasmussen. Reprinted by permission of the Estate of Knud Rasmussen.

Ian Hamilton Finlay, for "Ocean Stripe Series 2" and "Patch" from *6 Small Songs in 3's* by Ian Hamilton Finlay; and for "Semi-idiotic Poem" by Ian Hamilton Finlay. Reprinted by permission of the author.

John Furnival, for "Semi-erotic Poem" by John Furnival. Reprinted by permission of the author.

Donald Gallup and the Estate of Gertrude Stein, for "Listen to Me" from *Last Operas and Plays* by Gertrude Stein. Reprinted by permission of the Estate of Gertrude Stein and Donald Gallup as Literary Agent.

Allen Ginsberg, for "Psalm IV" by Allen Ginsberg. Reprinted by permission of the author.

Gotenburg Ethnographical Museum, for excerpts from *Inatoipippiler*, translated by Nils M. Homer. Reprinted by permission of the publisher.

Government Printer of the Republic of South Africa, for excerpts from *Contributions Towards Venda, History, Religion and Tribal Ritual* by N. J. van Warmelo. Reproduced under the Government Printer of the Republic of South Africa. Copyright Authority No. 3793 dated 11/1/1967.

Grossman Publishers, for excerpts from *The Incas* by Garcilaso de la Vega. Reprinted by permission of the publishers.

Harcourt, Brace & World, Inc., for "A Phantom Bird" from *The African Saga* by Blaise Cendrars. Reprinted by permission of the publisher.

Harper and Row, for adaptations from *A Black Civilization*, Illustrated, Revised Edition by W. Lloyd Warner. Copyright 1937 by Harper & Row, Publishers, Incorporated. Copyright © 1958 by W. Lloyd Warner. Reprinted by permission of the publisher.

Hawk's Well Press, for "Sightings VI" by Jerome Rothenberg and "New Moon Over Whaleback" by Robert Kelly, from *Sightings/Lunes* by Jerome Rothenberg and Robert Kelly; for "The Stars," "The Annunciation," "The Killer," "A Poison Arrow," "The Seven," "Ghosts and Shadows," "Return of the Warriors," "A Dead Hunter Speaks Through the Voice of a Shaman," "A Poem for the Ascent of Mount Carmel" (St. John of the Cross), translated and adapted by Jerome Rothenberg; "Free Union" by André Breton, translated by David Antin; "Ioanna Raving" by Takis Sinopoulos, translated by George Economou; "To the God of Fire" and "To the God of Fire as a Horse" from the Rig-Veda, adapted by Robert Kelly; "The Goddess" by Denise Levertov; all from *Poems from the Floating World*, edited by Jerome Rothenberg; and for "Imagine a Margin" from *O!* by Jess Collins (1960). All reprinted by permission of Hawk's Well Press.

Richard Higgins, for excerpts from *Clown's Way*. Reprinted by permission of the publisher.

Houghton Mifflin Company, for excerpts from Coolidge's *The Navaho Indians*. Reprinted by permission of the publisher.

Indiana University Press, for excerpts from *Translations from the Tamil* by A. K. Ramanujan. Reprinted by permission of the publisher.

John Day Company, Inc., for excerpts from *The Winged Serpent* by Margot Astrov. Copyright 1946 by Margot Astrov. Reprinted by permission of the publisher.

Johnson Reprint Corporation and Stackpole Books, for "Gassire's Lute" from *African Genesis* by Leo Frobenius and Douglas C. Fox. Copyright 1937 by Stackpole Sons. Reprinted by permission of the publishers.

Alfred A. Knopf, Inc., for "Ploughing on Sunday" copyright 1923 by Wallace Stevens. Renewed, 1951. From *The Collected Poems of Wallace Stevens*. Reprinted by permission of the publisher.

Librairie Orientaliste, Paul Geuthner, for excerpts from *La Vie de Marpa* by J. Bacot; and for excerpts from *Babylonian Penitential Psalms,* by S. Langdon. Reprinted by permission of the publisher.

David P. McAllester, for "War God's Horse Song (II), translated by David P. McAllester. Reprinted by permission of the translator.

Michael McClure, for excerpts from *Ghost Tantras ﹟1* by Michael McClure. Reprinted by permission of the author.

David McKay Company, Inc., for excerpts from *The Pyramid Texts in Translation and Commentary* by S. A. B. Mercer. Copyright 1952 by S. A. B. Mercer. Reprinted by permission of the publisher.

Jackson Mac Low, for "First Light Poem: For Iris—June 10, 1962" by Jackson Mac Low. Reprinted by permission of the author.

Macmillan & Company, Ltd., for excerpts from *Life of a South African Tribe* by Henri Junod. Reprinted by permission of the publisher.

The Medici Society Ltd., for excerpts from *The Papyrus of Ani,* by Sir E. Wallis Budge (1913). Reprinted by permission of the publisher.

Ben Moses, for "A Charm to Cause the Gangosa That Eats Away the Nose," adaptations by Ben Moses. Reprinted by permission of the author.

John Murray (Publishers), Ltd., for excerpts from *The Message of Milarepa* by Sir Humphrey Clarke; and for excerpts from *The Baiga* by Verrier Elwin. Reprinted by permission of the publisher.

New Directions Publishing Corporation and Russell Edson, for "Air Baby" from *The Very Thing That Happens* by Russell Edson. Copyright © 1960 by Russell Edson. Reprinted by permission of the publisher and the author.

New Directions Publishing Corporation, Jonathan Cape, Ltd. and Denise Levertov, for "The Artist" and "The Goddess" from Denise Levertov, *With Eyes at the Back of Our Heads.* Copyright © 1958, 1959 by Denise Levertov. Reprinted by permission of the publishers and author.

New Directions Publishing Corporation and Faber & Faber, Ltd., for selections from *Love Poems of Ancient Egypt,* translated by Ezra Pound and Noel Stock. Copyright © 1960 by Ezra Pound, © 1962 by Noel Stock and New Directions Publishing Corporation; and for "Papyrus" from Ezra Pound, *Personae.* Copyright 1926, 1954 by Ezra Pound. All reprinted by permission of the publishers.

New Directions Publishing Corporation and MacGibbon & Kee, Ltd., for "The Destruction of Tenochtitlan" from William Carlos Williams, *In the American Grain.* Copyright 1933 by William Carlos Williams. Reprinted by permission of the publishers.

New Directions Publishing Corporation and James Wright, for "El canto quiere ser luz" translated by James Wright, from Federico García Lorca, *Obras Completas,* © Aguilar. Copyright © 1962 by James Wright. All rights reserved. Reprinted by permission of the publisher, agents for the Estate of the Author, and the translator.

Origin Press and Robert Kelly, for "The Boar" by Robert Kelly. Copyright © 1962 by Cid Corman. Reprinted by permission of the publisher and the author.

Rochelle Owens, for adaptations of "Words from Seven Magic Songs" and "A Song of Men's Impotence and the Beasts They Hunted"; and for "Song of Meat, Madness and Travel" by Rochelle Owens. Reprinted by permission of the author.

Oxford University Press, for excerpts from *Nine Dayak Nights* by W. R. Geddes. Reprinted by permission of the publisher.

Oxford University Press and the International African Institute, for excerpts from *Social and Ritual Life of the Ambo* by Bronislaw Stefaniszyn. Reprinted by permission of the publisher and the International African Institute.

Penguin Books, Ltd., for excerpts from *The Epic of Gilgamesh,* translated by N. K. Sandars. Reprinted by permission of the publisher.

Philosophical Library and Routledge & Kegan Paul, Ltd., for excerpts from *Djanggawul* by R. M. Berndt (1953). Reprinted by permission of the publishers.

Pogamoggan, for "A Shaman Climbs Up the Sky," translated by Jerome Rothenberg. Reprinted by permission of the publisher.

Princeton University Press, for excerpts from *Ancient Near Eastern Texts Relating to the Old Testament,* by J. B. Pritchard. Reprinted by permission of the publisher.

Queen's Printer, Ottawa, Canada, for excerpts from Marius Barbeau, *Medicine Men of the North Pacific Coast,* Bulletin No. 152, Anthropological Series No. 42, 1958. Reprinted by permission of the publisher.

Jerome Rothenberg, for "Child of an Idumean Night" by Jerome Rothenberg, from *The Gorky Poems,* El Corno Emplumado. Reprinted through the courtesy of Margaret Randall and Sergio Mondragón.

Armand Schwerner, for excerpts from *The Tablets* by Armand Schwerner. Reprinted by permission of the author.

Charles Scribner's Sons and Robert Creeley, for "I Know a Man" from *For Love* by Robert Creeley. Copyright © 1959, 1962 by Robert Creeley. Reprinted by permission of the publisher and the author.

The Something Else Press, Inc., for *Ritual: A Book of Primitive Rites & Events* by Jerome Rothenberg; for excerpts from *Some Recent Happenings* by Allan Kaprow; for excerpts from *By Alison Knowles* by Alison Knowles; and for excerpts from *Berlin & Phenomena* by Wolf Vostell. All reprinted by permission of the publisher.

The Sixties Press and Robert Bly, for "Ode to My Socks" by Pablo Neruda, translated by Robert Bly. Reprinted by permission of the publisher and the translator.

Gary Snyder, for "1st Shaman Song" and "Sand" by Gary Snyder. Reprinted by permission of the author.

Studia Instituti Anthropos, for excerpts from Joseph F. Rock's *The Zhi mä Funeral Ceremony of the Na-Khi of Southwest China.* Reprinted by permission of the publisher.

Universidad Nacional Autónoma de Mexico, for excerpts from *Epica Nahuatl* and *Poesía Indígena de la Altiplanicie* by A. M. Garibay K. Translated and adapted by Jerome Rothenberg by permission of the Universidad Nacional Autónoma de Mexico.

University of California Press, for excerpts from *Cherokee Dance and Drama* by Frank Speck and Leonard Broom. Reprinted by permission of the publisher.

University of Chicago Press, for excerpts from *The Kumulipo* by Martha W. Beckwith. Reprinted by permission of the publisher.

The University of Chicago Press and Ure Smith Pty., Ltd., for excerpts from *World of the First Australians* by R. M. and C. H. Berndt. Reprinted by permission of the publishers.

University of Nebraska Press, for excerpts from *Black Elk Speaks* by John G. Neihardt. Reprinted by permission of the publisher.

A man child is born
May he live & be beautiful
A man child is born
May he become old, very old
Joy, joy, praise, praise

CONTENTS

Death & Defeat

The Book of Events (I)

The Book of Events (II)

Africa

Oceania

The Appendices

PRE-FACE

PRIMITIVE MEANS COMPLEX

That there are no primitive languages is an axiom of contemporary linguistics where it turns its attention to the remote languages of the world. There are no half-formed languages, no underdeveloped or inferior languages. Everywhere a development has taken place into structures of great complexity. People who have failed to achieve the wheel will not have failed to invent & develop a highly wrought grammar. Hunters & gatherers innocent of all agriculture will have vocabularies that distinguish the things of their world down to the finest details. The language of snow among the Eskimos is awesome. The aspect system of Hopi verbs can, by a flick of the tongue, make the most subtle kinds of distinction between different types of motion.

What is true of language in general is equally true of poetry & of the ritual-systems of which so much poetry is a part. It is a question of energy & intelligence as universal constants &, in any specific case, the direction that energy & intelligence (=imagination) have been given. No people today is newly born. No people has sat in sloth for the thousands of years of its history. Measure everything by the Titan rocket & the transistor radio, & the world is full of primitive peoples. But once change the unit of value to the poem or the dance-event or the dream (all clearly artifactual situations) & it becomes apparent what all those people have been doing all those years with all that time on their hands.

Poetry, wherever you find it among the "primitives"* (literally

* The word "primitive" is used with misgivings & put in quotes, but no way around it seems workable. "Non-technological" & "non-literate," which have often been suggested as alternatives, are too emphatic in pointing to supposed "lacks" &, though they feel precise to start with, are themselves open to question. Are the Eskimo snow-workers, e.g., really "non"- or "pre-technological"? And how does the widespread use of pictographs & pictosymbols, which can be "read" by later generations, affect their users' non-literate status? A major point throughout this book is that these peoples (& they're likely too diverse to be covered by a single name) are precisely "technicians" where it most concerns them— specifically in their relation to the "sacred" as something they can

everywhere), involves an extremely complicated sense of materials & structures. Everywhere it involves the manipulation (fine or gross) of multiple elements. If this isn't always apparent, it's because the carry-over (by translation or interpretation) necessarily distorts where it chooses some part of the whole that it can meaningfully deal with. The work is foreign & its complexity is often elusive, a question of gestalt or configuration, of the angle from which the work is seen. If you expect a primitive work to be simple or naïve, you will probably end up seeing a simple or naïve work; & this will be abetted by the fact that translation can, in general, only present as a single work, a part of what is actually there. The problem is fundamental for as long as we approach these works from the out-side—& we're likely fated to be doing that forever.

It's very hard in fact to decide what precisely are the boundaries of "primitive" poetry or of a "primitive" poem, since there's often no activity differentiated as such, but the words or vocables are part of a larger total "work" that may go on for hours, even days, at a stretch. What we would separate as music & dance & myth & painting is also part of that work, & the need for separation is a question of "our" interest & preconceptions, not of "theirs." Thus the picture is immediately complicated by the nature of the work & the media that comprise it. And it becomes clear that the "collective" nature of primitive poetry (upon which so much stress has been placed despite the existence of individualized poems & clearly identified poets) is to a great degree inseparable from the amount of materials a single work may handle.

Now all of this is, if so stated, a question of technology as well as inspiration; & we may as well take it as axiomatic for what follows that where poetry is concerned, "primitive" means complex.

WHAT IS A "PRIMITIVE" POEM?

Poems are carried by the voice & are sung or chanted in specific situations. Under such circumstances, runs the easy answer, the "poem" would simply be the words-of-the-song. But a little later on the question arises: what *are* the words & where do they begin

---

actively create or capture. That's the only way in fact that I'd hope to define "primitive": as a situation in which such conditions flourish & in which the "poets" are (in Eliade's phrase) the principal "technicians of the sacred."

& end? The translation, as printed, may show the "meaningful" element only, often no more than a single, isolated "line"; thus

A splinter of stone which is white (Bushman)
Semen white like the mist (Australian)
My-shining-horns (Chippewa: single word)
etc.

but in practice the one "line" will likely be repeated until its burden has been exhausted. (Is it "single" then?) It may be altered phonetically & the words distorted from their "normal" forms. Vocables with no fixed meanings may be intercalated. All of these devices will be creating a greater & greater gap between the "meaningful" residue in the translation & what-was-actually-there. We will have a different "poem" depending where we catch the movement, & we may start to ask: Is something within this work the "poem," or is everything?

Again, the work will probably not end with the "single" line & its various configurations—will more likely be preceded & followed by other lines. Are all of these "lines" (each of considerable duration) separate poems, or are they the component parts of a single, larger poem moving toward some specific (ceremonial) end? Is it enough, then, if the lines happen in succession & aren't otherwise tied? Will some further connection be needed? Is the group of lines a poem if "we" can make the connection? Is it a poem where no connection is apparent to "us"? If the lines come in sequence on a single occasion does the unity of the occasion connect them into a single poem? Can many poems be a single poem as well? (They often are.)

What's a sequence anyway?

What's unity?

THE UNITY OF "PRIMITIVE" THOUGHT & ITS SHATTERING

The anthology shows some ways in which the unity is achieved— in general by the imposition of some constant or "key" against which all disparate materials can be measured. A sound, a rhythm, a name, an image, a dream, a gesture, a picture, an action, a silence: any or all of these can function as "keys." Beyond that there's no need for consistency, for fixed or discrete meanings. An object is whatever it becomes under the impulse of the situation at hand. Forms are often open. Causality is often set aside. The poet (who may also be dancer, singer, magician, whatever the event demands of him) masters a series of techniques that can fuse the most seemingly contradictory propositions.

But above all there's a sense-of-unity that surrounds the poem, a reality concept that acts as a cement, a unification of perspective linking

> poet & man
> man & world
> world & image
> image & word
> word & music
> music & dance
> dance & dancer
> dancer & man
> man & world
> etc.

all of which has been put in many different ways—by Cassirer notably as a feeling for "the solidarity of all life" leading toward a "law of metamorphosis" in thought & word.

Within this undifferentiated & unified frame with its open images & mixed media, there are rarely "poems" as we know them—but we come in with our analytical minds & shatter the unity. It has in fact been shattered already by workers before us.

PRIMITIVE & MODERN: INTERSECTIONS & ANALOGIES

Like any collector, my approach to delimiting & recognizing what's a poem has been by analogy: in this case (beyond the obvious definition of poems as words-of-songs) to the work of modern poets. Since much of this work has been revolutionary & limit-smashing, the analogy in turn expands the range of what "we" can see as primitive poetry. It also shows some of the ways in which primitive poetry & thought are close to an impulse toward unity in our own time, of which the poets are forerunners. The important intersections (analogies) are:

(1) the poem carried by the voice: a "pre"-literate situation of poetry composed to be spoken, chanted or, more accurately, sung; compare this to the "post-literate" situation, in McLuhan's good phrase, or where-we-are-today;

       written poem as score
       public readings

       poets' theaters
       jazz poetry
       1960s rock poetry etc

(2) a highly developed process of image-thinking: concrete or non-causal thought in contrast to the simplifications of Aristotelian logic, etc., with its "objective categories" & rules of non-contradiction; a "logic" of polarities; creation thru dream, etc.; modern poetry (having had & outlived the experience of rationalism) enters a post-logical phase;

Blake's multi-images
symbolisme
surrealism

deep-image

random poetry
composition by field etc

(3) a "minimal" art of maximal involvement; compound elements, each clearly articulated, & with plenty of room for fill-in (gaps in sequence, etc.): the "spectator" as (ritual) participant who pulls it all together;

concrete poetry

(4) an "intermedia" situation, as further denial of the categories: the poet's techniques aren't limited to verbal maneuvers but operate also through song, non-verbal sound, visual signs, & the varied activities of the ritual event: here the "poem" = the work of the "poet" in whatever medium, or (where we're able to grasp it) the totality of the work;

picture poems
prose poems

happenings
total theater

poets as film-makers etc

(5) the animal-body-rootedness of "primitive" poetry: recognition of a "physical" basis for the poem within a man's body—or as an act of body & mind together, breath &/or spirit; in many cases too the direct & open handling of sexual imagery & (in the "events") of sexual activities as key factors in creation of the sacred;

dada
lautgedichte (sound poems)

beast language

line & breath
projective verse etc

sexual revolution etc

(6) the poet as shaman, or primitive shaman as poet & seer thru control of the means just stated: an open "visionary" situation prior to all system-making ("priesthood") in which the man creates thru dream (image) & word (song), "that Reason may have ideas to build on" (W. Blake).

Rimbaud's voyant
Rilke's angel
Lorca's duende

beat poetry
psychedelic see-in's, be-in's, etc

individual neo-shamanisms, etc works directly influenced by the "other" poetry or by analogies to "primitive art": ideas of negritude, tribalism, wilderness, etc.

What's more, the translations themselves may create new forms & shapes-of-poems with their own energies & interest—another intersection that can't be overlooked.

In all this the ties feel very close—not that "we" & "they" are identical, but that the systems of thought & the poetry they've achieved are, like what we're after, distinct from something in the "west," & we can now see & value them because of it. What's missing are the in-context factors that define them more closely group-by-group: the sense of the poems as part of an integrated social & religious complex; the presence in each instance of specific myths & locales; the fullness of the living culture. Here the going is rougher with no easy shortcuts through translation: no simple carry-overs. If our world is open to multiple influences & data, theirs is largely self-contained. If we're committed to a search for the "new," most of them are tradition-bound. (The degree to which "they" are can be greatly exaggerated.) If the poet's purpose among us is "to spread doubt [& create illusion]" (N. Calas), among them it's to overcome it.

That they've done so *without denying the reality* is also worth remembering.

THE BACKGROUND & STRUCTURE OF THIS BOOK

The present collection grew directly out of a pair of 1964 readings of "primitive & archaic* poetry" at The Poet's Hardware Theater & The Cafe Metro in New York. Working with me on those were the poets David Antin, Jackson Mac Low, & Rochelle Owens. The material, which I'd been assembling or translating over the previous several years, was arranged topically rather than geographically—an order preserved here in the first three sections of texts. The idea

---

* Throughout the book I use "archaic" to mean (1) the early phases of the so-called "higher" civilizations, where poetry & voice still hadn't separated or where the new writing was used for setting down what the voice had already made; (2) contemporary "remnant" cultures in which acculturation has significantly disrupted the "primitive modes"; & (3) a cover-all term for "primitive," "early high," & "remnant." The word is useful because of the generalization it permits (the variety of cultures is actually immense) & because it encompasses certain "mixed" cultural situations. My interest is in whether the poetry works, not in the "purity" of the culture from which it comes. I doubt, in fact, if there can be "pure" cultures.

for a "book of events" came from a discussion with Dick Higgins about what he was calling "near-poetry" & from my own sense of the closeness of primitive rituals (when stripped-down to the bare line of the activities) to the "happenings" & "events" he was presenting as publisher of *Something Else Press*. The last four sections roughly correspond to some kind of geographical reality—not that there aren't problems of overlap, etc., in a grouping by continents but simply that it provides an alternate way of bringing the materials together. (The reader may think of some others as well.) Certain omissions are also fairly obvious—notably that I haven't included any European works. Here the remnants were abundant enough, but, because of their absorption into precisely the stream-of-thought the anthology was countering, the distinctions were far from clear.

While the final gathering is several times its 1964 size, I don't see it in any sense as more than a beginning. My intention from the start was to find translations that would "translate," i.e., bring-the-work-across or be a living work in English, & that's a very different thing from (in the first place) looking for representative "masterpieces" & including them whatever the nature of the translations. I also have (no question about it) my own sense of what's worth it in poetry, & I've tried to work from that rather than against it. I haven't gone for "pretty" or "innocent" or "noble" poems so much as strong ones. Throughout I've kept the possibilities wide open: looking for new forms & media; hoping that what I finally assembled could be read as "contemporary," since so much of it is that in fact, still being created & used in a world we share. Where there was a choice of showing poems separately or in series (as described above), I've leaned toward the in-series presentation. Since I feel that the complexity & tough-mindedness of primitive poetry have never really been shown (& since I happen to like such qualities in poems), I've decided to stress them. I've kept in general within the domain of the book's title, though sometimes I did include poems for no other reason than that they sounded good to me or moved me.

The poems are first given without any comments or footnotes, & the reader who likes it like that doesn't have to go any further. (*He* won't, no matter what I say.) Taking poems straight in that sense is like the Australian aborigines who (wrote W. E. Roth) would borrow whole poems *verbatim* "in a language absolutely remote from (their) own, & not one word of which the audience or performers can understand the meaning of": an extreme case of out-of-context reading but (where the culture's alive to its own needs) completely legitimate. Even so I've provided a section of "commentaries," which try in each instance to fill-in the scene or to indicate a little of what the original poets would have expected their hearers to know—in other words, to sketch some of the elements for an in-context reading. These "commentaries," which the reader can approach from any direction he chooses, also show what the poems mean to me or to other poets in this century who have approached them out-of-context. In that sense they can be read (particularly those for the first three sections) as a running series of essays dealing wtth the questions about primitive poetry lightly touched-on in this introduction, or even as an approach to poetry in general. Where it seemed worthwhile I've also printed contemporary American & European poems as analogues to the "primitive" work, sometimes without further comment. As with modern & primitive art, these either show the direct influence of the other poetry or, much more frequently, a coincidence of forms arising from an analogous impulse.

I've tried to make the book usable for anyone who wants it. Likely there are places where I've explained too much (here the reader whose special knowledge exceeds my own will simply have to forgive me), & I've often included materials more from the point of descriptive interest (i.e., for the story) than of "scientific" accuracy. For the reader who wants to follow-up on what's given here, I've been as straightforward as possible about the sources, providing a running bibliography & cross-referencing where I could. Translations range from the very literal to the very free (there's no one method that insures a decent result in English), & the commentaries often point out how far (or not) the translator has gone. But the limits of any translation, in terms of the "information" it carries, are also obvious. Such "information" concerns the language itself as a medium, & the language of the translator can hardly be a guide, since it should (where he's giving a poem for a poem) be working from its own imperatives. Enough to say that the original poetries presented here range from those that lean heavily on an archaic or specialized vocabulary & syntax to those that turn the common language toward the purposes of song—& that the same is true of the verse, which includes everything from the very open to the very closed.

Distinctions of this kind are obviously important, but it's only been possible for me to show some of the more striking examples. In one of the appendices I've reproduced in detail a single poem-series from Australia that the translator (R. M. Berndt) reconstructs through presentation of the original text, literal translation, free working, & interpretive & stylistic notes. While it's a remarkable piece of work, the method is much too specialized & space-consuming to provide a workable carry-over in all instances. Another appendix presents a series of statements about poetics from a number of "primitive" poets & song-men, & other such statements are scattered throughout the commentaries. I've hoped by doing this to get-across the sense of these poets as individualized & functioning human beings. To this end also I've tried where possible to name the original poets—either those who delivered the poems or the ancient figures to whom the poems were attributed. Still another appendix gives my own notes for the Seneca Indian Eagle Dance (a loosely structured intermedia event) & the scenario of a performance piece (*Gift Event III, for Poets, Musicians & Dancers*) derived from its general ordering of activities.

Beyond that, it's up to the individual reader who may, like his "primitive" counterpart, enjoy finishing the work on-his-own, i.e., by filling-in what's missing.

THANKS & ACKNOWLEDGMENTS, ETC.

The problem is to remember all who were helpful, & even so there's not enough space to state the ways they were. Here are the names, anyway, with thanks & in the hope they'll understand: Jerry Bloedow, David Antin, Jackson Mac Low, Rochelle Owens, Harry Smith, James Laughlin, Sara Blackburn, Anne Freedgood, Dick Higgins, Emmett Williams, Gary Snyder, Jonathan Greene, David Wang, Stanley Diamond, Flicker Hammond, Michael McClure, Marcia Evans, Martha Neufeld, David P. McAllester, & various friends at the Coldspring Longhouse (Steamburg, N.Y.) who showed me what the sacred was.

There are also collections before this one, which were of value to me & will be I'm sure to others. The best worldwide anthology I know of—a remarkable book though much heavier on archaic & classical works than this one, & relatively lighter on the "primitive"—is the very full *Trésor de la poésie universelle,* edited by Roger Caillois & Jean-Clarence Lambert & published by Gallimard. C. M. Bowra's *Primitive Song*—though he restricts himself to a selected number of hunting-&-gathering groups, & though I disagree with him on *x* number of points—contains enough examples (& good ones) to be considered an anthology in itself. Among the very good regional collections, I particularly want to mention Margot Astrov's *The Winged Serpent* for the American Indians (but also George W. Cronyn's long-out-of-print *The Path on the Rainbow;* A. Grove Day's *The Sky Clears;* Angel M. Garibay K.'s great collections of archaic Mexican poetry; & the fantastic outpouring of myths & texts published—mostly early in this century—by the Bureau of American Ethnology & other museums, institutions, etc.). For Africa there are two good recent collections, Leonard W. Doob's *Ants Will Not Eat Your Fingers* & Ulli Beier's *African Poetry: Anthology of Traditional African Poems;* both editors were kind enough to let me see their work in advance & in both cases I've tried not to duplicate what they've given. I haven't been into anything from other regions as good or as contemporary-feeling as some of these—except for the scattered & hard-to-find collections from tribal India by Verrier Elwin & by W. G. Archer. But there are, of course, specific books on specific peoples (see the commentaries that follow) & other collections where the matter is rich but the language (for me at least) is out of earshot.

Behind the book also are a woman & a child, & I'm reminded again how central the-woman & the-child are to the "oldest" cultures that we know. The dedication of this book is therefore rightly theirs—in whose presence I've sometimes touched that oldest & darkest love.

Jerome Rothenberg

New York City
March 15, 1967

POST-SCRIPT TO PRE-FACE

Once having gotten here the question was WHERE NOW? I've been lucky since then to have been able to work with some of the materials at closer range, moving toward a collaboration with song-men & others who could open the languages to me—& the closer one gets the more pressing becomes the problem of how to understand & to translate the *sound* of the originals. It now seems possible to do it, to get at those "meanings" which are more than the meaning-of-the-words; possible & desirable too, for the greatest secret these poems still hold is in the actual relation between the words, the music, the dance, & the event, a relation which many among us have been trying to get at in our own work. Every new translation is the uncovering of a hidden form in the language of the translator, but at the same time the rediscovery of universal patterns that can be realized by any man still willing to explore them. In some future edition I hope to include the results of experimental work (by myself & others) in the *total translation* of these poetries. Because we have so much already, it is at last possible to have it all. *This post-script is an incitement to those who would join in the enterprise; it is in no sense a final word.*

J.R.

Allegany Reservation (Seneca)
Steamburg, N.Y.
September, 1, 1968

THE TEXTS

Come, ascend the ladder: all come in: all sit down.
We were poor, poor, poor, poor, poor,
When we came to this world through the poor place,
Where the body of water dried for our passing.
Banked up clouds cover the earth.
All come four times with your showers:
Descend to the base of the ladder & stand still:
Bring your showers & great rains.
All, all come, all ascend, all come in, all sit down.

                                    (Zuni Indian)

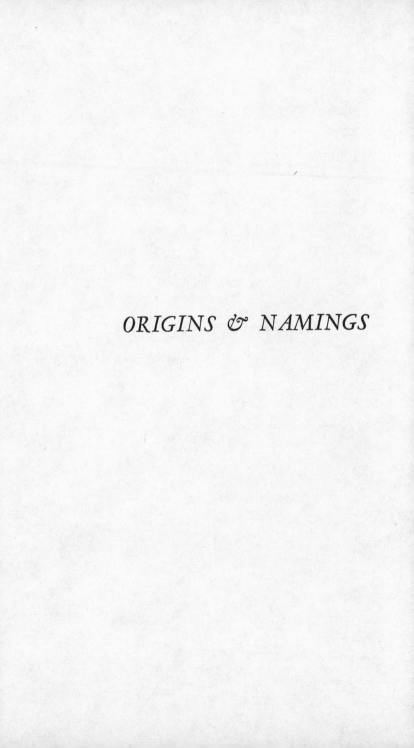

ORIGINS & NAMINGS

Genesis I

Water went they say. Land was not they say. Water only then, mountains were not, they say. Stones were not they say. Fish were not they say. Deer were not they say. Grizzlies were not they say. Panthers were not they say. Wolves were not they say. People were washed away they say. Grizzlies were washed away they say. Panthers were washed away they say. Deer were washed away they say. Coyotes were not then they say. Ravens were not they say. Herons were not they say. Woodpeckers were not they say. Then wrens were not they say. Then hummingbirds were not they say. Then otters were not they say. Then jack-rabbits, grey squirrels were not they say. Then long-eared mice were not they say. Then wind was not they say. Then snow was not they say. Then rain was not they say. Then it didn't thunder they say. Then trees were not when it didn't thunder they say. It didn't lighten they say. Then clouds were not they say. Fog was not they say. It didn't appear they say. Stars were not they say. It was very dark.

(Kato Indian)

Sounds

1

Dad a da da
Dad a da da
Dad a da da
Da kata kai

Ded o ded o
Ded o ded o
Ded o ded o
Da kata kai

(Australia)

2

heya heya heya·a yo·ho· yo·ho· yaha hahe·ya·an
ha·yahe· ha·wena
yo·ho· yo·ho· yaha hahe·ya·an
ha·yahe· ha·wena
he·yo· wena hahe·yahan
ha·yahe· ha·wena
he·yo· wena hahe·yahan
he he he he·yo
he·yo· wena hahe·yahan
he he he he·yo
he·yo· howo·   heyo
wana heya heya

(Navaho)

Genesis II

In the very beginning everything was resting in perpetual darkness: night oppressed all the earth like an impenetrable thicket.

(And) Karora was lying asleep, in everlasting night, at the very bottom of the soak of Ilbalintja: as yet there was no water in it, but all was dry ground.

Over him the soil was red with flowers & overgrown with many grasses: & a great pole was swaying above him.

. . . And Karora's head lay at the root of the great pole: he had rested thus ever from the beginning.

And Karora was thinking, & wishes & desires flashed through his mind. Bandicoots began to come out from his navel & from his arm-pits. They burst through the sod above & sprang into life.

And now dawn was beginning to break.

From all quarters men saw a new light appearing: the sun itself began to rise at Ilbalintja, & flooded everything with its light.

Then the gurra ancestor was minded to rise, now that the sun was mounting higher.

He burst through the crust that had covered him: & the gaping hole that he had left behind became the Ilbalintja Soak, filled with the sweet dark juice of honeysuckle buds.

(Australia: Aranda)

EGYPTIAN GOD NAMES

1

"It is Re who created his names out of his members"

—Chapter 17, *Book of the Dead*

2

These gods are like this in their caverns, which are in the Netherworld. Their bodies are in darkness.

The Upreared One.
Cat.
Terrible One.
Fat Face.
Turned Face.
The One belonging to the Cobra.

3

They are like this in their coffins. They are the rays of the Disk, their souls go in the following of the Great God.

The One of the Netherworld.
The Mysterious One.
The One of the Cavern.
The One of the Coffin.
She who combs.
The One of the Water.
The Weaver.

4

These gods are like this: they receive the rays of the Disk when it lights up the bodies of those of the Netherworld. When he passes by, they enter into darkness.

The Adorer.
Receiving Arm.
Arm of Light.
Brilliant One.
The One of the Rays.
Arm of Dawn.

5

Salutations to Osiris.

Osiris, the Gold of Millions.
Osiris, the Great Saw.
Osiris the Begetter.
Osiris the Scepter.
Osiris the King.
Osiris on the Sand.
Osiris in all the Lands.
Osiris at the head of the Booth of the distant Marshlands.
Osiris in his places which are in the South.
Osiris at the head of his town.

6

The Cat.

Head of Horus.
Face of Horus.
Neck of Horus.
Throat of Horus.
Iii.
The Gory One.

7

The Swallower of Millions.

Genesis III

1

From the conception the increase.
From the increase the swelling.
From the swelling the thought.
From the thought the remembrance.
From the remembrance the desire.

2

The word became fruitful:
It dwelt with the feeble glimmering:
It brought forth night:
The great night, the long night,
The lowest night, the highest night,
The thick night to be felt,
The night to be touched, the night unseen.
The night following on,
The night ending in death.

3

From the nothing the begetting:
From the nothing the increase:
From the nothing the abundance:
The power of increasing, the living breath
It dwelt with the empty space,
It produced the firmament which is above us.

4

The atmosphere which floats above the earth.
The great firmament above us, the spread-out space dwelt
    with the early dawn.
Then the moon sprang forth.
The atmosphere above dwelt with the glowing sky.
Then the sun sprang forth.
They were thrown up above as the chief eyes of heaven.
Then the sky became light.
The early dawn, the early day.
The midday. The blaze of day from the sky.

(New Zealand: Maori)

IMAGES

(1)

An Eskimo Poem for the Sun

The sun up there, up there.

(2)

A Dama Poem for the Ha-Tree

O the ha-tree, O the hard tree!

(3)

A Bushman Poem for the Jackal

Canter for me, little jackal, O little jackal,
   little jackal.

(4)

An Eskimo Poem against Death

I watched the white dogs of the dawn.

(5)

A Chippewa Song for the Crow

I am the crow—I am the crow—his skin is my body.

(6)

A Bushman Poem for the Blue Crane

A splinter of stone which is white.

(7)

A Yuma Indian Poem about the Water-Bug

The water-bug is drawing the shadows of evening
    toward him across the water.

Bantu Combinations

1.

I am still carving an ironwood stick.
I am still thinking about it.

2.

The lake dries up at the edges.
The elephant is killed by a small arrow.

3.

The little hut falls down.
Tomorrow, debts.

4.

The sound of a cracked elephant tusk.
The anger of a hungry man.

5.

Is there someone on the shore?
The crab has caught me by one finger.

6.

We are the fire which burns the country.
The Calf of the Elephant is exposed on the plain.

(Africa)

CORRESPONDENCES

from *The Book of Changes*

The Creative is heaven. It is round, it is the prince, the father, jade, metal, cold, ice; it is deep red, a good horse, an old horse, a lean horse, a wild horse, tree fruit.

The Receptive is the earth, the mother. It is cloth, a kettle, frugality, it is level, it is a cow with a calf, a large wagon, form, the multitude, a shaft. Among the various kinds of soil, it is the black.

The Arousing is thunder, the dragon. It is dark yellow, it is a spreading out, a great road, the eldest son. It is decisive & vehement; it is bamboo that is green & young, it is reed & rush.

Among horses it signifies those which can neigh well, those with white hind legs, those which gallop, those with a star on the forehead.

Among useful plants it is the pod-bearing ones. Finally, it is the strong, that which grows luxuriantly.

The Gentle is wood, wind, the eldest daughter, the guideline, work; it is the white, the long, the high; it is advance & retreat, the undecided, odor.

Among men it means the gray-haired; it means those with broad foreheads; it means those with much white in their eyes; it means those close to gain, so that in the market they get threefold value. Finally, it is the sign of vehemence.

The Abysmal is water, ditches, ambush, bending & straightening out, bow & wheel.

Among men it means the melancholy, those with sick hearts, with earache.

It is the blood sign; it is red.

Among horses it means those with beautiful backs, those with wild courage, those which let their heads hang, those with thin hoofs, those which stumble.

Among chariots it means those with many defects.

It is penetration, the moon.

It means thieves.

Among varieties of wood it means those which are firm & have much pith.

The Clinging is fire, the sun, lightning, the middle daughter.

It means coats of mail & helmets; it means lances & weapons. Among men it means the big-bellied.

It is the sign of dryness. It means the tortoise, the crab, the snail, the mussel, the hawkbill tortoise.

Among trees it means those which dry out in the upper part of the trunk.

Keeping Still is the mountain; it is a bypath; it means little stones, doors & openings, fruits & seeds, eunuchs & watchmen, the fingers; it is the dog, the rat, & the various kinds of black-billed birds.

Among trees it signifies the firm & gnarled.

The Joyous is the lake, the youngest daughter; it is a sorceress; it is mouth & tongue. It means smashing & breaking apart; it means dropping off & bursting open. Among the kinds of soil it is the hard & salty. It is the concubine. It is the sheep.

(China)

GENESIS IV

And I commanded in the very lowest parts that visible things should come from invisible, & Adoil came down very great, & I beheld, & look! it was a belly of great light.

And I said: 'Spread apart, & let the visible come out of thee.'

And it spread apart, & a great light came out. And I was in the center of the light, & as light is born from light, an age came out, a great age, & it showed me all the creation I had thought to make.

And I saw that it was good.

And I set a throne up for myself, & took my seat on it, & I said to the light: 'Go up higher & fix yourself high above the throne, & be a foundation for the highest things.'

And above the light there is nothing else, & then I leaned back & I looked up from my throne.

And I commanded the lowest a second time, & I said: 'Let Archas come forth hard,' & it came forth hard from the invisible.

And it came forth hard, heavy & very red.

And I said: 'Be opened, Archas, & let there be born from thee,' & it became open, an age came out, a very great, a very dark age, bearing the creation of all lower things, & I saw that it was good & said:

'Go down below, & make yourself firm & be a foundation for the lower things,' & it happened, & it went down & fixed itself, & became the foundation for the lower things, & below the darkness there is nothing else.

(Hebrew)

Aztec Definitions

Ruby-Throated Hummingbird

It is ashen, ash colored. At the top of its head & the throat, its feathers are flaming, like fire. They glisten, they glow.

Amoyotl (a water-strider)

It is like a fly, small & round. It has legs, it has wings; it is dry. It goes on the surface of the water; it is a flyer. It buzzes, it sings.

Bitumen (a shellfish)

It falls out on the ocean shore; it falls out like mud.

Little Blue Heron

It resembles the brown crane in color; it is ashen, grey. It smells like fish, rotten fish, stinking fish. It smells of fish, rotten fish.

Seashell

It is white. One is large, one is small. It is spiraled, marvelous. It is that which can be blown, which resounds. I blow the seashell. I improve, I polish the seashell.

A Mushroom

It is round, large, like a severed head.

The Avocado Tree

The leaves, the foliage are brown. Its fruit is black, dark; it shines. Within, it is herb-green. Its base is thin, the top rounded, round. It is oily; it has moisture; it has a center.

Elocpulin (*a tree*)

Its foliage, its leaves, its fruit: broad, thick, fat, ball-like; each one ball-like, large, pulpy, breakable into small pieces, watery. . . . They fill one's mouth, satisfy one, taste good to one, make one covet them, make one want them, are constantly required. The center is fat; they fill one's mouth; they satisfy one.

Pine

The pine tree is tender, verdant, very verdant. It has particles of (dried) pine (resin). It has cones—pine cones; it has a bark, a thick skin. It has pine resin, a resin. (The wood) can be broken, shattered. The pine is embracing. It is a provider of light, a means of seeing, a resinous torch. It is spongy, porous, soft. It forms a resin; drops stand formed; they stand sputtering. They sputter. It burns, it illuminates things, it makes a resin; a resin exudes. It turns into a resin. Resin is required.

A Mountain

High, pointed; pointed on top, pointed at the summit, towering; wide, cylindrical, round; a round mountain, low, low-ridged; rocky, with many rocks; craggy with many crags; rough with rocks; of earth; with trees; grassy; with herbs; with shrubs; with water; dry; white; jagged; with a sloping plain, with gorges, with caves; precipitous, having gorges; canyon land, precipitous land with boulders.

I climb the mountain; I scale the mountain. I live on the mountain. I am born on the mountain. No one becomes a mountain—no one turns himself into a mountain. The mountain crumbles.

Another Mountain

It is wooded; it spreads green.

Forest

It is a place of verdure, of fresh green; of wind—windy places, in wind, windy; a place of cold: it becomes cold; there is much frost; it is a place which freezes. It is a place from which misery comes, where it exists; a place where there is affliction—a place of affliction, of lamentation, a place of affliction, of weeping; a place where there is sadness, a place of compassion, of sighing; a place which arouses sorrow, which spreads misery.

It is a place of gorges, gorge places; a place of crags, craggy places; a place of stony soil, stony-soiled places; in hard soil, in clayey soil, in moist & fertile soil. It is a place among moist & fertile lands, a place of moist & fertile soil, in yellow soil.

It is a place with cuestas, cuesta places; a place with peaks, peaked places; a place which is grassy, with grassy places; a place of forests, forested places; a place of thin forest, thinly forested places; a place of thick forest, thickly forested places; a place of jungle, of dry tree stumps, of underbrush, of dense forest.

It is a place of stony soil, stony-soiled places; a place of round stones, round-stoned places; a place of sharp stones, of rough stones; a place of crags, craggy places; a place of *tepetate;* a place with clearings, cleared places; a place of valleys, of coves, of places with coves, of cove places; a place of boulders, bouldered places; a place of hollows.

It is a disturbing place, fearful, frightful; home of the savage beast, dwelling-place of the serpent, the rabbit, the deer; a place from which nothing departs, nothing leaves, nothing emerges. It is a place of dry rocks, of boulders; bouldered places; boulder land, a land of bouldered places. It is a place of caves, cave places, having caves—a place having caves.

It is a place of wild beasts; a place of wild beasts—of the ocelot, the *cuitlachtli,* the bobcat, the serpent, the spider, the rabbit, the deer; of stalks, grass, prickly shrubs: of the mesquite, of the pine. It is a place where wood is owned. Trees are felled. It is a place where trees are cut, where wood is gathered, where there is chopping, where there is logging: a place of beams.

It becomes verdant, a fresh green. It becomes cold, icy. Ice forms & spreads; ice lies forming a surface. There is wind, a crashing wind; the wind crashes, spreads whistling, forms whirlwinds. Ice is blown by the wind; the wind glides.

There is no one; there are no people. It is desolate; it lies desolate. There is nothing edible. Misery abounds, misery emerges, misery spreads. There is no joy, no pleasure. It lies sprouting; herbs lie sprouting; nothing lies emerging; the earth is pressed down. All die of thirst. The grasses lie sprouting. Nothing lies cast about. There is hunger; all hunger. It is the home of hunger; there is death from hunger. All die of cold; there is freezing; there is trembling; there is the clattering, the chattering of teeth. There are cramps, the stiffening of the body, the constant stiffening, the stretching out prone.

There is fright, there is constant fright. One is devoured; one is slain by stealth; one is abused; one is brutally put to death; one is tormented. Misery abounds. There is calm, constant calm, continuing calm.

Mirror Stone

Its name comes from nowhere. This can be excavated in mines; it can be broken off. Of these mirror stones, one is white, one black. The white one—this is a good one to look into: the mirror, the clear, transparent one. They named it mirror of the noblemen, the mirror of the ruler.

The black one—this one is not good. It is not to look into; it does not make one appear good. It is one (so they say) which contends with one's face. When someone uses such a mirror, from it is to be seen a distorted mouth, swollen eyelids, thick lips, a large mouth. They say it is an ugly mirror, a mirror which contends with one's face.

Of these mirrors, one is round; one is long: they call it *acaltezcatl*. These mirror stones can be excavated in mines, can be polished, can be worked.

I make a mirror. I work it. I shatter it. I form it. I grind it. I polish it with sand. I work it with fine abrasive sand. I apply to it a glue of bat shit. I prepare it. I polish it with a fine cane. I make it shiney. I regard myself in the mirror. I appear from there in my looking-mirror; from it I admire myself.

Secret Road

Its name is secret road, the one which few people know, which not all people are aware of, which few people go along. It is good, fine; a good place, a fine place. It is where one is harmed, a place of harm. It is known as a safe place; it is a difficult place, a dangerous place. One is frightened. It is a place of fear.

There are trees, crags, gorges, rivers, precipitous places, places of precipitous land, various places of precipitous land, various precipitous places, gorges, various gorges. It is a place of wild animals, a place of wild beasts, full of wild beasts. It is a place where one is put to death by stealth; a place where one is put to death in the jaws of the wild beasts of the land of the dead.

I take the secret road. I follow along, I encounter the secret road. He goes following along, he goes joining that which is bad, the corner, the darkness, the secret road. He goes to seek, to find, that which is bad.

The Cave

It becomes long, deep; it widens, extends, narrows. It is a constricted place, a narrowed place, one of the hollowed-out places. It forms hollowed-out places. There are roughened places; there are asperous places. It is frightening, a fearful place, a place of death. It is called a place of death because there is dying. It is a place of darkness; it darkens; it stands ever dark. It stands wide-mouthed, it is wide-mouthed. It is wide-mouthed; it is narrow-mouthed. It has mouths which pass through.

I place myself in the cave. I enter the cave.

The Precipice

It is deep—a difficult, a dangerous place, a deathly place. It is dark, it is light. It is an abyss.

Genesis V

1

In the beginning the word gave origin to the father.

2

A phantasm, nothing else existed in the beginning: the Father touched an illusion, he grasped something mysterious. Nothing existed. Through the agency of a dream our Father Nai-mu-ena kept the mirage to his body, & he pondered long & thought deeply.

Nothing existed, not even a stick to support the vision: our Father attached the illusion to the thread of a dream & kept it by the aid of his breath. He sounded to reach the bottom of the appearance, but there was nothing. Nothing existed.

Then the Father again investigated the bottom of the mystery. He tied the empty illusion to the dream thread & pressed the magical substance upon it. Then by the aid of his dream he held it like a wisp of raw cotton.

Then he seized the mirage bottom & stamped upon it repeatedly, sitting down at last on his dreamed earth.

The earth-phantasm was his now, & he spat out saliva repeatedly so that the forests might grow. Then he lay down on his earth & covered it with the roof of heaven. As he was the owner of the earth he placed above it the blue & the white sky.

Thereupon Rafu-ema, the-man-who-has-the-narratives, sitting at the base of the sky, pondered, & he created this story so that we might listen to it here upon earth.

(Colombia: Uitoto Indians)

The Pictures

1.

(Passamaquoddy Indian)

2.

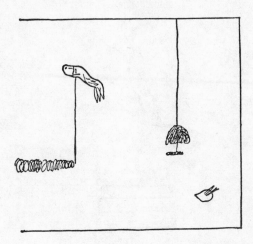

(Skokomish Indian)

3.

—Red Corn (Osage)

4. *The Supplication*

(Alaskan)

5.

(Nicobar)

6.

(Easter Island)

The Girl of the Early Race Who Made the Stars

(by ‖kábbo)

My mother was the one who told me that the girl arose; she put her hands into the wood ashes; she threw up the wood ashes into the sky. She said to the wood ashes: "The wood ashes which are here, they must altogether become the Milky Way. They must white lie along in the sky, that the stars may stand outside of the Milky Way, while the Milky Way is the Milky Way, while it used to be wood ashes." They the ashes altogether become the Milky Way. The Milky Way must go round with the stars; while the Milky Way feels that, the Milky Way lies going around; while the stars sail along; therefore, the Milky Way, lying, goes along with the Stars. The Milky Way, when the Milky Way stands upon the earth, the Milky Way turns across in front, while the Milky Way means to wait, while the Milky Way feels that the Stars are turning back; while the Stars feel that the Sun is the one who has turned back; he is upon his path; the Stars turn back; while they go to fetch the daybreak; that they may lie nicely, while the Milky Way lies nicely. The Stars shall also stand nicely around. They shall sail along upon their footprints, which they, always sailing along, are following. While they feel that, they are the Stars which descend.

The Milky Way lying comes to its place, to which the girl threw up the wood ashes, that it may descend nicely; it had lying gone along, while it felt that it lay upon the sky. It had lying gone round, while it felt that the Stars also turned round. They turning round passed over the sky. The sky lies still; the Stars are those which go along; while they feel that they sail. They had been setting; they had, again, been coming out; they had, sailing along, been following their footprints. They become white, when the Sun comes out. The Sun sets, they stand around above; while they feel that they did turning follow the Sun.

The darkness comes out; they the Stars wax red, while they had at first been white. They feel that they stand brightly around; that they may sail along; while they feel that it is night. Then, the people go by night; while they feel that the ground is made light. While they feel that the Stars shine a little. Darkness is upon the ground. The Milky Way gently glows; while it feels that it is wood ashes. Therefore, it gently glows. While it feels that the girl was the one who said that the Milky Way should give a little light for the people, that they might return home by night, in the middle of the night. For, the earth would not have been a little light, had not the Milky Way been there. It and the Stars.

(Africa: Bushman)

THE FRAGMENTS

(1)

....
command...
....
.... of the boat of the evening...
....
....
Thy face is like.................................
....
....
....
....

(2)

To say: ....for me three meals
one in heaven, two on earth.
A lion-helmet............green......................

(3)

......................four.........................
.... a point.....................
.... darkness.....................
.... be not......................
come...

(4)

In my wearied......, me.......
In my inflamed nostril, me........
Punishment, sickness, trouble.......me
A flail which wickedly afflicts,......me

A lacerating rod..........me

A.......hand.......me
A terrifying message.......me
A stinging whip...........me

....
.............in pain I *faint* (?)

....

ALL LIVES, ALL DANCES, & ALL IS LOUD

The fish does . . . HIP
The bird does . . . VISS
The marmot does . . . GNAN

I throw myself to the left,
I turn myself to the right,
I act the fish,
Which darts in the water, which darts
Which twists about, which leaps—
All lives, all dances, & all is loud.

The fish does . . . HIP
The bird does . . . VISS
The marmot does . . . GNAN

The bird flies away,
It flies, flies, flies,
Goes, returns, passes,
Climbs, soars & drops.
I act the bird—
All lives, all dances, & all is loud.

The fish does . . . HIP
The bird does . . . VISS
The marmot does . . . GNAN

The monkey from branch to branch,
Runs, bounds & leaps,
With his wife, with his brat,
His mouth full, his tail in the air,
There goes the monkey! There goes the Monkey!
All lives, all dances, & all is loud.

(Africa: Gabon Pygmy)

Yoruba Praises

1

Shango is the death who kills money with a big stick
The man who lies will die in his home
Shango strikes the one who is stupid
He wrinkles his nose & the liar runs off
Even when he does not fight, we fear him
But when war shines in his eye
His enemies & worshippers run all the same
Fire in the eye, fire in the mouth, fire on the roof
The leopard who killed the sheep & bathed in its blood
The man who died in the market & woke up in the house

2

Shango is an animal like the gorilla
A rare animal in the forest
As rare as the monkey who is a medicine man
Shango, do not give me a little of your medicine
Give me all! So that I can spread it over my face & mouth
Anybody who waits for the elephant, waits for death
Anybody who waits for the buffalo, waits for death
Anybody who waits for the railway, waits for trouble
He says we must avoid the thing that will kill us
He says we must avoid trouble
He is the one who waited for the things we are running away
  from

(Africa: Yoruba)

WAR GOD'S HORSE SONG I

(Words by Tall Kia ahni. Interpreted by Louis Watchman)

I am the Turquoise Woman's son.
On top of Belted Mountain
beautiful horses—slim like a weasel!
My horse with a hoof like a striped agate,
with his fetlock like a fine eagle plume:
my horse whose legs are like quick lightning
whose body is an eagle-plumed arrow:
my horse whose tail is like a trailing black cloud.
The Little Holy Wind blows thru his hair.
My horse with a mane made of short rainbows.
My horse with ears made of round corn.
My horse with eyes made of big stars.
My horse with a head made of mixed waters.
My horse with teeth made of white shell.
The long rainbow is in his mouth for a bridle
          & with it I guide him.
When my horse neighs, different-colored horses follow.
When my horse neighs, different-colored sheep follow.
          I am wealthy because of him.

          Before me peaceful
          Behind me peaceful
          Under me peaceful
          Over me peaceful—
          Peaceful voice when he neighs.
I am everlasting & peaceful.
I stand for my horse.

                                        (Navaho Indian)

War God's Horse Song II
(by Frank Mitchell)

With their voices they are calling me,
With their voices they are calling me!

I am the child of White Shell Woman,
 With their voices they are calling me,
I am the son of the Sun,
 With their voices they are calling me,
I am Turquoise Boy,
 With their voices they are calling me!

From the arching rainbow, turquoise on its outer edge,
 from this side of where it touches the earth,
 With their voices they are calling me,
Now the horses of the Sun-descended-boy,
 With their voices they are calling me!

The turquoise horses are my horses,
 With their voices they are calling me,
Dark stone water jars their hooves,
 With their voices they are calling me,
Arrowheads the frogs of their hooves,
 With their voices they are calling me,
Mirage-stone their striped hooves,
 With their voices they are calling me,
Dark wind their legs,
 With their voices they are calling me,
Cloud shadow their tails,
 With their voices they are calling me,
All precious fabrics their bodies,
 With their voices they are calling me,

Dark cloud their skins,
  With their voices they are calling me,
Scattered rainbow their hair,
  With their voices they are calling me,
Now the Sun rises before them to shine on them,
  With their voices they are calling me!

New moons their cantles,
  With their voices they are calling me,
Sunrays their backstraps,
  With their voices they are calling me,
Rainbows their girths,
  With their voices they are calling me,
They are standing, waiting, on rainbows,
  With their voices they are calling me,
The dark-rain-four-footed-ones, their neck hair falling in a wave,
  With their voices they are calling me!

Sprouting plants their ears,
  With their voices they are calling me,
Great dark stars their eyes,
  With their voices they are calling me,
All kinds of spring waters their faces,
  With their voices they are calling me,
Great shell their lips,
  With their voices they are calling me,
White shell their teeth,
  With their voices they are calling me,
There is flash-lightning in their mouths,
  With their voices they are calling me,
Dark-music sounds from their mouths,
  With their voices they are calling me,
They call out into the dawn,
  With their voices they are calling me,
Their voices reach all the way out to me,
  With their voices they are calling me,

Dawn-pollen is in their mouths,
    With their voices they are calling me,
Flowers and plant-dew are in their mouths,
    With their voices they are calling me!

Sunray their bridles,
    With their voices they are calling me,
To my right arm, beautifully to my hand they come,
    With their voices they are calling me,
This day they become my own horses,
    With their voices they are calling me,
Ever increasing, never diminishing,
    With their voices they are calling me,
My horses of long life and happiness,
    With their voices they are calling me,
I, myself, am the boy of long life and happiness,
    With their voices they are calling me!

With their voices they are calling me,
With their voices they are calling me!

                      (Navaho Indian)

To the God of Fire as a Horse

Your eyes do not make mistakes.
Your eyes have the sun's seeing.
Your thought marches terribly in the night
blazing with light & the fire
breaks from your throat as you whinny in battle.

This fire was born in a pleasant forest
This fire lives in ecstasy somewhere in the night.

His march is a dagger of fire
His body is enormous
His mouth opens & closes as he champs on the world
He swings the axe-edge of his tongue
    smelting & refining the raw wood he chops down.

He gets ready to shoot & fits arrow to bowstring
He hones his light to a fine edge on the steel
He travels through night with rapid & various movements
His thighs are rich with movement.
    He is a bird that settles on a tree.

(India)

To the God of Fire

He hides himself like a thief in the hidden cave
  in darkness with the cow of vision.
It is to him we always surrender:
  he carries our surrender with him.

His movements are the law of the working of truth
He circles the world & the sea swells him up with its song:
  the flame of truth burns in the heart of water.

He is earth & the wide fields we grow festive in,
The pleasure of running water, the hill we climb,
The clean air at its peak from which we watch
Invincible horses gallop along unbroken rivers that he runs
                                    beside.

  And he eats the forests of earth:
The wind breathes him out & he perches in the branches
And he scorches the hair of earth's body with his flame.

And he breathes on the water like a gull in the trough of
                           the wave,
And he wakes at daybreak to begin the recitation of the word,
And he is like a god of wine & like a white cow with her calf,
And he spreads out over the world,
  and his light can be seen very far.

                                 (India)

THE STARS

For we are the stars. For we sing.
For we sing with our light.
For we are birds made of fire.
For we spread our wings over the sky.
Our light is a voice.
We cut a road for the soul
for its journey through death.
For three of our number are hunters.
For these three hunt a bear.
For there never yet was a time
when these three didn't hunt.
For we face the hills with disdain.
This is the song of the stars.

(Passamaquoddy Indian)

VISIONS & SPELS

The Annunciation
(by Marpa)

*

a man born from a flower in space a man
riding a colt foaled from a sterile mare
his reins are formed from the hair of a tortoise

    a rabbit's horn for a dagger he
    strikes down his enemies

a man without lips who is speaking who
sees without eyes a man without ears
who listens who runs without legs

the sun & the moon dance
& blow trumpets

a young child touches
the wheel-of-the-law

    which turns over

*

: secret of the body
    : of the word
        : of the heart of the gods

the inner breath is the horse of the bodhisattvas

whipped by compassion it
rears it drives the old yak
from the path of madness

               (Tibet)

How Isaac Tens Became a Shaman

Thirty years after my birth was the time.

*

I went up into the hills to get firewood. While I was cutting up the wood into lengths, it grew dark towards the evening. Before I had finished my last stack of wood, a loud noise broke out over me, chu––––––, & a large owl appeared to me. The owl took hold of me, caught my face, & tried to lift me up. I lost consciousness. As soon as I came back to my senses I realized that I had fallen into the snow. My head was coated with ice, & some blood was running out of my mouth.

*

I stood up & went down the trail, walking very fast, with some wood packed on my back. On my way, the trees seemed to shake & to lean over me; tall trees were crawling after me, as if they had been snakes. I could see them.

*

At my father's home . . . I fell into a sort of trance. It seems that two shamans were working over me to bring me back to health. . . . When I woke up & opened my eyes, I thought that flies covered my face completely. I looked down, & instead of being on firm ground, I felt that I was drifting in a huge whirlpool. My heart was thumping fast.

*

Another time, I went to my hunting grounds on the other side of the river. . . . I caught two fishers in my traps, took their pelts, & threw the flesh & bones away. Farther along I looked for a bear's den amid the tall trees. As I glanced upwards, I saw an owl, at the top of a high cedar. I shot it, & it fell down in the bushes close to me. When I went to pick it up, it had disappeared. Not a feather was left; this seemed very strange. I walked down to the river, crossed over the ice, & returned to the village at Gitenmaks. Upon arriving at my fishing station on the point, I heard the noise of a crowd of people around the smoke-house, as if I were being chased away, pursued. I dared not look behind to find out what all this was about, but I hurried straight ahead. The voices followed in my tracks & came very close behind me. Then I wheeled around & looked back. There was no one in sight, only trees. A trance came over me once more, & I fell down, unconscious. When I came to, my head was buried in a snowbank.

*

I got up & walked on the ice up the river to the village. There I met my father who had just come out to look for me, for he had missed me. We went back together to my house. Then my heart started to beat fast, & I began to tremble, just as had happened before, when the shamans were trying to fix me up. My flesh seemed to be boiling, & I could hear s^n————————. My body was quivering. *While I remained in this state, I began to sing. A chant was coming out of me without my being able to do anything to stop it. Many things appeared to me presently: huge birds & other animals. . . . These were visible only to me, not to the others in my house. Such visions happen when a man is about to become a shaman; they occur of their*

*own accord. The songs force themselves out complete without
any attempt to compose them. But I learned & memorized
those songs by repeating them.*

First Song

Death of the salmon,
my death

but the city
finds life in it

the salmon floats
in the canyon

ghosts in the city
below me

the robin cries over
my head &

this robin, the
woman I fly with

Second Song

where the dead sing, where
the grizzly

hides in the sky
& I watch him circle

the door to my house
swings shut   fires

are burning
beneath it   hard

vision, their faces
of faces in a crowd

Third Song

in mud to my knees,
a lake

where the shellfish
holds me, is

cutting my ankles,
in death

Fourth Song

a boat, a stranger's
boat, a canoe

& myself inside it, a
stranger inside it

it floats past trees,
past water

runs among
whirlpools

Fifth Song

& vision: beehives
were stinging my body

or the ghosts of bees,
giants

& the old woman
working me

until I grew   listened
in dreams, in her head

(Gitksan Indian)

A Shaman Climbs Up the Sky

.

The Shaman mounts a scarecrow in the shape of a goose
above the white sky
beyond the white clouds
above the blue sky
beyond the blue clouds

this bird climbs the sky

..

The Shaman offers horse meat to the chief drummer
the master of the six-knob
drum he takes a small piece
then he draws closer he
brings it to me in his hand

when I say "go" he bends
first at the knees when I
say "scat" he takes it all

whatever I give him

...

The Shaman fumigates nine robes
gifts no horse can carry
that no man can lift &
robes with triple necks
to look at & to touch
three times: to use this
as a horse blanket

                sweet
prince ulgan

you are my prince
my treasure

you are my joy

....

Invocation to Markut, the bird of heaven

this bird of heaven who keeps
   five shapes & powerful
   brass claws (the moon

has copper claws the moon's
beak is made of ice) whose

   wings are powerful &
   strike the air whose tail

is power & a heavy wind

markut whose left wing
   hides the moon whose
      right wing hides the sun

      who never gets lost who flies
     past that-place nothing tires her
who comes toward this-place

in my house I listen
for her singing I wait
the game begins

falling past my right eye landing
here
on my right shoulder

markut is the mother of five eagles

The Shaman reaches the 1st sky

my shadow on the landing
I have climbed to (have reached
this place called sky
& struggled with its summit)
I who stand here
higher than the moon

full moon my shadow

.

The Shaman pierces the 2d sky

to reach the second landing
this further level

look!

the floor below us
lies in ruins

..

At the End of the Climb: Praise to Prince Ulgan

three stairways lead
to him three flocks
sustain him PRINCE ULGAN!

blue hill where no hill
was before: blue sky
everywhere: a blue cloud
turning swiftly

that no one can reach:
a blue sky that no one
can reach (to reach it
to journey a year by water

then to bow before him
three times to exalt him)
for whom the moon's edge
shines forever PRINCE ULGAN!

you have found use for the hoofs
of our horses you who give us
flocks who keep pain from us

                    sweet

prince ulgan

for whom the stars & the sky
are turning a thousand times
turning a thousand times over

                    (Altaic)

From THE GREAT VISION

(by Black Elk)

I.

It was the summer when I was nine years old, and our people were moving slowly toward the Rocky Mountains. We camped one evening in a valley beside a little creek just before it ran into the Greasy Grass, and there was a man by the name of Man Hip who liked me and asked me to eat with him in his tepee.

While I was eating, a voice came and said: "It is time; now they are calling you." The voice was so loud and clear that I believed it, and I thought I would just go where it wanted me to go. So I got right up and started. As I came out of the tepee, both my thighs began to hurt me, and suddenly it was like waking from a dream, and there wasn't any voice. So I went back into the tepee, but I didn't want to eat. Man Hip looked at me in a strange way and asked me what was wrong. I told him that my legs were hurting me.

The next day the camp moved on to where the different bands of our people were coming together, and I rode in a pony drag, for I was very sick. Both my legs and both my arms were swollen badly and my face was all puffed up.

When we had camped again, I was lying in our tepee and my mother and father were sitting beside me. I could see out through the opening, and there two men were coming from the clouds, headfirst like arrows slanting down, and I knew they were the same that I had seen before. Each now carried a long spear, and from the points of these a jagged lightning flashed. They came clear down to the ground this time and stood a little way off and looked at me and said: "Hurry! Come! Your Grandfathers are calling you!"

Then they turned and left the ground like arrows slanting upward from the bow. When I got up to follow, my legs did not hurt me any more and I was very light. I went outside the tepee, and yonder where the men with flaming spears were going, a little cloud was coming very fast. It came and stooped and took me and turned back to where it came from, flying fast.

2.

Now suddenly there was nothing but a world of cloud, and we three were there alone in the middle of a great white plain with snowy hills and mountains staring at us; and it was very still; but there were whispers.

Then the two men spoke together and they said: "Behold him, the being with four legs!"

I looked and saw a bay horse standing there, and he began to speak: "Behold me!" he said. "My life-history you shall see." Then he wheeled about to where the sun goes down, and said: "Behold them! Their history you shall know."

I looked, and there were twelve black horses all abreast with necklaces of bison hoofs, and they were beautiful, but I was frightened, because their manes were lightning and there was thunder in their nostrils.

Then the bay horse wheeled to where the great white giant lives (the north) and said: "Behold!" And there were twelve white horses all abreast. Their manes were flowing like a blizzard wind and from their noses came a roaring, and all about them white geese soared and circled.

Then the bay wheeled round to where the sun shines continually (the east) and bade me look; and there twelve sorrel horses, with necklaces of elk's teeth, stood abreast with eyes that glimmered like the day-break star and manes of morning light.

Then the bay wheeled once again to look upon the place where you are always facing (the south), and yonder stood twelve buckskins all abreast with horns upon their heads and manes that lived and grew like trees and grasses.

And when I had seen all these, the bay horse said: "Your Grandfathers are having a council. These shall take you; so have courage."

Then all the horses went into formation, four abreast—the blacks, the whites, the sorrels, and the buckskins—and stood behind the bay, who turned now to the west and neighed; and yonder suddenly the sky was terrible with a storm of plunging horses in all colors that shook the world with thunder, neighing back.

Now turning to the north the bay horse whinnied, and yonder all the sky roared with a mighty wind of running horses in all colors, neighing back.

And when he whinnied to the east, there too the sky was filled with glowing clouds of manes and tails of horses in all colors singing back. Then to the south he called, and it was crowded with many colored, happy horses, nickering.

Then the bay horse spoke to me again and said: "See how your horses all come dancing!" I looked, and there were horses, horses everywhere—a whole skyful of horses dancing round me.

"Make haste!" the bay horse said; and we walked together side by side, while the blacks, the whites, the sorrels, and the buckskins followed, marching four by four.

I looked about me once again, and suddenly the dancing horses without number changed into animals of every kind and into all the fowls that are, and these fled back to the four quarters of the world from which the horses came, and vanished.

Then as we walked, there was a heaped up cloud ahead that changed into a tepee, and a rainbow was the open door of it; and through the door I saw six old men sitting in a row.

The two men with the spears now stood beside me, one on either hand, and the horses took their places in their quarters, looking inward, four by four. And the oldest of the Grandfathers spoke with a kind voice and said: "Come right in and do not fear." And as he spoke, all the horses of the four quarters neighed to cheer me. So I went in and stood before the six, and they looked older than men can ever be—old like hills, like stars.

The oldest spoke again: "Your Grandfathers all over the world are having a council, and they have called you here to teach you." His voice was very kind, but I shook all over with fear now, for I knew that these were not old men, but the Powers of the World. And the first was the Power of the West; the second, of the North; the third, of the East; the fourth, of the South; the fifth, of the Sky; the sixth, of the Earth. I knew this, and was afraid, until the first Grandfather spoke again: "Behold them yonder where the sun goes down, the thunder beings! You shall see, and have from them my power; and they shall take you to the high and lonely center of the earth that you may see; even to the place where the sun continually shines, they shall take you there to understand."

And as he spoke of understanding, I looked up and saw the rainbow leap with flames of many colors over me.

Now there was a wooden cup in his hand and it was full of water and in the water was the sky.

"Take this," he said. "It is the power to make live, and it is yours."

Now he had a bow in his hands. "Take this," he said. "It is the power to destroy, and it is yours."

Then he pointed to himself and said: "Look close at him who is your spirit now, for you are his body and his name is Eagle Wing Stretches."

And saying this, he got up very tall and started running toward where the sun goes down; and suddenly he was a black horse that stopped and turned and looked at me, and the horse was very poor and sick; his ribs stood out.

Then the second Grandfather, he of the North, arose with a herb of power in his hand, and said: "Take this and hurry." I took and held it toward the black horse yonder. He fattened and was happy and came prancing to his place again and was the first Grandfather sitting there.

The second Grandfather, he of the North, spoke again: "Take courage, younger brother," he said; "on earth a nation you shall make live, for yours shall be the power of the white giant's wing, the cleansing wind." Then he got up very tall and started running toward the north; and when he turned toward me, it was a white goose wheeling. I looked about me now, and the horses in the west were thunders and the horses of the north were geese. And the second Grandfather sang two songs that were like this:

> "They are appearing,
> They are appearing,
> The thunder nation is appearing.
>
> They are appearing,
> They are appearing,
> The white geese nation is appearing."

And now it was the third Grandfather who spoke, he of where the sun shines continually. "Take courage, younger brother," he said, "for across the earth they shall take you!" Then he pointed to where the daybreak star was shining, and beneath the star two men were flying. "From them you shall have power," he said, "from them who have awakened all the beings of the earth with roots and legs and wings." And as he said this, he held in his hand a peace pipe which had a spotted eagle outstretched upon the stem; and this eagle seemed alive, for it was poised there, fluttering, and its eyes were looking at me. "With this pipe," the Grandfather said, "you shall walk upon the earth, and whatever sickens there you shall make well." Then he pointed to a man who was bright red all over, the color of good and of plenty, and as he pointed, the red man lay down and rolled and changed into a bison that got up and galloped toward the sorrel horses of the east, and they too turned to bison, fat and many.

And now the fourth Grandfather spoke, he of the place where you are always facing (the south), whence comes the power to grow. "Younger brother," he said, "with the powers of the four quarters you shall walk, a relative. Behold, the living center of a nation I shall give you, and with it many you shall save." And I saw that he was holding in his hand a bright red stick that was alive, and as I looked it sprouted at the top and sent forth branches, and on the branches many leaves came out and murmured and in the leaves the birds began to sing. And then for just a little while I thought I saw beneath it in the shade the circled villages of people and every living thing with roots or legs or wings, and all were happy. "It shall stand in the center of the nation's circle," said the Grandfather, "a cane to walk with and a people's heart; and by your powers you shall make it blossom."

Then he rose very tall and started running toward the south, and was an elk; and as he stood among the buckskins yonder, they too were elks.

Now the fifth Grandfather spoke, the oldest of them all, the Spirit of the Sky. "My boy," he said, "I have sent for you and you have come. My power you shall see!" He stretched his arms and turned into a spotted eagle hovering. "Behold," he said, "all the wings of the air shall come to you, and they and the winds and the stars shall be like relatives. You shall go across the earth with my power." Then the eagle soared above my head and fluttered there; and suddenly the sky was full of friendly wings all coming toward me.

Now I knew the sixth Grandfather was about to speak, he who was the Spirit of the Earth, and I saw that he was very old, but more as men are old. His hair was long and white, his face was all in wrinkles and his eyes were deep and dim. I stared at him, for it seemed I knew him somehow; and as I stared, he slowly changed, for he was growing backwards into youth, and when he had become a boy, I knew that he was myself with all the years that would be mine at last. When he was old again, he said: "My boy, have courage, for my power shall be yours, and you shall need it, for your nation on the earth will have great troubles. Come."

He rose and tottered out through the rainbow door, and as I followed I was riding on the bay horse who had talked to me at first and led me to that place.

3.

I looked below me where the earth was silent in a sick green light, and saw the hills look up afraid and the grasses on the hills and all the animals; and everywhere about me were the cries of frightened birds and sounds of fleeing wings. I was the chief of all the heavens riding there, and when I looked behind me, all the twelve black horses reared and plunged and thundered and their manes and tails were whirling hail and their nostrils snorted lightning. And when I looked below again, I saw the slant hail falling and the long, sharp rain, and where we passed, the trees bowed low and all the hills were dim.

Now the earth was bright again as we rode. I could see the hills and valleys and the creeks and rivers passing under. We came above a place where three streams made a big one—a source of mighty waters—and something terrible was there. Flames were rising from the waters and in the flames a blue man lived. The dust was floating all about him in the air, the grass was short and withered, the trees were wilting, two-legged and four-legged beings lay there thin and panting, and wings too weak to fly.

Then the black horse riders shouted "Hoka hey!" and charged down upon the blue man, but were driven back. And the white troop shouted, charging, and was beaten; then the red troop and the yellow.

And when each had failed, they all cried together: "Eagle Wing Stretches, hurry!" And all the world was filled with voices of all kinds that cheered me, so I charged. I had the cup of water in one hand and in the other was the bow that turned into a spear as the bay and I swooped down, and the spear's head was sharp lightning. It stabbed the blue man's heart, and as it struck I could hear the thunder rolling and many voices that cried "Un-hee!," meaning I had killed. The flames died. The trees and grasses were not withered any more and murmured happily together, and every living being cried in gladness with whatever voice it had. Then the four troops of horsemen charged down and struck the dead body of the blue man, counting coup; and suddenly it was only a harmless turtle.

(Sioux Indian)

The Dream of Enkidu

Enkidu slept alone in his sickness & he poured out his heart to Gilgamesh, 'Last night I dreamed again, my friend. The heavens moaned & the earth replied; I stood alone before an awful being; his face was sombre like the black bird of the storm. He fell upon me with the talons of an eagle & he held me fast, pinioned with his claw, till I smothered; then he transformed me so that my arms became wings covered with feathers. He turned his stare towards me, & he led me away to the palace of Irkalla, the Queen of Darkness, to the house from which none who enters ever returns, down the road from which there is no coming back.

'There is the. house whose people sit in darkness; dust is their food & clay their meat. They are clothed like birds with wings for covering, they see no light, they sit in darkness. I entered the house of dust & I saw the kings of the earth, their crowns put away forever; rulers & princes, all those who once wore kingly crowns & ruled the world in the days of old. They who had stood in the place of the gods, like Anu & Enlil, stood now like servants to fetch baked meats in the house of dust, to carry cooked meat & cold water from the water-skin.

'In the house of dust which I entered were high-priests & acolytes, priests of the incantation & of ecstasy; there were servers of the temple, & there was Etana, that king of Kish whom the eagle carried to heaven in the days of old. I saw also Samuqan, god of cattle, & there was Ereshkigal the Queen of the Underworld; & Belit-Sheri squatted in front of her, she who is recorder of the gods & keeps the book of death. She held a tablet from which she read. She raised her head, she saw me & spoke: "Who has brought this one here?"

'Then I awoke like a man drained of blood who wanders alone
in a waste of rushes; like one whom the bailiff has seized &
his heart pounds with terror. O my brother, let some great
prince, some other, come when I am dead, or let some god
stand at your gate, let him obliterate my name & write his
own instead.'

Enkidu had peeled off his clothes & flung himself down, &
Gilgamesh listened to his words & wept quick tears, Gilgamesh
listened & his tears flowed. He opened his mouth & spoke to
Enkidu: 'Who is there in strong-walled Uruk who has wisdom
like this? *Strange things have been spoken, why does your
heart speak strangely? The dream was marvelous but the terror was great; we must treasure the dream whatever the terror; for the dream has shown that misery comes at last to the
healthy man, the end of life is sorrow.*'

And Gilgamesh lamented, 'Now I will pray to the great gods,
for my friend had an ominous dream.'

(Mesopotamia)

Pyramid Texts

1

To say: Face falls on face; face sees face.
A knife, colored black & green, goes out against it, until
  it has swallowed that
which it has licked.

(Utterance 228)

2

To say: Unas, I have trampled the mud of the water
  courses. Thot is the protector of Unas
when it is dark, when it is dark.

(Utterance 279)

3

To say: Doer, doer; passer, passer;
thy face behind thee; guard thyself against the great
  door.

(Utterance 280)

4

To say: A vulture has become pregnant with Unas in
  the night;
he is on thy horn, O pregnant cow.
If thou art green, well, Unas will be green, green as
  living plants.

(Utterance 351)

5

To say: This is the eye of Horus which he gave to
    Osiris,
thou has given it back to him, that he may equip
    his face with it;
but this is this eye of sweet odor—concerning which
    Horus spoke in the presence of Geb—
of incense & flame.
One pellet of incense;
three pellets of incense;
a bow.

(Utterance 598)

(Egypt)

THE KILLER
(after A'yu^{n}ini)

          Careful: my knife drills your soul
                    listen, whatever-your-name-is
                    One of the wolf people
          listen   I'll grind your saliva into the earth
          listen   I'll cover your bones with black flint
          listen   ″   ″   ″   ″   ″   ″   feathers
          listen   ″   ″   ″   ″   ″   ″   rocks
          Because you're going where it's empty
                    Black coffin out on the hill
          listen   the black earth will hide you, will
                    find you a black hut
                    Out where it's dark, in that country
          listen   I'm bringing a box for your bones
                    A black box
                    A grave with black pebbles
          listen   your soul's spilling out
          listen   it's blue

                              (Cherokee Indian)

A POISON ARROW

Enough poison to make
your head spin, & chains
to pin you down, & once
they've shot the arrow
& once it lands, well
it's just like the fly & the horse:
I mean a fly that's bitten one horse
will damn sure go after another
& I mean too that this arrow's
like a pregnant woman
            hungry for some meat
& even if it doesn't break your skin
            you die
& if it gets in & does its stuff
            you die
& if it sort of touches you & drops right out
            you die
      & as long as you stay out of my blood
      what do I care whose blood you get in
            kill him
      I won't stand in the way

This is a fire that I'm setting off
& this is a fire that I'm lifting up
& this is a shadow that's burning
& this is the sun that's burning
Because the poison I've got is stronger than bullets
      & it's louder than thunder
      & it's hotter than fire
& what do I care who it gets, kill him!
                  I won't stand in the way
As long as you stay out of my blood

                  (Africa: Hausa)

A Charm: To Cause the Gangosa That Eats Away the Nose

hornbill who lives at siga siga
hornbill who lives at siga siga
  in the lowana treetop
    he cuts he cuts
    he tears open
    standing he cuts
    he cuts flying
    he cuts from the nose
    from the temples
    he slices
    he cuts he cuts
    he tears open
    from the throat
    from the hip
    from the root of the tongue
    he tears open
    flying he cuts

hornbill who lives at darubia
hornbill who lives at darubia
  in the lowana treetop
    he slices it up
    he booms crying droning
    he cuts
    he tears open
    flying he cuts
    from the side of the body
    from the back of the neck
    from the root of the tongue

from the temples
flying he cuts
he cuts standing

hornbill who lives at lamona
hornbill who lives at lamona
  in the lowana treetop
    he booms crying droning
    he tears open
    flying he cuts
    he crouches bent over
    he crouches hands over kidneys
    he crouches head bent in arms
    he slices it up
    from the back of the neck
    from the navel
    from the small of the back
    he crouches hand over kidneys
    he booms crying droning
    he cuts
    he tears open
    flying he cuts
    he cuts standing
    from the root of the tongue
    from the throat
    from the kidneys
    from the guts
    he tears open
    flying he tears it

where?
    in what place?
for a ghost?
    for a woman?
for your skin?
    for mine?

for my vision?
my vision deceives me
    your shadow
    your spirit
I hide it   I bag it away
& they stagger back staggering stricken
they crouch   their heads in their arms
    & it comes at them
    howling & shrieking
& flying   it comes at them

(New Guinea: Dobu)

Snake Chant / Storm Chant

1

Winding throwing forward
writhing throwing forward
skin of snake rising
to heaven rising
heart beats continuously
tail wants to exterminate
tail wants to exterminate
tail wants to move
trembling.

2

In the West the clouds vegetate
in the East they are scattered
flowers unfold
white cloud unfolds
mistletoe branches ooze
lightning falls on mistletoe branches
ooze ibaratree tuffed
killed
weeping
paralyzed.
Crushed fire extending
fire having watched fire extending
wood for the fire
bends expands

lightning
beats breaks
water on the surface of clay
where the clouds were together
roaring
continuously
lightning.

(Africa: Kijoku)

Offering Flowers

(The Aztecs had a feast which fell out in the ninth month & which they called: The Flowers Are Offered)

& two days before the feast, when flowers were sought, all scattered over the mountains, that every flower might be found

& when these were gathered, when they had come to the flowers & arrived where they were, at dawn they strung them together; everyone strung them

& when the flowers had been threaded, then these were twisted & wound in garlands—long ones, very long, & thick—very thick

& when morning broke the temple guardians then ministered to Uitzilopochtli; they adorned him with garlands of flowers; they placed flowers upon his head

& before him they spread, strewed & hung rows of all the various flowers, the most beautiful flowers, the threaded flowers

then flowers were offered to all the rest of the gods

they were adorned with flowers; they were girt with garlands of flowers

flowers were placed upon their heads, there in the temples

& when midday came, they all sang & danced

quietly, calmly, evenly they danced

they kept going as they danced

. .

  .

I offer flowers. I sow flower seeds. I plant flowers. I assemble flowers. I pick flowers. I pick different flowers. I remove flowers. I seek flowers. I offer flowers. I arrange flowers. I thread a flower. I string flowers. I make flowers. I form them to be extending, uneven, rounded, round bouquets of flowers.

I make a flower necklace, a flower garland, a paper of flowers, a bouquet, a flower shield, hand flowers. I thread them. I string them. I provide them with grass. I provide them with leaves. I make a pendant of them. I smell something. I smell them. I cause one to smell something. I cause him to smell. I offer flowers to one. I offer him flowers. I provide him with flowers. I provide one with flowers. I provide one with a flower necklace. I provide him with a flower necklace. I place a garland on one. I provide him a garland. I clothe one in flowers. I clothe him in flowers. I cover one with flowers. I cover him with flowers. I destroy one with flowers. I destroy him with flowers. I injure one with flowers. I injure him with flowers.

I destroy one with flowers; I destroy him with flowers; I injure one with flowers: with drink, with food, with flowers, with tobacco, with capes, with gold. I beguile, I incite him with flowers, with words; I beguile him, I say, "I caress him with flowers. I seduce one. I extend one a lengthy discourse. I induce him with words."

I provide one with flowers. I make flowers, or I give them to one that someone will observe a feastday. Or I merely continue to give one flowers; I continue to place them in one's hand, I continue to offer them to one's hands. Or I provide one with a necklace, or I provide one with a garland of flowers.

(Aztec)

From THE NIGHT CHANT
(after Bitahatini)

In Tsegihi
In the house made of the dawn
In the house made of evening twilight
In the house made of dark cloud
In the house made of rain & mist, of pollen, of
   grasshoppers
Where the dark mist curtains the doorway
The path to which is on the rainbow
Where the zigzag lightning stands high on top
Where the he-rain stands high on top

O male divinity
With your moccasins of dark cloud, come to us
With your mind enveloped in dark cloud, come to us
With the dark thunder above you, come to us soaring
With the shapen cloud at your feet, come to us soaring
With the far darkness made of the dark cloud over your
   head, come to us soaring
With the far darkness made of the rain & mist over your
   head, come to us soaring
With the zigzag lightning flung out high over your head
With the rainbow hanging high over your head, come to us
   soaring
With the far darkness made of the rain & the mist on the ends
   of your wings, come to us soaring
With the far darkness of the dark cloud on the ends of your
   wings, come to us soaring
With the zigzag lightning, with the rainbow high on the ends
   of your wings, come to us soaring

With the near darkness made of the dark cloud of the rain & the
    mist, come to us
With the darkness on the earth, come to us

With these I wish the foam floating on the flowing water over
    the roots of the great corn
I have made your sacrifice
I have prepared a smoke for you
My feet restore for me
My limbs restore, my body restore, my mind restore, my voice
    restore for me
Today, take out your spell for me

Today, take away your spell for me
Away from me you have taken it
Far off from me it is taken
Far off you have done it

Happily I recover
Happily I become cool

My eyes regain their power, my head cools, my limbs regain their
    strength, I hear again

Happily the spell is taken off for me
Happily I walk, impervious to pain I walk, light within I walk,
    joyous I walk

Abundant dark clouds I desire
An abundance of vegetation I desire
An abundance of pollen, abundant dew, I desire

Happily may fair white corn come with you to the ends of the
    earth
Happily may fair yellow corn, fair blue corn, fair corn of all
    kinds, plants of all kinds, goods of all kinds, jewels of all kinds,
    come with you to the ends of the earth

With these before you, happily may they come with you
With these behind, below, above, around you, happily may they
   come with you
Thus you accomplish your tasks

Happily the old men will regard you
Happily the old women will regard you
The young men & the young women will regard you
The children will regard you
The chiefs will regard you

Happily as they scatter in different directions they will regard
   you
Happily as they approach their homes they will regard you

May their roads home be on the trail of peace
Happily may they all return

In beauty I walk
With beauty before me I walk
With beauty behind me I walk
With beauty above me I walk
With beauty above & about me I walk
It is finished in beauty
It is finished in beauty

                                        (Navaho Indian)

DEATH & DEFEAT

When Hare heard of Death, he started for his lodge & arrived there crying, shrieking, *My uncles & my aunts must not die!* And then the thought assailed him: *To all things death will come!* He cast his thoughts upon the precipices & they began to fall & crumble. Upon the rocks he cast his thoughts & they became shattered. Under the earth he cast his thoughts & all the things living there stopped moving & their limbs stiffened in death. Up above, towards the skies, he cast his thoughts & the birds flying there suddenly fell to the earth & were dead.

After he entered his lodge he took his blanket &, wrapping it around him, lay down crying. *Not the whole earth will suffice for all those who will die. Oh there will not be enough earth for them in many places!* There he lay in his corner wrapped up in his blanket, silent.

(Winnebago Indian)

Poem from A DISPUTE OVER SUICIDE

....

Behold, my name stinks
more than the odor of carrion birds
on summer days when the heaven is hot.

Behold, my name stinks
more than the odor of fishermen
& the shores of the pools they have fished.

Behold, my name stinks
more than that of a woman
of whom slander has been spoken concerning a man.

....

To whom should I speak today?
Brothers are evil
the friends of today love not.

To whom should I speak today?
Hearts are covetous
every man plundereth the goods of his fellow.

To whom should I speak today?
Yesterday is forgotten
men do not as they were done by nowadays.

To whom should I speak today?
There is no heart of man
whereon one might lean.

To whom should I speak today?
The righteous are no more
the land is given over to evil-doers.

To whom should I speak today?
There is a lack of companions
men have recourse to a stranger to tell their troubles.

To whom should I speak today?
I am heavy-laden with misery
& without a comforter.

. . . .

Death is in my eyes today
as when a sick man becomes whole
as the walking abroad after illness.

Death is in my eyes today
like the scent of myrrh
like sitting beneath the boat's sail on a breezy day.

Death is in my eyes today
like the smell of water-lilies
like sitting on the bank of drunkenness.

Death is in my eyes today
like a well-trodden road
as when men return home from a foreign campaign.

Death is in my eyes today
like the unveiling of the heaven
as when a man attains to that which he knew not.

Death is in my eyes today
like the desire of a man to see his home
when he hath passed many years in captivity.

(Egypt)

A Peruvian Dance Song

Wake up, woman
Rise up, woman
In the middle of the street
A dog howls

May the death arrive
May the dance arrive

Comes the dance
You must dance
Comes the death
You can't help it!

Ah! what a chill
Ah! what a wind

(Ayacucho Indian)

Death Song
by Juana Manwell (Owl Woman)

In the great night my heart will go out
Toward me the darkness comes rattling
In the great night my heart will go out

(Papago Indian)

The Relations of Wind, Rain, & Cloud to Human Beings after Death

(by Día!kwain)

1

The wind does thus when we die, our own wind blows; for we, who are human beings, we possess wind; we make clouds, when we die. Therefore, the wind does thus when we die, the wind makes dust, because it intends to blow, taking away our footprints, with which we had walked about while we still had nothing the matter with us; & our footprints, which the wind intends to blow away, would otherwise still lie plainly visible. For the thing would seem as if we still lived. Therefore, the wind intends to blow, taking away our footprints.

And, our gall, when we die, sits in the sky; it sits green in the sky, when we are dead.

2

For, mother & the others used to tell us about it, that girls are those whom the Rain carries off; & the girls remain at that water, to which the rain had taken them, girls with whom the Rain is angry. The Rain lightens, killing them; they become stars, while their appearance has been changed. They become stars. For, mother & the others used to tell us about it, that a girl, when the Rain has carried her off, becomes like a flower which grows in the water.

We who do not know are apt to do thus when we perceive them, as they stand in the water, when we see that they are so beautiful; we think, 'I will go & take the flowers which are standing in the water. For they are not a little beautiful.' Mother & the others said to us about it, that the flower—

when it saw that we went towards it—would disappear in the water. We should think, 'The flowers which were standing here, where are they? Why is it that I do not perceive them at the place where they stood, here?' It would disappear in the water, when it saw that we went towards it; we should not perceive it, for it would go into the water.

Therefore, mother & the others said to us about it, that we ought not to go to the flowers which we see standing in the water, even if we see their beauty. For they are girls whom the Rain has taken away, they resemble flowers; for they are the water's wives, & we look at them, leaving them alone. For we should also be like them in what they do.

3

The hair of our head will resemble clouds, when we die, when we in this manner make clouds. These things are those which resemble clouds; & we think that they are clouds. We, who do not know, we are those who think in this manner, that they are clouds. We, who know, when we see that they are like this, we know that they are a person's clouds; that they are the hair of his head. We, who know, we are those who think thus, while we feel that we seeing recognize the clouds, how the clouds do in this manner form themselves.

(Africa: Bushman)

THE MOURNING SONG OF SMALL-LAKE-UNDERNEATH

(by Hayi-a'k!ᵘ)

I always compare you to a drifting log with iron
    nails in it.
Let my brother float in, in that way.
Let him float ashore on a good sandy beach.
I always compare you, my mother, to the sun passing
    behind the clouds.
That is what makes the world dark.

(Tlingit Indian)

LAMENTATION

It is he, it is he,
The person with the spirit of an owl
It is he, it is he,
The person with the spirit of an owl
It is he, it is he

All the manitous are weeping
Because I go around weeping
Because I go around weeping
All the manitous are weeping

The sky will weep
The sky
At the end of the earth
The sky will weep

(Fox Indian)

The Flight of Quetzalcoatl

*

Then the time came for Quetzalcoatl too, when he felt the darkness twist in him like a river, as though it meant to weigh him down, & he thought to go then, to leave the city as he had found it & to go, forgetting there ever was a Tula

Which was what he later did, as people tell it who still speak about the Fire: how he first ignited the gold & silver houses, their walls speckled with red shells, & the other Toltec arts, the creations of man's hands & the imagination of his heart

& hid the best of them in secret places, deep in the earth, in mountains or down gullies, buried them, took the cacao trees & changed them into thorned acacias

& the birds he'd brought there years before, that had the richly colored feathers & whose breasts were like a living fire, he sent ahead of him to trace the highway he would follow towards the seacoast

When that was over he started down the road

*

A whole day's journey, reached

THE JUNCTURE OF THE TREE
(so-called)

> fat prominence of bark
> sky branches

I sat beneath it
saw my face/cracked
mirror

An old man
                       & named it
                       TREE OF OLD AGE

thus to name
it to raise stones
to wound the bark
with stones

to batter it with
stones the stones to
cut the bark to fester
in the bark

                   TREE OF OLD AGE

stone patterns: starting
from the roots they
reach the highest leaves

*

The next day gone with walking
Flutes were sounding in his ears

                   Companions' voices

He squatted on a rock to rest
he leaned his hands against the rock

                   Tula shining in the distance

: which he saw he
saw it & began to cry

he cried the cold sobs cut his throat

> A double thread of tears, a hailstorm
> beating down his face, the drops
> burn through the rock
> The drops of sorrow fall against the stone
> & pierce its heart

& where his hands had rested
shadows lingered on the rock: as if
his hands had pressed soft clay
As if the rock were clay

The mark too of his buttocks in the rock,
embedded there forever

The hollow of his hands preserved forever

> A place named TEMACPALCO

*

To Stone Bridge next

water swirling in the riverbed
a spreading turbulence of water

: where he dug a stone up
made a bridge across
> & crossed it

*

: who kept moving until he reached the Lake of Serpents,
   the elders waiting for him there, to tell him he would
   have to turn around, he would have to leave their country & go home

: who heard them ask where he was bound for, cut off from all a man remembers, his city's rites long fallen into disregard

: who said it was too late to turn around, his need still driving him, & when they asked again where he was bound, spoke about a country of red daylight & finding wisdom, who had been called there, whom the sun was calling

: who waited then until they told him he could go, could leave his Toltec things & go (& so he left those arts behind, the creations of man's hands & the imagination of his heart; the crafts of gold & silver, of working precious stones, of carpentry & sculpture & mural painting & book illumination & featherweaving)

: who, delivering that knowledge, threw his jewelled necklace in the lake, which vanished in those depths, & from then on that place was called The Lake of Jewels

*

Another stop along the line

    This time
    THE CITY OF THE SLEEPERS

And runs into a shaman

Says, you bound for somewhere honey

Says, the country of Red Daylight know it? expect to land there probe a little wisdom maybe

Says, no fooling try a bit of pulque brewed it just for you

Says, most kind but awfully sorry scarcely touch a drop you know

Says, perhaps you've got no choice perhaps I might not let you go now you didn't drink perhaps I'm forcing you against your will might even get you drunk come on honey drink it up

Drinks it with a straw

> So drunk he falls down fainting
> on the road & dreams &
> snores his snoring echoes very far

& when he wakes finds silence
& an empty town, his face
reflected & the hair shaved off

> Then calls it
> CITY OF THE SLEEPERS

*

There is a peak between Old Smokey
& The White Woman

Snow is falling
& fell upon him in those days

> & on his companions
> who were with him, on
> his dwarfs, his clowns
> his gimps

> It fell

till they were frozen
lost among the dead

The weight oppressed him
& he wept for them

He sang

> The tears are endless
> & the long sighs
> issue from my chest

Further out
THE HILL OF MANY COLORS

which he sought

Portents everywhere, those
dark reminders
of the road he walks

*

It ended on the beach
It ended with a hulk of serpents formed into a boat
& when he'd made it, sat in it & sailed away
A boat that glided on those burning waters, no one knowing when
    he reached the country of Red Daylight
It ended on the rim of some great sea
It ended with his face reflected in the mirror of its waves
The beauty of his face returned to him
& he was dressed in garments like the sun
It ended with a bonfire on the beach where he would hurl him-
    self
& burn, his ashes rising & the cries of birds
It ended with the linnet, with the birds of turquoise color, birds
    the color of wild sunflowers, red & blue birds
It ended with the birds of yellow feathers in a riot of bright gold
Circling till the fire had died out
Circling while his heart rose through the sky
It ended with his heart transformed into a star
It ended with the morning star with dawn & evening
It ended with his journey to Death's Kingdom with seven days of
    darkness
With his body changed to light
A star that burns forever in that sky

                                   (Aztec)

A Sequence of Songs
of the Ghost Dance Religion

1

My children,
When at first I liked the whites,
I gave them fruits,
I gave them fruits.

—Nawat, "Left Hand"
(Southern Arapaho)

2

Father have pity on me,
I am crying for thirst,
All is gone,
I have nothing to eat.

—Anon.
(Arapaho)

3

The father will descend
The earth will tremble
Everybody will arise,
Stretch out your hands.

—Anon.
(Kiowa)

4

The Crow—*Ehe'eye!*
I saw him when he flew down,
To the earth, to the earth.
He has renewed our life,
He has taken pity on us.

> —Moki, "Little Woman"
> (Cheyenne)

5

I circle around
The boundaries of the earth,
Wearing the long wing feathers
As I fly.

> —Anon.
> (Arapaho)

6

I'yehe! my children—
My children,
We have rendered them desolate.
The whites are crazy—Ahe'yuhe'yu!

> —"Sitting Bull" (Arapaho
> "Apostle of the Dance")

7

We shall live again.
We shall live again.

> —Anon.
> (Comanche)

THE STRING GAME

(by Día!kwain, after Xaa-ttin)

These were people
Who broke the string for me.
  Therefore
This place became like this for me,
On account of it.
Because the string broke for me,
  Therefore
The place does not feel to me
As the place used to feel to me,
  On account of it.
The place feels as if it stood open before me,
Because the string has broken for me.
  Therefore
The place does not feel pleasant to me
  Because of it.

                                (Africa: Bushman)

The Abortion

1

East, west, north, south
Tell me in which river
We shall put away the child
With rotting thatch below it
And jungly silk above
We will have it put away
You at the lower steps
I at the upper
We will wash & go to our homes
You by the lower path
I by the upper
We will go to our homes

2

O my love
My mind has broken
For the spring has ceased its flow
In the gully by the plantain
Drink cups of medicine
Swallow down some pills
Like a black cow
That has never had a calf
You will again be neat & trim

3

Like a bone
Was the first child born
And the white ants have eaten it

O my love, do not weep
Do not mourn
We two are here
And the white ants have eaten it

4

The field has not been ploughed
The field is full of sand
Little grandson
Why do you linger?
From a still unmarried girl
A two-months child has slipped
And that is why they stare

5

You by the village street
I by the track in the garden
We will take the child away
To the right is a bent tree
To the left is a stump
O my love
We will bury it between them

6

In the unploughed rice field, elder brother
What birds are hovering?
At midnight, the headman's middle daughter
Has taken it away
They are tearing the after-birth to pieces

(India: Santal)

The Tale of a Dog Which Made a Song
(by Unoko Masila)

It happened long ago when the country was desolate, during the war between Umatiwane & Umpangazita, the hoes rattled as the people were digging. They looked up, & the hoes said, What are you looking up at? It's only us hoes. Then a dog sat down on his buttocks & said:

Madhladhla! you have no pity
for my treasure.
Sing with me, Father
about the son of Ukadhlakadhla
his only son!

The people said, on hearing that song of the dog, This country
is dead.

(Africa: Zulu)

DEATH RITES I

Leader: The gates of Dan are shut.

Company: Shut are the gates of Dan.

Leader: The spirits of the dead flit hurrying there.
             Their crowd is like the flight of mosquitoes.
             The flight of mosquitoes which dance in the
                evening.

Company: Which dance in the evening.

Leader: The flight of mosquitoes which dance in the
                evening.
             When the night has turned completely black.
             When the sun has vanished.
             When the sun has turned completely black.
             The dance of the mosquitoes.
             The whirlwind of dead leaves.
             When the storm has growled.

Company: When the storm has growled.

Leader: They await him who will come.

Company: Him who will come.

Leader: Him who will say: You, come, you, go away!

Company: Him who will say: Come, go!

Leader: And Khvum will be with his children.

Company: With his children.

All: And this is the end.

                                    (Africa: Gabon Pygmy)

THE BOOK OF EVENTS (I)

LILY EVENTS

(1) A man and woman looking for lilies.

(2) All the people going down to look for lilies.

(3) Mud taken up looking for lilies.

(4) Washing the lilies in the water to remove the mud.

(5) Washing themselves off after the mud has got on them.

(6) Lilies in a basket.

(7) Walking from the lily place "to go look for a dry place to sit down."

(Australia: Arnhem Land)

Garbage Event

1. Pigs and chickens feed on the grass in an inhabited area until it is bare of grass.

2. Garbage is added to the area.

3. The participants defend the "abandoned beauty" and "town-quality" of the environment against all critics.

> *Sample defense:*
> *Critic.* This place is dirty.
> *Answer.* It is filthy.
>
> *Critic.* Why don't you clean it up?
> *Answer.* We like it the way it is.
>
> *Critic.* Garbage is unhealthy.
> *Answer.* The pigs feed better in it.
>
> *Critic.* It breeds mosquitoes.
> *Answer.* There are more mosquitoes in a jungle.

(Borneo: Dayak)

Beard Event

The men shave and fashion "Van Dyke" beards. The women paint.

(Australia: Arnhem Land)

Stone Fire Event

The old men build a stone fire and the men inhale the smoke and squat over the fire in order to allow the smoke to enter their anuses.

> *Realization.* All the men divide into groups around the various stone fires the old men have made. The women dance around them. All the men hold their heads over the fires and inhale the smoke and heat. They also squat over the fire to allow the smoke to enter the anal opening. Men, women and young boys then paint themselves with red ocher and kangaroo grease.

(Australia: Arnhem Land)

Climbing Event I

A great jar is set up with two small ladders leaning against its sides. The performers climb up one of the ladders & down the other throughout a whole night.

(Sarawak)

Climbing Event II
(Variation of Climbing Event I)

The performer lies on his back under a tree, sends a cord up & climbs up on it to a nest on top of the tree, then across to other trees, & at sunset down to the first tree again.

(Australia)

GIFT EVENT I

Bestow a gift on someone, to be repaid by an equivalent counter-gift after a lapse of time. Let as much as a year or more elapse between payments.

(New Guinea: Trobriand Islands)

GIFT EVENT II

Start by giving away different colored glass bowls.
Have everyone give everyone else a glass bowl.
Give away handkerchiefs and soap and things like that.
Give away a sack of clams and a roll of toilet paper.
Give away teddybear candies, apples, suckers and oranges.
Give away pigs and geese and chickens, or pretend to do so.
Pretend to be different things.
Have the women pretend to be crows, have the men pretend to be something else.
Talk Chinese or something.
Make a narrow place at the entrance of a house and put a line at the end of it that you have to stoop under to get in.
Hang the line with all sorts of pots and pans to make a big noise.
Give away frying pans while saying things like "Here is this frying pan worth $100 and this one worth $200."
Give everyone a new name.
Give a name to a grandchild or think of something and go and get everything.

(Kwakiutl Indian)

Marriage Event

for Carolee Schneemann

(1) Large quantities of food & cloth are piled in a heap.

(2) The Bridegroom appears outside his own house, where a continuous stream of human bodies leads from his doorway to that of his Father-in-Law.

(3) As many people as there are permit him to walk over their backs as they lie prostrate on the ground.*

(4) When the Bridegroom reaches the Father-in-Law's house, three old women prostrate themselves so as to form a living chair for him.

(5) A fish is brought forward &, with the aid of a sharp stick, is cut up & diced on a human body. It is presented to the Bridegroom who eats it raw.

(6) The piles of food & cloth are distributed to as many people as there are, & the food is eaten. Afterwards the street of human bodies is again formed for the return.

(7) The Bridegroom's family perform the same event for the bride.

(Polynesia: Hervey Islands)

* Should the numbers be insufficient to reach the Father-in-Law's house, those first walked-on rise up quickly & run through the crowd, again to take their places in front.

GOING-AROUND EVENT

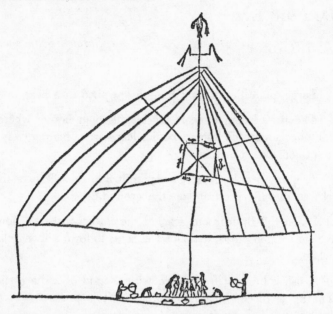

1. A long pole is fixed in the middle of a house, the upper end of which protrudes from the vent-hole. On it are two double tassels & a seal-skin float, to the flippers of which are fastened the pelt of a fox & an iron kettle. A square frame made of paddles surmounted by several wooden images of manned boats & whales is suspended halfway up the pole, by means of which people may turn the pole with the frame. Several walrus-heads form the central object of the event.

2. The wheel is turned around as quickly as possible, & in the direction of the sun's course, by people of both sexes, while several other persons beat the drum. All sing various tunes of their own choice. At last those turning the wheel stop; & the men, still running in the same direction, begin to seize women from all over the house. Every man has the right to sleep that night with the woman he has caught.

(Asiatic Eskimo)

LANGUAGE EVENT I

Abolish words bearing any affinities with the names of the participants, and substitute new ones in their stead.

(Paraguay: Abipone Indian)

LANGUAGE EVENT II

Imply in speech some physical characteristic of the person addressed or spoken of, partly by means of suffixed elements, partly by means of "consonantal play."* The physical classes indicated by these methods may include children, unusually fat or heavy people, unusually short adults, those suffering from some defect of the eye, hunchbacks, those that are lame, left-handed persons, and circumcised males.

(British Columbia: Nootka Indian)

* Consonantal play consists either in altering certain consonants of a word to other consonants that are phonetically related to them, or in inserting meaningless consonants or consonant clusters in the body of the word.

LANGUAGE EVENT III

All parts of a hut are named, and the names have references to the sexual relations between man and woman.

Question. What is the doorstep?
Answer. The doorstep is a woman.

Q. And the crossbar over the door, what is that?
A. The crossbar is a man.

Q. When the door is being put in, what is that?
A. That is when the man comes.

Q. And the hingepin on the door?
A. His penis.

Q. What is the ceiling of the hut and the floor beneath?
A. A boy and a girl who are mating.

Q. And the grass bundles hanging down above them?
A. The python.

Q. Then what is the beaten floor?
A. That is my aunt.

Q. Who has been beating the floor then?
A. A hand.

Q. But what is the door?
A. The door is the crocodile.

Q. And if the door is closed, what is that?
A. The crocodile stretching out.

Q. What is the door from the outside?
A. The crocodile's back.

Q. And if that one is closed?
A. A pregnant woman.

Q. Then what is a door that is open?
A. The woman after delivery.

Q. What are the two sides of the river?
A. A boy and a girl when they meet.

Q. But which one is the crocodile that bites?
A. That is the top one, the one below has no sense.

Q. What is the wall in front of you?
A. A man that is virile.

Q. And the wall behind you?
A. A man who is impotent.

Q. Then what is this housepost?
A. A man who rips a girl apart.

Q. And that one?
A. The striker of the thighs, the crusher of the little ribs.

(Africa: Venda)

FRIENDSHIP DANCE

Preparation

Men participants form a single file and are joined by women who dance in front of them as partners. During the song they dance counterclockwise with a shuffling trot, and in the intervals walk in a circle. At the song, when the leader begins to insert words suggestive of intimacy (see translations below), the humorous gestures and acts of the pantomime begin.

Song & Pantomime

A free rendering of the song is as follows: "Ha!-Ha! I am called an old man [poor and ugly] but I am not this. I am going to take this woman home with me, as I did not know that there was such a good shell-shaker, none like her. I'll take her home to my town."

During the song the leader may raise his hands, palms in, to shoulder height, at times turning halfway to the left and moving sideways. Throughout he is imitated by the men. Toward the end, the leader reaches the climax of his humor in the following phrase, "Ha!-Ha! We are going to touch each other's privates"; the men, holding their partners' hands, suit actions to words.

Movements (Sequence of Intimacy)

1. Greeting, holding hands facing.
2. Side by side, holding hands crossed.
3. Facing, putting palms upon partners' palms.
4. Placing hands on partners' shoulders while facing.
5. Placing arms over partners' shoulders while side by side.
6. Placing hats on women partners' heads while facing.

7. Stroking partners under chin while facing.
8. Putting hands on female partners' breasts while side by side.
9. Touching the clothing over the partners' genitals while side by side.

(Cherokee Indian)

GREASE FEAST EVENT

A great fire is lighted in the center of the host's house. The flames leap up to the roof and the guests are almost scorched by the heat, but they do not stir, else the host's fire has conquered them. Even when the roof begins to burn and the fire attacks the rafters, they must appear unconcerned. The host alone has the right to send a man up to the roof to put out the fire. While the feast is in progress the host sings a scathing song ridiculing his rival and praising himself. Then the grease is filled in large spoons and passed to the guests first. If a person thinks he has given a greater grease feast than that offered by the host, he refuses the spoon. Then he runs out of the house to fetch a copper plate "to squelch with it the fire." The host proceeds at once to tie a copper plate to each of his houseposts. If he should not do so, the person who refused the spoon would on returning strike the posts with the copper plate, which is considered equal to striking the host's face. Then the man who went to fetch his plate breaks it and gives it to the host. This is called "squelching the host's fire."

Squelching Song

1. I thought another one was causing the smoky weather. I am the only one on earth—the only one in the world who makes thick smoke rise from the beginning of the year to the end.

2. What will my rival say now—that "spider woman"; what will he pretend to do next? The words of that "spider woman" do not go a straight way. Will he not brag that he is going to give away canoes, that he is going to break coppers, that he is going to give a grease feast? Such will be the words of the "spider woman," and therefore your face is dry and mouldy, you who are standing in front of the stomachs of your guests.

3. Nothing will satisfy you; but sometimes I treated you so roughly that you begged for mercy. Do you know what you will be like? You will be like an old dog, and you will spread your legs before me when I get excited. This I throw into your face, you whom I always tried to vanquish; whom I have mistreated; who does not dare to stand erect when I am eating.

(Kwakiutl Indian)

Peacemaking Event

Preparations

An open area of ground is set aside, and across it is erected what is called a *koro-cop*. Posts are put up in a line, to the tops of these is attached a length of strong cane, and from the cane are suspended bundles of shredded palm leaf (*koro*). The "visitors" are the forgiving party, while the home party are those who have committed the last act of hostility.

Movements

The visitors enter dancing, the step being that of the ordinary dance. The women of the home party mark the time by clapping their hands on their thighs. The visitors dance forward in front of the men standing at the *koro-cop,* and then, still dancing all the time, pass backwards and forwards between the standing men, bending their heads as they pass beneath the suspended cane. The visitors may make threatening gestures at the men standing at the *koro-cop*, and every now and then break into a shrill shout. The men at the *koro* stand silent and motionless.

After dancing thus for a little time, the leader of the visitors approaches the man at one end of the *koro* and, taking him by the shoulders from the front, leaps vigorously up and down to the time of the dance, thus giving the man he holds a good shaking. The leader then passes on to the next man in the row while another of the visitors goes through the same performance with the first man. This is continued until each of the dancers has "shaken" each of the standing men. The dancers then pass under the *koro* and shake their enemies in the same manner from the back. After a little more shaking the dancers retire, and the women of the visiting group come forward and dance in much the same way, each woman giving each man of the other group a good shaking.

When the women have been through their dance the two parties of men and women sit down and weep together.

(Andaman Islands)

Booger Event

Participants

A company of four to ten or more masked men (called "boogers"), occasionally a couple of women companions. Each dancer is given a personal name, usually obscene; for example:

    Black Man
    Black Ass
    Frenchie
    Big Balls
    Asshole
    Rusty Asshole
    Burster (penis)
    Swollen Pussy
    Long Prick
    Sweet Prick
    Piercer
    Fat Ass
    Long Haired Pussy
    Etcetera.

Prelude

The dancers enter. The audience and the dancers break wind.

First Action

The masked men are systematically malignant. They act mad, fall on the floor, hit at the spectators, push the men spectators as though to get at their wives and daughters, etc.

Second Action

The boogers demand "girls." They may also try to fight and dance. If they do, the audience tries to divert them.

Third Action

Booger Dance Song. The name given to the booger should be taken as the first word of the song. This is repeated any number of times, while the owner of the name dances a solo, performing as awkward and grotesque steps as he possibly can. The audience applauds each mention of the name, while the other dancers indulge in exhibitionism, e.g., thrusting their buttocks out and occasionally displaying toward the women in the audience large phalli concealed under their clothing. These phalli may contain water, which is then released as a spray.

Interlude

Everyone smokes.

Fourth Action

A number of women dancers, equaling the number of boogers, enter the line as partners. As soon as they do, the boogers begin their sexual exhibitions. They may close upon the women from the rear, performing body motions in pseudo-intercourse; as before, some may protrude their large phalli and thrust these toward their partners with appropriate gestures and body motions.

Postlude

The rest of the performance consists of miscellaneous events chosen by the audience.

(Cherokee Indian)

Sea Water Event

The tides of the ocean and the floods are danced; certain birds and animals are included.

(Australia: Arnhem Land)

FURTHER SEA WATER EVENTS

(1) An island far out in the sea.

(2) Lightning that strikes out in the middle ocean and in the east.

(3) Black cloud.

(4) A wind coming in from the sea.

(5) Calm sea water.

(6) Heavy waves on the surface of the sea.

(7) A small bird that dives into the sea for fish.

(8) Kingfish.

(9) A flat white fish.

(10) Whale.

(11) Diamond fish.

(12) Crocodile.*

(13) A plank floating on the tide and coming toward the shore.

(14) A hollow log floating on the incoming tide.

(15) A small oyster found on the plank.

(16) Coconuts floating on an incoming tide.

(17) The country where the coconut, hollow log and plank come from.

(18) The back of a turtle (near land).

(19) The head of a tortoise-shell turtle.

(20) People where the coconuts come from.

(21) Paddle.

(22) Canoe.

(23) Noise the paddle makes on the gunwale.

* Further Directions. "The crocodile sings lightning when it comes in the east and that's when the crocodile lays his eggs and that's when the sting ray gets fat and good to eat. When that lightning comes and the rain comes that makes the sting ray fat, that makes the crocodile lay his eggs."

(24) A small bird crying out on the beach when it sees the people coming in.

(25) Paddle.

(26) The paddles being thrown on the beach.

(27) Canoe rolling about on the beach with the sea hitting against it.

(28) Men walking along on the beach.

(29) Men looking for turtle eggs in the sand beach.

(30) Men following the tracks of turtles going toward the nest.

(31) The turtle nest.

(32) Turtle eggs.
The men drink the white of the turtle egg.

(33) Basket.
The men put the eggs in the basket.

(34) Putting the basket on the shoulder and carrying it down to the shade.

(35) Putting the eggs down in the shade.

(36) Walking fast down the large path to the well.

(37) Cleaning the dirt and refuse out of the well.

(38) Washing oneself with the water because of the dirt on the body from cleaning out the well.

(39) Taking off ornaments and drying them on the well.

(40) Going back to the turtle beach, cleaning off dirt under the big trees.

(41) Gathering wood for a fire.

(42) Fire burning.

(43) Coals of a fire smoking.

(44) People are sleepy and they sleep.

(45) Waking up.

(46) Smoking a cigarette.

(47) Red cloud.

(Australia: Arnhem Land)

Noise Event

1. Make a joyful noise unto the Lord, all the earth: make a loud noise, and rejoice, and sing praise.

2. Sing unto the Lord with the harp; with the harp, and the voice of a psalm.

3. With trumpets and sound of cornet make a joyful noise before the Lord.

4. Let the sea roar, and the fullness thereof; the world, and they that dwell therein.

5. Let the floods clap their hands: let the hills be joyful together.

(Hebrew)

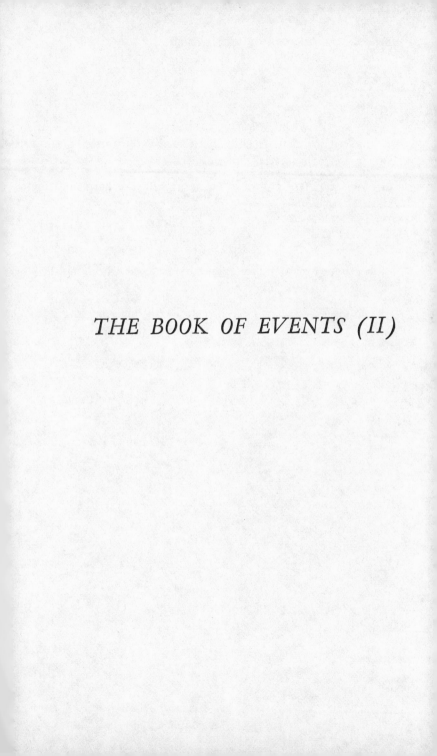

THE BOOK OF EVENTS (II)

TAMING THE STORM

A Two-Shaman Vision & Event

I

[On the third evening of the storm we were solemnly invited to
attend a shaman seance in one of the snow houses. The man who
invited us was a pronouncedly blond Eskimo, bald & with a
reddish beard, as well as a slight tinge of blue in his eyes. His
name was Kigiuna, "sharp tooth."]

The hall consisted of two snow huts built together, the entrance leading on to the middle of the floor, & the two snow-
built platforms on which one slept were opposite one another.
One of the hosts, Tamuánuaq, "the little mouthful," received
me cordially & conducted me to a seat. The house, which was
four meters wide & six meters long, had such a high roof that
the builder had had to stay it with two pieces of driftwood,
which looked like magnificent pillars in the white hall of snow.
And there was so much room on the floor that all the neighbors'
little children were able to play "catch" round the pillars during
the opening part of the festival.

The preparations consisted of a feast of dried salmon, blubber
& frozen, unflensed seal carcasses. They hacked away at the
frozen dinner with big axes & avidly swallowed the lumps of
meat after having breathed upon them so that they should not
freeze the skin off lips & tongue.

"Fond of food, hardy & always ready to feast," whispered
"Eider Duck" to me, his mouth full of frozen blood.

2

The shaman of the evening was Horqarnaq, "Baleen," a young
man with intelligent eyes & swift movements. There was no de-
ceit in his face, & perhaps for that reason it was long before he
fell into a trance. He explained before commencing that he had
few helpers. There was his dead father's spirit & its helping
spirit, a giant with claws so long that they could cut a man right
through simply by scratching him; & then there was a figure
that he had created himself of soft snow, shaped like a man—
a spirit who came when he called. A fourth & mysterious helping spirit was Aupilalánguaq, a remarkable stone he had once
found when hunting caribou; it had a lifelike resemblance to a
head & neck, & when he shot a caribou near to it he gave it a
head-band of the long hairs from the neck of the animal.

He was now about to summon these helpers, & all the women
of the village stood around in a circle & encouraged him.

"You can & you do it so easily because you are so strong,"
they said flatteringly, & incessantly he repeated:

*"It is a hard thing to speak the truth. It is difficult to make
hidden forces appear."*

But the women around him continued to excite him, & at
last he slowly became seized with frenzy. Then the men joined
in, the circle around him became more & more dense, & all
shouted inciting things about his powers & his strength.

Baleen's eyes become wild. He distends them & seems to be
looking out over immeasurable distance; now & then he spins
round on his heel, his breathing becomes agitated, & he no
longer recognizes the people around him: *"Who are you?"* he
cries.

"Your own people!" they answer.

"Are you all here?"

"Yes, except those two who went east on a visit."

Again Baleen goes round the circle, looks into the eyes of all, gazes ever more wildly about him, & at last repeats like a tired man who has walked far & at last gives up:

"*I cannot. I cannot.*"

At that moment there is a gurgling sound, & a helping spirit enters his body. A force has taken possession of him & he is no longer master of himself or his words. He dances, jumps, throws himself over among the clusters of the audience & cries to his dead father, who has become an evil spirit. It is only a year since his father died, & his mother, the widow, still sorrowing over the loss of her provider, groans deeply, breathes heavily & tries to calm her wild son; but all the others cry in a confusion of voices, urging him to go on, & to let the spirit speak.

3

The seance has lasted an hour, an hour of howling & invoking of unknown forces, when something happens that terrifies us, who have never before seen the storm-god tamed. Baleen leaps forward & seizes good-natured old Kigiuna, who is just singing a pious song to the Mother of the Sea Beasts, grips him swiftly by the throat & brutally flings him backwards & forwards in the midst of the crowd. At first both utter wailing, throaty screams, but little by little Kigiuna is choked & can no longer utter a sound; but suddenly there is a hiss from his lips, & he too has been seized with ecstasy. He no longer resists, but follows Baleen, who still has him by the throat, & they tumble about, quite out of their minds. The men of the house have to stand in front of the big blubber lamps to prevent their being broken or upset; the women have to help the children up on to the platform to save them from being knocked down in the scrimmage; and so it goes on for a little while, until Baleen has squeezed all the life out of his opponent, who is now being dragged after him like a lifeless bundle. Only then does he release his hold, & Kigiuna falls heavily to the floor.

There is a deathly silence in the house. Baleen is the only one who continues his wild dance, until in some way or other his

eyes become calm & he kneels in front of Kigiuna & starts to rub
& stroke his body to revive him. Slowly Kigiuna is brought back
to life, very shakily he is put back on his feet, but scarcely has
he come to his senses again when the same thing is repeated.
Three times he is killed in this manner! But when Kigiuna comes
to life for the third time, it is he who falls into a trance &
Baleen who collapses. The old seer rises up in his curious, much
too obese might, yet rules us by the wildness in his eyes & the
horrible, reddish-blue sheen that has come over his face through
all the ill-usage he has been subjected to. All feel that this is a
man whom death has just touched, & they involuntarily step
back when, with his foot on Baleen's chest, he turns to the
audience & announces the vision he sees. With a voice that
trembles with emotion he cries out over the hall:

*"The sky is full of naked beings rushing through the air.
Naked people, naked men, naked women, rushing along &
raising gales & blizzards.*

*"Don't you hear the noise? It swishes like the beating of the
wings of great birds in the air. It is the fear of naked people, it is
the flight of naked people!*

*"The weather spirit is blowing the storm out, the weather
spirit is driving the weeping snow away over the earth, & the
helpless storm-child Narsuk shakes the lungs of the air with his
weeping.*

*"Don't you hear the weeping of the child in the howling of the
wind?*

*"And look! Among all those naked crowds, there is one, one
single man, whom the wind has made full of holes. His body is
like a sieve & the wind whistles through the holes: Tju, Tju-u,
Tju-u-u! Do you hear him? He is the mightiest of all the wind-
travellers.*

*"But my helping spirit will stop him, will stop them all. I see
him coming calmly towards me. He will conquer, will conquer!
Tju, tju-u! Do you hear the wind? Sst, sst, ssst! Do you see the*

*spirits, the weather, the storm, sweeping over us with the swish
of the beating of great birds' wings?"*

At these words Baleen rises from the floor, & the two shamans,
whose faces are now transfigured after this tremendous storm
sermon, sing with simple, hoarse voices a song to the Mother of
the Sea Beasts:

> *Woman, great woman down there*
> *Send it back, send it away from us, that evil!*
> *Come, come, spirit of the deep!*
> *One of your earth-dwellers*
> *Calls to you,*
> *Asks you to bite his enemies to death!*
> *Come, come, spirit of the deep!*

When the two had sung the hymn through, all the other voices
joined in, a calling, wailing chorus of distressed people. No one
knew for what he was calling, no one worshipped anything; but
the ancient song of their forefathers put might into their minds.

And suddenly it seemed as if nature around us became alive.
We saw the storm riding across the sky in the speed & thronging
of naked spirits. We saw the crowd of fleeing dead men come
sweeping through the billows of the blizzard, & all visions &
sounds centered in the wing-beats of the great birds for which
Kigiuna had made us strain our ears.

(Copper Eskimo)

CORONATION EVENT & DRAMA

CAST

Horus	The new king
Corpse of Osiris	Mummy representing the old king
Thoth	The chief officiant
Isis & Nephthys	Two wailing women
Followers of Horus	Princes; staff of embalmers, morticians, etc.
Set & henchmen	Temple & sacral personnel

SCENE I

(ACTION): THE CEREMONIAL BARGE IS EQUIPPED.

Horus requests his Followers to equip him with the Eye of power.

(ACTION): THE LAUNCHING OF THE BARGE MARKS THE OPENING UP OF THE NILE & INAUGURATES THE CEREMONY OF INSTALLING OR RECONFIRMING THE KING.

Horus (to his Followers):
Bring me the EYE
whose spel
opens this river.

Horus also instructs his Followers to bring upon the scene the god Thoth, who is to act as master of ceremonies, & the corpse of his father, Osiris.

(ACTION): BEER IS PROFFERED.

SCENE II

(ACTION): THE ROYAL PRINCES LOAD EIGHT mnsh JARS INTO THE BOW OF THE BARGE.

Thoth loads the corpse of Osiris upon the back of Set, so that it may be carried up to heaven.

Thoth (to Set):
  See, you cannot
  match this
  god, the stronger.
    (to Osiris):
  As your Heart masters his Cold.

  (ACTION): THE ELDERS OF THE COURT ARE MUSTERED.

SCENE III

(ACTION): A RAM IS SENT RUSHING FROM THE PEN, TO
SERVE AS A SACRIFICE IN BEHALF OF THE KING. MEAN-
WHILE—AS AT ALL SUCH SACRIFICES—THE EYE OF HORUS
IS DISPLAYED TO THE ASSEMBLY.

Isis appears on the scene.

Isis (to Thoth):
  That your
  lips
  may open
  that the Word may
  come
  may give the EYE
  to Horus.

  (ACTION): THE ANIMAL IS SLAUGHTERED. ITS MOUTH
  FALLS OPEN UNDER THE KNIFE.

Isis (to Thoth):
  Open thy mouth—
  the Word!

SCENE IV

(ACTION): PRIESTS SLAUGHTER THE RAM. THE CHIEF OFFI-
CIANT HANDS A PORTION TO THE KING & FORMALLY PRO-
CLAIMS HIS ACCESSION.

Thoth conveys the Eye to Horus.

Thoth (to Horus):
   Son takes his
   father's
   place: the Prince
   is Lord.

   (ACTION): THE KING IS ACCLAIMED BY THE ASSEMBLY.

SCENE V

   (ACTION): GRAIN IS STREWN UPON THE THRESHING
   FLOOR.

Horus requests his followers to convey to him the Eye which survived the combat with Set.

Horus (to his Followers):
   Bringing your wheat
   to the barn
   or bringing me
   THE EYE
   wrenched from Set's
   clutches.

SCENE VI

   (ACTION): THE CHIEF OFFICIANT HANDS TWO LOAVES
   TO THE KING.

The two loaves symbolize the two eyes of Horus: the one retained by Set, & the one restored to Horus by Thoth.

Thoth (to Horus):
   See, this is THE EYE
   I bring you:
   EYE-YOU-WILL-NEVER-LOSE.

   (ACTION): DANCERS ARE INTRODUCED.

Horus (to Thoth):
   My EYE that dances for joy before you.

SCENE VII

(ACTION): A FRAGRANT BOUGH IS HOISTED ABOARD THE
BARGE.

*The corpse of Osiris is hoisted onto the back of Set, his van-
quished assailant.*

The Gods (to Set):
O Set! who never will escape
The-one-who-masters-masters-thee.

Horus (gazing on the corpse of Osiris):
O this noble
body, this
lovely beautiful
body.

(ACTION): THE WORKMEN STAGGER UNDER THE WEIGHT
OF THE BOUGH.

Horus (to Set):
You bend under him, you plot no more against him!

(Egypt)

Dance Scene: The Death of Tlacahuepan

Poet:

In the flower-covered Hall of the Eagles
Teoxinmac makes his song :   his beautiful song.

My Prince Motecuzoma:
Are they there now, lined up
in the realm of death?
Do they still weep on the jade staircase
by the shore of sacred water?

Like bunches of emeralds, the quetzal plumes grow green again.
The hearts of gold flowers open in your house.

My Prince Motecuzoma:
Are they there now, lined up
in the realm of death?
Do they still weep on the jade staircase
by the shore of sacred water?

So you must record and remember of the wall of Acapechopan:
The adornments of quetzal plumes fly there.
In Matlacueye's skirt the final disgrace followed:
there the Chichimeca Princes wept.

Motecuzoma:

Thus I came to life
and thus I was born.
I am Motecuzoma:
with my needle of cactus
with my darts in rain
with my white bracelets.

Another Singer:

Could it be true that nothing matters to us?
They search for fragrant flowers:
they are much desired.
There is death in flowering water
there is death in delicious water:
Tlacahuepan and Ixtilcuechahuac!

(*There follows an interlude of song without words.*)

How well the White Eagle
is colored by smoke.
Now the quetzal and red quacamaya
are colored by smoke within the sky:
they are Tlacahuepan and Ixtilcuechahuac!

(*Interlude of song without words.*)

Chorus:

Where are you going? Where are you going?

The Heroes:

To war. To the divine water:
there where men color our Mother Itzpapálotl.
To the battlefield.

Chorus:

Dust rises
in the blazing water:
Camaxtil's heart is full of pain.
Matlacueyetzin, Macuilmalinaltzin:
the battle is like a flower:
it is placed in your hands
it is placed there now.

The Poet:

Where will we go where there is no death?
My heart weeps for this.
    Be strong:
    no one must live here.
Then the Princes go to death.
My heart is humbled!
    Be strong:
    no one must live here.

Second Part. A Poet Alone:

Inside the flower-covered place
golden and red flowers have been woven together.
Fragrant flowers are distributed and scattered:
they fall like rain in the flowery place.
With them the men are decorated
with them you are made happy
here in the flowery patio.
Now the flowers of sadness sadly are spilled.
Now they are enjoying themselves.

Now is sung:

Your heart is a rose jade and a book of pictures
oh Chichimeca Motecuzoma.
Precious golden and red birds
fly over the flowering water.
Rest now and amuse yourself
oh displeased Motecuzoma:
among the precious flowers is the flower of life.
Precious golden and red birds
fly over the flowering water.

Still sung:

Oh Motecuzoma! Gaze at the great temple:
see where the beautiful plumes are hanging.
Coming down now are men who have flowers the color of gold.
Now the Otami sings: now he is weeping for you.
You are a Chichimeca.
Green lights shine over the mountains.
See, fellow Tlaxcaltecas:
our Father God is stretched out.
Motecuzoma, you rule over
the many-colored flowers.
And this is the house of God:
he who dwells within the sky.

Motecuzoma:

My acacia flowers
my cactus flowers:
their hearts are opening.

(Aztec)

AFRICA

GHOSTS & SHADOWS

> The soul is a dark forest.
> —D. H. Lawrence

Ghosts in this forest, shadows
thrown back by the night
Or in daylight
  like bats that drink from our veins
  & hang from moist walls, in deep caves
Behind this green moss, these awful white stones
We pray to know who has seen them
  Shadows thrown back by the night
We pray to know who has seen them

(Gabon Pygmy)

THE CHAPTER OF CHANGING INTO PTAH

1

I eat bread.

I drink ale.

I hoist up my garments.

I cackle like the Smen goose.

I land on that place hard by the Sepulchre for the festival of the Great God.

All that is abominable, all that is abominable I will not eat.

Shit is abominable, I will not eat it.

All that is abominable to my Ka will not enter my body.

I will live on what the gods live.

I will live & I will be master of their cakes.

And I will eat them under the trees of the dweller in the house of Hathor My Lady.

I will make an offering.

My cakes are in Busiris, my offerings are in Heliopolis.

I wrap a robe around me woven by the goddess Tait.

I will stand up & sit down wherever it pleases me.

My head is like the head of Ra.

I am complete like Tem.

2

I will come forth.

My tongue is like the tongue of Ptah

& my throat like that of Hathor.

With my mouth I remember the words of Tem my father.

Tem forced the woman, the wife of Keb

& broke the heads of those around him

so that people were afraid of him

& proclaimed him

& made me his heir on Keb's earth.
Then I mastered their women.
Keb refreshed me.
Keb lifted me up to his throne.
Those in Heliopolis bowed their heads to me.
I am their bull.
I am stronger than the Lord-of-the-Hour.
I have fucked all their women.
I am Master for millions of years.

(Egypt)

Prayer to Thot

Be praised Lord of the house
You white haired monkey, beautiful in body
And gentle in mind, beloved by everyone.

My God Thot is of precious stones,
He lights up the earth with his sparkle,
The moon disc on his head is of red jasper,
His phallus is of quartz.

His love leaps on his eyebrows;
He opens his mouth to give life;
My house is full of joy since Thot entered,
It thrives and flourishes since he dwells here.

Thot, I fear nothing,
Since you became my strength.

(Egypt)

THE CANNIBAL HYMN

The sky is heavy, it is raining stars.
The arches of the sky are cracking; the bones of the earthgod
 tremble;
The Pleiads are struck dumb by the sight of Unas
Who rises towards the sky, transfigured like a god,
Who lives off his father and eats his mother.
He is the bull of the sky; his heart lives off the divine beings;
He devours their intestines, when their bodies are charged with
 magic.
It is he who passes judgment, when the elders are slaughtered.
He is Lord over all meals.
He ties the sling with which he catches his prey,
He prepares the meal himself.
It is he who eats men and lives off the gods.
He has servants who execute his orders.
Skullgrabber catches them for him, like bulls with a lasso.
Headerect watches them for him and brings them to him;
Willow-croucher binds them
And tears their intestines from their body,
Winepresser slaughters them
And cooks a meal for him in his evening pots.
Unas swallows their magic powers
He relishes their glory.
The large ones among them are his morning meal,
the medium size are his lunch,
The small ones among them he eats for supper.
Their senile men and women he burns as incense.
The great ones in the North sky lay the fire for him
With the bones of the elders,
Who simmer in the cauldrons themselves;
Look, those in the sky work and labor for Unas.
They polish the cookingpots for him with thighs of their wives.

O Unas has reappeared in the sky,
He is crowned as Lord of the Horizon,
Those he meets in his path he swallows raw.
He has broken the joints of the gods,
Their spines and their vertebrae.
He has taken away their hearts,
He has swallowed the red crown
He has eaten the green crown,
He feeds on the lungs of the Wise,
He feasts, as he now lives on hearts,
And on the power they contain.
He thrives luxuriously, for all their power is in his belly,
His nobility can no longer be taken away.
He has consumed the brain of every god,
His life time is eternity,
His limit is infinity.

(Egypt)

INCANTATION BY ISIS
FOR REVIVAL OF THE DEAD OSIRIS

come to thy beloved one

BEAUTIFUL BEING   triumphant!

come to Thy sister   come to thy wife
Arise! Arise! Glorious Brother!
from thy bier that I may
hover near thy genital
forever

Beautiful Boy my brother come to my breasts
take there of that milk to thy fill
thy nuts will I guard upon
nor shall the Fiends of Darkness tear at your Eye

come to your house   come to your house

BEAUTIFUL BEING   !Boy Body!

that your cock glide forward in radiance
to our pavilion

          Osiris!   Osiris!

when the Ra- (Disc) glides onward in the Sun-boat

  ∫ flamespurts spew off the prow

                O may I catch thy spurts o brother
                    as the shrieking human
                          catches the sun!

                          (Egypt)

Conversations in Courtship

. . . .

He says:

I adore the gold-gleaming Goddess,
                    Hathor the dominant,
                                and I praise her.
I exalt the Lady of Heaven,
     I give thanks to the Patron.
She hears my invocation
     and has fated me to my lady,
Who has come here, herself, to find me.
     What felicity came in with her!
I rise exultant
     in hilarity
               and triumph when I have said:
                              Now,
And behold her.
     Look at it!
                    The young fellows fall at her feet.
Love is breathed into them.

I make vows to my Goddess,
     because she has given me this girl for my own.
I have been praying three days,
     calling her name.
For five days she has abandoned me.

She says:

I went to his house, and the door was open.
     My beloved was at his ma's side
          with brothers and sisters about him.

Everybody who passes has sympathy for him,
   an excellent boy, none like him,
      a friend of rare quality.
He looked at me when I passed
   and my heart was in jubilee.
If my mother knew what I am thinking
   she would go to him at once.

O Goddess of Golden Light,
     put that thought into her,
        Then I could visit him
And put my arms round him while people were looking
And not weep because of the crowd,
     But would be glad that they knew it
       and that you know me.
What a feast I would make to my Goddess,
     My heart revolts at the thought of exit,
If I could see my darling tonight,
      Dreaming is loveliness.

He says:

Yesterday. Seven days and I have not seen her.
      My malady increases;
         limbs heavy!
             I know not myself any more.
High priest is no medicine, exorcism is useless:
   a disease beyond recognition.

I said: She will make me live,
   her name will rouse me,
Her messages are the life of my heart
   coming and going.
My beloved is the best of medicine,
   more than all pharmacopoeia.
My health is in her coming,
   I shall be cured at the sight of her.

Let her open my eyes
  and my limbs are alive again;
Let her speak and my strength returns.
Embracing her will drive out my malady.
  Seven days and
              she has abandoned me.

(Egypt)

Egyptian Remedies

(1) TO ALLAY ITCHING

Cyperus-from-the-meadow
Onion-meal
Incense
Wild date-juice

Make it into one and apply to the scurvy place.

Look to it because this is the true remedy. It was found among the proven remedies in the temple of the god, Osiris.

It is a remedy which drives away the scurf in every limb of a person.

Yes, it heals at once,
You see.

(2) REMEDY FOR BALDNESS PREPARED FOR SES, MOTHER OF HIS MAJESTY THE KING OF UPPER AND LOWER EGYPT, TETA, DECEASED

Toes-of-a-dog
Refuse-of-dates
Hoof-of-an-ass

(3) TO STOP THE CRYING OF A CHILD

Pods-of-the-poppy-plant
Fly-dirt-which-is-on-the-wall

Make it into one, strain, and take for four days.

It acts at once!

(4) WORDS TO DRIVE OUT THE WHITE GROWTH IN THE EYES

A formula to repeat over the brain of a tortoise that is mixed in honey, and then laid on the eyes.

There is a shouting in the southern sky in the darkness.
There is an uproar in the northern sky.
The hall of pillars falls into the waters.
The ship-folk of the sun-god beat their oars so that the heads at his side fall into the water.
Who leads hither what he finds?

I lead forth what I find.
I lead forth your heads.
I lift up your necks.
I fasten what has been cut from you in its place.
I lead you forth to drive away the god of fevers and all possible deadly arts.

FIVE AMBO GHOST SONGS

1

The dove stays in the garden.
Oh, you dove,
Oh, that dove.

2

I have no rattles—
am shabby for the shades.

3

The ghost is gone in rags,
The ghost is gone in rags,
And the ghost in rags,
The ghost is gone in rags.

4

See how it circles—
the airplane on its airdrome.

5

Ah! the roofs,
Ah! Ah! Ah! Ah! Ah! Ah!
She climbs the roofs,
Our mother.
My friends?
Why do you call me?
The boy sleeps in the bush,
Oh . . . Oh . . . Oh
This is like a swing.

(Northern Rhodesia)

THE COMET

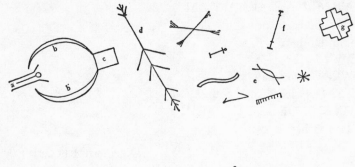

(a) A stranger enters a town. He walks up the main street between two rows of houses (b b) till he comes to the Egbo House (c).

(d) Is a comet which has lately been seen by the townspeople.

(e) Property is strewn about in disorder—denoting confusion.

(f) A seat before the Chief's house.

(g) The arm-chair in which the body of the Head Chief has been set. His death was foretold by the comet.

(hh) Two claimants to the office of Head Chief now vacant. The townsfolk have collected in the Egbo House to decide between the rivals.

(Ekoi, Nigeria)

THE TRIAL

A Judge's House

|||| Men standing outside

Men sit outside

The prisoner

Irons or chains

Sign to shew that the man has got into trouble through a love affair.

Sign which shews that the prisoner has the reputation of being an inconstant lover

Other love affairs which are brought up against the prisoner –

Sign for a man who stands quite a long way off and says:
'I have nothing to do with the case'

(Ekoi, Nigeria)

THE LOVERS

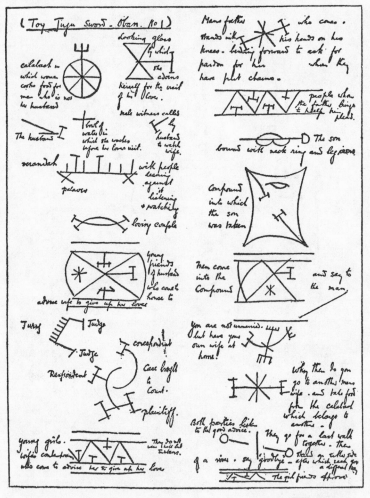

(Ekoi, Nigeria)

DRUM POEM #7

M–M–M–FF M–M F M–F,
MF M M–F,
M–F–F–F–F F–M–F M,
M–M–F M–M–F M,
M F FM M M–M–M,
F–F F–F F–F,
M–M–M–FF M–FM M–M–M–F–F,
M–M–M–FF M–FM M–M–M–F–F,
M–F–F–F–F F–M–F M,
M–M–F M–M–F M,
M F FM M M–M–M,
F–F F–F F–F,
M M M–F F,
F–F F F F.

Oh Witch, don't kill me, Witch
Please spare me, Witch
This Holy Drummer swears to you that
When he rises up some morning
He will sound his drums for you some morning
Very early
Very early
Very early
Oh Witch that kills our children very early
Oh Witch that kills our children very early
This Holy Drummer swears to you that
When he rises up some morning
He will sound his drums for you some morning
Very early
Very early
Very early
Hear me talking to you
Try & understand

(Ashanti)

ORIKI OGUN

1

Ogun kills on the right & destroys on the right
Ogun kills on the left & destroys on the left
Ogun kills suddenly in the house & suddenly in the field
Ogun kills the child with the iron with which it plays
Ogun kills in silence
Ogun kills the thief & the owner of the stolen goods
Ogun kills the owner of the slave—& the slave runs away
Ogun kills the owner of the house & paints the hearth with his
    blood
Ogun is the death who pursues a child until it runs into the bush
Ogun is the needle that pricks at both ends
Ogun has water but he washes in blood

2

Ogun sacrifices an elephant to his head
Master of iron, head of warriors
Ogun, great chief of robbers
Ogun wears a bloody cap
Ogun has four hundred wives & one thousand four hundred
    children
Ogun the fire that sweeps the forest
Ogun's laughter is no joke
Ogun eats two hundred earthworms & does not vomit

3

Ogun has many gowns, he gives them all to the beggars
He gives one to the woodcock—the woodcock dyes it indigo
He gives one to the coucal—the coucal dyes it in camwood
He gives one to the cattle egret—the cattle egret leaves it white

Ogun is not like something you can throw into your cap
Do you think you can put on your cap & walk away with him?

Ogun scatters his enemies
When the butterflies arrive at the place where the cheetah shits
they scatter in all directions.

The light shining on Ogun's face is not easy to behold
Ogun, let me not see the red of your eye

(Yoruba)

HYENA

My father came in the darkness
And I left in the darkness
Saying, "I do not walk by moonlight—I'm no scared child."
Hyena, my name is not spoken in the nighttime,
I just might come around,
The prowler, the croucher,
Son of the darkness walker.

(Hurutshe)

CATTLE

Powerful body and causer of fights
Cook of the good white water
Long- and straight-nosed God:
When it goes "moo,"
The women say, "it goes 'moo,'"
But the men say, "It says 'to arms!'"
O my father's animal, you red woman,
Wet-nosed God you give a sip of something hot.
You have devoured my father and will devour me.
Wet-nosed animal
All my roads lead to the land of the Ndebele, those rustlers.
Last night I slept with a blue crane in the trunk of a white thorn
    tree
And I listened for your sounds.
It takes a man with many sons to handle them.

(Hurutshe)

THE TRAIN

Iron thing coming from Pompi, from the round-house
Where Englishmen smashed their hands on it,
It has no front it has no back.
Rhino Tshukudu going that way.
Rhino Tshukudu no, coming this way.
I'm no greenhorn, I'm a strong, skillful man.
Animal coming from Pompi, from Moretele.
It comes spinning out a spider's web under a cloud of gnats
Moved by the pulling of a teat, animal coming from Kgobola-
   diatla
Comes out of the big hole in the mountain, mother of the great
   woman,
Coming on iron cords.
I met this woman of the tracks curving her way along the river
   bank and over the river.
I thought I'd snatch her
So I said
"Out of the way, son of Mokwatsi, who stands there at the teat."
The stream of little red and white birds gathered up all of its
   track
Clean as a whistle.
Tshutshu over the dry plains
Rhino Tshukudu out of the high country
Animal from the south, steaming along
It comes from Pompi, the round-house, from Kgobola-diatla.

(Hurutshe)

THE ELEPHANT I

Elephant, who brings death.
Elephant, a spirit in the bush.
With a single hand
he can pull two palm trees to the ground.
If he had two hands
he would tear the sky like an old rag.
The spirit who eats dog,
the spirit who eats ram,
the spirit who eats
a whole palm fruit with its thorns.
With his four mortal legs
he tramples down the grass.
Wherever he walks
the grass is forbidden to stand up again.

(Yoruba)

The Elephant II

Elephant hunter, take your bow!
Elephant hunter, take your bow!

In the weeping forest, under the wing of the evening
the night all black has gone to rest happy:
in the sky the stars have fled trembling,
fireflies shine vaguely & put out their lights:
above us the moon is dark, its white light is put out.
The spirits are wandering.

Elephant hunter, take your bow!
Elephant hunter, take your bow!

In the frightened forest the tree sleeps, the leaves are dead
the monkeys have closed their eyes, hanging from the branches
    above us:
the antelopes slip past with silent steps
eat the fresh grass, prick their ears
lift their heads & listen frightened:
the cicada is silent, stops his grinding song.

Elephant hunter, take your bow!
Elephant hunter, take your bow!

In the forest lashed by the great rain
Father elephant walks heavily, *baou, baou*
careless, without fear, sure of his strength
Father elephant, whom no one can vanquish:
among the trees which he breaks he stops & starts again:
he eats, roars, overturns trees & seeks his mate:
Father elephant, you have been heard from far.

Elephant hunter, take your bow!
Elephant hunter, take your bow!

In the forest where no one passes but you
hunter, lift up your heart, leap & walk:
meat in front of you, the huge piece of meat
the meat that walks like a hill
the meat that makes the heart glad
the meat that we'll roast on our coals
the meat into which our teeth sink
the fine red meat & the blood we drink smoking.

Elephant hunter, take your bow!
Elephant hunter, take your bow!

(Gabon Pygmy)

DEATH RITES II

The animal runs, it passes, it dies. And it is the great cold.
It is the great cold of the night, it is the dark.
The bird flies, it passes, it dies. And it is the great cold.
It is the great cold of the night, it is the dark.
The fish flees, it passes, it dies. And it is the great cold.
It is the great cold of the night, it is the dark.
Man eats & sleeps. He dies. And it is the great cold.
It is the great cold of the night, it is the dark.
There is light in the sky, the eyes are extinguished, the star shines.
The cold is below, the light is on high.
The man has passed, the shade has vanished, the prisoner is free!

   Khvum, Khvum, come in answer to our call!

                                        (Gabon Pygmy)

A Song of Changes

The light becomes dark.
The night, & again the night,
The day with hunger tomorrow.
The Maker is angry with us.
The Old Ones have passed away,
Their bones are far off, below.
Their spirits are wandering—
Where are their spirits wandering?
Perhaps the passing wind knows.
Their bones are far off, below.
Are they below, the spirits? Are they here?
Do they see the offerings set out?
Tomorrow is empty & naked
For the Maker is no more there,
Is no more the host seated at the hearth.

(Gabon Pygmy)

THE PRAISES OF THE FALLS

A bo phela a morapeli, Malaola
tse phelang le tse shoeleng.

He will live who knows how to
pray. Divining the things alive
& dead.

The Fall of the Little Creeper

(1)   is one called "rascal of the circle"
(2)   is a calf that doesn't frolic, doesn't come
out of the village
(3)   then it frolics & goes back to its post

The Rise of the Little Creeper of the White Clay

(1)   the little creeper
(2)   of the white clay makes them kill each other
(3)   then they die, they kill each other in the
chief's village
I the white ox die
am dying for the land
(4)   the creeper's calf is full of power
(5)   doesn't frolic when it comes out of the
village
(6)   then it frolics & goes back to its post

The Fall of the Napjane of the Hyena

(1)   of the wild beast roaming around at night
(2)   of the white hair
(3)   Son of Malimane
(4)   while you were thinking of the road from
town
(5)   the question should be: *what?*
(6)   that I should save the pity for myself

(7)   for being born alone
(8)   if we were only two
(9)   sons of a single father
(10)   one would kill, one would follow stabbing
(11)   one would take the fire with a dry plant
(12)   would move far from town
(13)   out where the fire's burning

The Rise of the Lamentation
(1)   of the strong man
(2)   not to pursue a man at night
(3)   who turns & hits you with a stone

The Swimming of Rangoako
(1)   Rangoako is crying
(2)   on account of things forgotten
(3)   a child's cradle
(4)   which isn't lost
            which was sighted
(5)   at the boundary of someone else's field

The Swimming of the Sunbird
(1)   Sunbird
        secret & daring
(2)   when you take up a piece of straw
(3)   & say you imitate the hammerhead
(4)   though nobody can imitate the hammerhead
(5)   bird
        of those who take new clothes
        into deep waters
(6)   you are taking up pieces of straw
        one by one
(7)   you build above pools
(8)   the little sunbird
        mustn't fall

(9)   that falls & goes *phususu*
        in the pool
(10)   the patient man
        is sitting on the drift
(11)   watching his sins pass by
(12)   & sees the river reed
        mocking
        the reed of the plain
(13)   saying:
        when the grass is burning
(14)   the other one laughing also
        saying:
        when the river fills up

The Swimming of the Red Sparrow
(1)   Red sparrow,
        never be a stranger
(2)   Stranger with stunted horns
(3)   & open guilt
(4)   This big turd was the stranger's
(5)   Our headsman's
        turd
        is such a
        paltry thing

The Fall or Swimming of the Molele
(1)   of
        mothers
        of "give me some fat
        to smear myself"
(2)   & fat to smear it on the road
(3)   to wait
        a long time, not to
        smear
        if going to your husband
(4)   the smooth face of some monkey

(5)   & the space in front of him
(6)   those shining stones

The Fall of Shaping the Hammer
(1)   some irons eating
        some others
        in the pincers
(2)   the positions of the bushmen's huts
(3)   the bushman's son
        throwing
        his arrow
        is turning his back
(4)   & hits the eland in the udder
(5)   & these attract crowds
        & are facing each other
(6)   one died at the drift
(7)   & one in the public places
(8)   take their hoes
        & spades
(9)   let's bury the witchdoctors

*Of the Witchdoctor Who Stopped the Pig by
His Cleverness*
(1)   The sky is eating
        is whispering
(2)   & eating
        it roots in the straw
(3)   that the asparagus may stay with its garbage
(4)   sky
        of distant lands
        & of the hearth
(5)   now that the sky has stopped
        raining
        joy, joy
        cries the pig

(6)   & is an animal
        that grows fat
        in fair weather

The Masibo Plant of the Power
   (1)   Who doesn't belong to the powerful
           doesn't grow from the power
   (2)   This is the eland
           & the small antelope
   (3)   & the beast with a mane
   (4)   This eland has bewitched
           the eland of the shepherds
   (5)   has arisen
           has taken a new skin
   (6)   Does the cow suck power from her calf?
   (7)   The woman sucks power from her child

The Famous Masibo of the Swimming
   (1)   Swim on the deep waters
           lie upon them
   (2)   who have no hippos & no little things
   (3)   no beast of prey
           biting
           while it moves
   (4)   & coiling itself in a corner
   (5)   only the little hippos were swimming
   (6)   the big ones
           never swim here anymore
   (7)   Why are the crocodiles
           fighting in the water?
   (8)   They are fighting for an old
           crocodile
   (9)   for many talks in the water
   (10)   which says: I do not
           bite, I only
           play

(11)   will bite some other year
(12)   when the mimosa
        & the willow tree
        are growing

The Famous Moremoholo

(1)   O the monkey of the fall
(2)   the shield is shining
       on the mountain
(3)   the woman with the hairy
       foot
(4)   who hides the fire
       from her husband
(5)   O the monkey is a man
       has learned the rain

The Finding of the Donga

(1)   of the child's fear
       in his bed
(2)   the fear of the hands of shepherds
(3)   of pigeons
(4)   who flap their wings
       returning
(5)   the fear of your brother
       the bat
(6)   when he runs with the cattle

The Fame of the Lamp

(1)   O mother elephant
(2)   O mother elephant, I'm going blind
(3)   O mother elephant, I came here in secret
(4)   O mother elephant, their road was red
(5)   O mother elephant, there was blood & disorder
(6)   O mother elephant, who shakes her ear
       O running elephant

The Fame of the Creepers
- (1)   This is the big creeper
- (2)   whose leaves have fallen
- (3)   We warm ourselves
  at its embers
  We use it again
- (4)   You are light
  the lamp
- (5)   which says:
  make light for us

  poor people

The Appearance of the Orchis of the Basutos
- (1)   of the children of one clan
- (2)   & of one who distributes
  posterity
- (3)   & of the white calabash
  for remembrance
- (4)   & the distribution of meat
- (5)   of sheep & of kids
- (6)   of the springboks
  bringing hunger
  to our bellies

The Lamp of the Seers
- (1)   The angry man
  fights with his mother-in-law
- (2)   What was the good of those lamps?
- (3)   Seeing wonders
  every morning
- (4)   your sins passed by
  & you saw them
- (5)   & saw the child of a cow
  & of a human being

(6)   saw them, could tell them
        apart

        from the entrails

The Rise of the Cobra
  (1)   He fell on the rock
          & lay down
  (2)   but he got up with his luggage
  (3)   got up & shook off
          the dust
  (4)   White head?
          Wear ornaments
  (5)   White hair is a sign
  (6)   something
          the ancestors long for
  (7)   fur from the head
          of a hare
          would make it
  (8)   This is the last time

                                    (Basuto)

A Phantom Bird

A man who had killed a big bird took off its skin & put it to dry on the roof. Then the owner of the skin went into the garden, but this skin then changed itself into the same bird, made a drum, called all the chickens & danced the Chelecheteche.

> A na ngo tu ng'ande
> Chelecheteche,
> Che, che, che,
> Chelecheteche,
> Che, che, che,
> A ne ngo ku tu ng'ande.

When it was over, he caught hold of a chicken to eat it.

The next day the owner of this bird skin went into the garden. This skin again changed itself into the same bird: it called the chickens, it danced the Chelecheteche. The people had hidden themselves to see how it managed to eat all the chickens: they saw this big bird, the transformed one, & they killed it.

I have ground the bean soup, on my knees, before the door, & I enter. Take the potatoes from the fire; they are burning!

(Chinyanja)

The Story of the Leopard Tortoise
(by !kwéiten ta ‖ken, after ‡kamme-an)

The people had gone hunting: she was ill; and she perceived
a man who came up to her hut; he had been hunting around.

She asked the man to rub her neck a little with fat for
her; for, it ached. The man rubbed it with fat for her. And
she altogether held the man firmly with it. The man's hands
altogether decayed away in it.

Again, she espied another man, who came hunting. And she
also spoke, she said: "Rub me with fat a little."

And the man whose hands had decayed away in her neck,
he was hiding his hands, so that the other man should not
perceive them, namely, that they had decayed away in it. And
he said: "Yes; O my mate! rub our elder sister a little with
fat; for, the moon has been cut, while our elder sister lies ill.
Thou shalt also rub our elder sister with fat." He was hiding
his hands, so that the other one should not perceive them.

The Leopard Tortoise said: "Rubbing with fat, put thy hands
into my neck." And he, rubbing with fat, put in his hands
upon the Leopard Tortoise's neck; and the Leopard Tortoise
drew in her head upon her neck; while his hands were altogether in her neck; and he dashed the Leopard Tortoise upon
the ground, on account of it; while he desired, he thought,
that he should, by dashing it upon the ground, break the
Leopard Tortoise. And the Leopard Tortoise held him fast.

The other one had taken out his hands from behind his
back; and he exclaimed: "Feel thou that which I did also
feel!" and he showed the other one his hands; and the other
one's hands were altogether inside the Leopard Tortoise's neck.
And he arose, he returned home. And the other one was dashing
the Leopard Tortoise upon the ground; while he returning

went; and he said that the other one also felt what he had felt. A pleasant thing it was not, in which he had been! He yonder returning went; he arrived at home.

The people exclaimed: "Where hast thou been?" And he, answering, said that the Leopard Tortoise had been the one in whose neck his hands had been; that was why he had not returned home. The people said: "Art thou a fool? Did not thy parents instruct thee? The Leopard Tortoise always seems as if she would die; while she is deceiving us."

(Bushman)

GASSIRE'S LUTE

Four times Wagadu stood there in all her splendor. Four times Wagadu disappeared and was lost to human sight: once through vanity, once through falsehood, once through greed and once through dissension. Four times Wagadu changed her name. First she was called Dierra, then Agada, then Ganna, then Silla. Four times she turned her face. Once to the north, once to the west, once to the east and once to the south. For Wagadu whenever men have seen her, has always had four gates: one to the north, one to the west, one to the east and one to the south. Those are the directions whence the strength of Wagadu comes, the strength in which she endures no matter whether she be built of stone, wood and earth or lives but as a shadow in the mind and longing of her children. For really, Wagadu is not of stone, not of wood, not of earth. Wagadu is the strength which lives in the hearts of men and is sometimes visible because eyes see her and ears hear the clash of swords and ring of shields, and is sometimes invisible because the indomitability of men has overtired her, so that she sleeps. Sleep came to Wagadu for the first time through vanity, for the second time through falsehood, for the third time through greed and for the fourth time through dissension. Should Wagadu ever be found for the fourth time, then she will live so forcefully in the minds of men that she will never be lost again, so forcefully that vanity, falsehood, greed and dissension will never be able to harm her.

Hoooh! Dierra, Agada, Ganna, Silla! Hoooh! Fasa!

Every time that the guilt of man caused Wagadu to disappear she won a new beauty which made the splendor of her next appearance still more glorious. Vanity brought the song of the bards which all peoples (of the Sudan) imitate and value today. Falsehood brought a rain of gold and pearls. Greed brought writing as the Burdama still practice it today and which in Wagadu was the business of the women. Dissension will enable the fifth Wagadu to be as enduring as the rain of the south and as the rocks of the Sahara, for every man will then have Wagadu in his heart and every woman a Wagadu in her womb.

Hoooh! Dierra, Agada, Ganna, Silla! Hoooh! Fasa!

Wagadu was lost for the first time through vanity. At that time Wagadu faced north and was called Dierra. Her last king was called Nganamba Fasa. The Fasa were strong. But the Fasa were growing old. Daily they fought against the Burdama and the Boroma. They fought every day and every month. Never was there an end to the fighting. And out of the fighting the strength of the Fasa grew. All Nganamba's men were heroes, all the women were lovely and proud of the strength and the heroism of the men of Wagadu.

All the Fasa who had not fallen in single combat with the Burdama were growing old. Nganamba was very old. Nganamba had a son, Gassire, and he was old enough, for he already had eight grown sons with children of their own. They were all living and Nganamba ruled in his family and reigned as a king over the Fasa and the doglike Boroma. Nganamba grew so old that Wagadu was lost because of him and the Boroma became slaves again to the Burdama who seized power with the sword. Had Nganamba died earlier would Wagadu then have disappeared for the first time?

Hoooh! Dierra, Agada, Ganna, Silla! Hoooh! Fasa!

Nganamba did not die. A jackal gnawed at Gassire's heart. Daily Gassire asked his heart: "When will Nganamba die? When will Gassire be king?" Every day Gassire watched for the death of his father as a lover watches for the evening star to rise. By day, when Gassire fought as a hero against the Burdama and drove the false Boroma before him with a leather girth, he thought only of the fighting, of his sword, of his shield, of his horse. By night, when he rode with the evening into the city and sat in the circle of men and his sons, Gassire heard how the heroes praised his deeds. But his heart was not in the talking; his heart listened for the strains of Nganamba's breathing; his heart was full of misery and longing.

Gassire's heart was full of longing for the shield of his father, the shield which he could carry only when his father was dead, and also for the sword which he might draw only when he was king. Day by day Gassire's rage and longing grew. Sleep passed him by. Gassire lay, and a jackal gnawed at his heart. Gassire felt the misery climbing into his throat. One night Gassire sprang out of bed, left the house and went to an old wise man, a man who knew more than other people. He entered the wise man's house and asked: "Kiekorro! When will my father, Nganamba, die and leave me his sword and shield?" The old man said: "Ah, Gassire, Nganamba will die; but he will not leave you his sword and shield! You will carry a lute. Shield and sword shall others inherit. But your lute shall cause the loss of Wagadu! Ah, Gassire!" Gassire said: "Kiekorro, you lie! I see that you are not wise. How can Wagadu be lost when her heroes triumph daily? Kiekorro, you are a fool!" The old wise man said: "Ah, Gassire, you cannot believe me. But your path will lead you to the partridges in the fields and you will understand what they say and that will be your way and the way of Wagadu."

Hoooh! Dierra, Agada, Ganna, Silla! Hoooh! Fasa!

The next morning Gassire went with the heroes again to do battle against the Burdama. Gassire was angry. Gassire called to the heroes: "Stay here behind. Today I will battle with the Burdama alone." The heroes stayed behind and Gassire went on alone to do battle with the Burdama. Gassire hurled his spear. Gassire charged the Burdama. Gassire swung his sword. He struck home to the right, he struck home to the left. Gassire's sword was as a sickle in the wheat. The Burdama were afraid. Shocked, they cried: "That is no Fasa, that is no hero,

that is a Damo [a being unknown to the singer himself]."
The Burdama turned their horses. The Burdama threw away
their spears, each man his two spears, and fled. Gassire called
the knights. Gassire said: "Gather the spears." The knights
gathered the spears. The knights sang: "The Fasa are heroes.
Gassire has always been the Fasa's greatest hero. Gassire has
always done great deeds. But today Gassire was greater than
Gassire!" Gassire rode into the city and the heroes rode behind
him. The heroes sang: "Never before has Wagadu won so
many spears as today."

Gassire let the women bathe him. The men gathered. But
Gassire did not seat himself in their circle. Gassire went into
the fields. Gassire heard the partridges. Gassire went close to
them. A partridge sat under a bush and sang: "Hear the *Dausi!*
Hear my deeds!" The partridge sang of its battle with the
snake. The partridge sang: "All creatures must die, be buried
and rot. Kings and heroes die, are buried and rot. I, too,
shall die, shall be buried and rot. But the *Dausi*, the song of
my battles, shall not die. It shall be sung again and again and
shall outlive all kings and heroes. Hoooh, that I might do such
deeds! Hoooh, that I may sing the *Dausi!* Wagadu will be
lost. But the *Dausi* shall endure and shall live!"

Hoooh! Dierra, Agada, Ganna, Silla! Hoooh! Fasa!

Gassire went to the old wise man. Gassire said: "Kiekorro!
I was in the fields. I understood the partridges. The partridge
boasted that the song of its deeds would live longer than
Wagadu. The partridge sang the *Dausi*. Tell me whether men
also know the *Dausi* and whether the *Dausi* can outlive life
and death?" The old wise man said: "Gassire, you are hastening
to your end. No one can stop you. And since you cannot be
a king you shall be a bard. Ah! Gassire. When the kings of the
Fasa lived by the sea they were also great heroes and they
fought with men who had lutes and sang the *Dausi*. Oft struck
the enemy *Dausi* fear into the hearts of the Fasa, who were
themselves heroes. But they never sang the *Dausi* because they

were of the first rank, of the Horro, and because the *Dausi* was only sung by those of the second rank, of the Diare. The Diare fought not so much as heroes for the sport of the day but as drinkers for the fame of the evening. But you, Gassire, now that you can no longer be the second of the first [i.e. King], shall be the first of the second. And Wagadu will be lost because of it." Gassire said: "Wagadu can go to blazes!"

Hoooh! Dierra, Agada, Ganna, Silla! Hoooh! Fasa!

Gassire went to a smith. Gassire said: "Make me a lute." The smith said: "I will, but the lute will not sing." Gassire said: "Smith, do your work. The rest is my affair." The smith made the lute. The smith brought the lute to Gassire. Gassire struck on the lute. The lute did not sing. Gassire said: "Look here, the lute does not sing." The smith said: "That's what I told you in the first place." Gassire said: "Well, make it sing." The smith said: "I cannot do anything more about it. The rest is your affair." Gassire said: "What can I do, then?" The smith said: "This is a piece of wood. It cannot sing if it has no heart. You must give it a heart. Carry this piece of wood on your back when you go into battle. The wood must ring with the stroke of your sword. The wood must absorb down-dripping blood, blood of your blood, breath of your breath. Your pain must be its pain, your fame its fame. The wood may no longer be like the wood of a tree, but must be penetrated by and be a part of your people. Therefore it must live not only with you but with your sons. Then will the tone that comes from your heart echo in the ear of your son and live on in the people, and your son's life's blood, oozing out of his heart, will run down your body and live on in this piece of wood. But Wagadu will be lost because of it." Gassire said: "Wagadu can go to blazes!"

Hoooh! Dierra, Agada, Ganna, Silla! Hoooh! Fasa!

Gassire called his eight sons. Gassire said: "My sons, today we go to battle. But the strokes of our swords shall echo no

longer in the Sahel alone, but shall retain their ring for the
ages. You and I, my sons, will that we live on and endure
before all other heroes in the *Dausi*. My oldest son, today
we two, thou and I, will be the first in battle!"

Gassire and his eldest son went into the battle ahead of the
heroes. Gassire had thrown the lute over his shoulder. The
Burdama came closer. Gassire and his eldest son charged. Gassire and his eldest son fought as the first. Gassire and his
eldest son left the other heroes far behind them. Gassire fought
not like a human being, but rather like a Damo. His eldest
son fought not like a human being, but like a Damo. Gassire
came into a tussle with eight Burdama. The eight Burdama
pressed him hard. His son came to help him and struck four
of them down. But one of the Burdama thrust a spear through
his heart. Gassire's eldest son fell dead from his horse. Gassire
was angry. And shouted. The Burdama fled. Gassire dismounted
and took the body of his eldest son upon his back. Then he
mounted and rode slowly back to the other heroes. The eldest
son's heart's blood dropped on the lute which was also hanging
on Gassire's back. And so Gassire, at the head of his heroes,
rode into Dierra.

Hoooh! Dierra, Agada, Ganna, Silla! Hoooh! Fasa!

Gassire's eldest son was buried. Dierra mourned. The urn
in which the body crouched was red with blood. That night
Gassire took his lute and struck against the wood. The lute
did not sing. Gassire was angry. He called his sons. Gassire said
to his sons: "Tomorrow we ride against the Burdama."

For seven days Gassire rode with the heroes to battle. Every
day one of his sons accompanied him to be the first in the
fighting. And on every one of these days Gassire carried the
body of one of his sons, over his shoulder and over the lute,
back into the city. And thus, on every evening, the blood of
one of his sons dripped on to the lute. After the seven days of
fighting there was a great mourning in Dierra. All the heroes
and all the women wore red and white clothes. The blood of

the Boroma (in sacrifice) flowed everywhere. All the women wailed. All the men were angry. Before the eighth day of the fighting all the heroes and the men of Dierra gathered and spoke to Gassire: "Gassire, this shall have an end. We are willing to fight when it is necessary. But you, in your rage, go on fighting without sense or limit. Now go forth from Dierra! A few will join you and accompany you. Take your Boroma and your cattle. The rest of us incline more to life than fame. And while we do not wish to die fameless we have no wish to die for fame alone."

The old wise man said: "Ah, Gassire! Thus will Wagadu be lost today for the first time."

Hoooh! Dierra, Agada, Ganna, Silla! Hoooh! Fasa!

Gassire and his last, his youngest, son, his wives, his friends and his Boroma rode out into the desert. They rode through the Sahel. Many heroes rode with Gassire through the gates of the city. Many turned. A few accompanied Gassire and his youngest son into the Sahara.

They rode far: day and night. They came into the wilderness and in the loneliness they rested. All the heroes and all the women and all the Boroma slept. Gassire's youngest son slept. Gassire was restive. He sat by the fire. He sat there long. Presently he slept. Suddenly he jumped up. Gassire listened. Close beside him Gassire heard a voice. It rang as though it came from himself. Gassire began to tremble. He heard the lute singing. The lute sang the *Dausi*.

When the lute had sung the *Dausi* for the first time, King Nganamba died in the city Dierra; when the lute had sung the *Dausi* for the first time, Gassire's rage melted; Gassire wept. When the lute had sung the *Dausi* for the first time, Wagadu disappeared—for the first time.

Hoooh! Dierra, Agada, Ganna, Silla! Hoooh! Fasa!

Four times Wagadu stood there in all her splendor. Four times Wagadu disappeared and was lost to human sight: once through vanity, once through falsehood, once through greed and once through dissension. Four times Wagadu changed her name. First she was called Dierra, then Agada, then Ganna, then Silla. Four times she turned her face. Once to the north, once to the west, once to the east and once to the south. For Wagadu, whenever men have seen her, has always had four gates: one to the north, one to the west, one to the east and one to the south. Those are the directions whence the strength of Wagadu comes, the strength in which she endures no matter whether she be built of stone, wood or earth or lives but as a shadow in the mind and longing of her children. For, really, Wagadu is not of stone, not of wood, not of earth. Wagadu is the strength which lives in the hearts of men and is sometimes visible because eyes see her and ears hear the clash of swords and ring of shields, and is sometimes invisible because the indomitability of men has overtired her, so that she sleeps. Sleep came to Wagadu for the first time through vanity, for the second time through falsehood, for the third time through greed and for the fourth time through dissension. Should Wagadu ever be found for the fourth time, then she will live so forcefully in the minds of men that she will never be lost again, so forcefully that vanity, falsehood, greed and dissension will never be able to harm her.

Hoooh! Dierra, Agada, Ganna, Silla! Hoooh! Fasa!

Every time that the guilt of man caused Wagadu to disappear she won a new beauty which made the splendor of her next appearance still more glorious. Vanity brought the song of the bards which all peoples imitate and value today. Falsehood brought a rain of gold and pearls. Greed brought writing as the Burdama still practice it today and which in Wagadu was the business of the women. Dissension will enable the fifth Wagadu to be as enduring as the rain of the south and as the rocks of the Sahara, for every man will then have Wagadu in his heart and every woman a Wagadu in her womb.

Hoooh! Dierra, Agada, Ganna, Silla! Hoooh! Fasa!

(Soninke)

AMERICA

THREE MIDĒ SONGS & PICTURE-SONGS

(1st Set)

An Imploration for Clear Weather

I swing the spirit like a child

The sky is what I was telling you
about

We have lost the sky

I am helping you

Have I made an error?

(Silence)

I am using my heart

What are you saying to me & am I
in-my-senses?

The spirit wolf

I didn't know where I was going

I depend on the clear sky

I give you the-other-village,
spirit that you are

The thunder is heavy

We are talking to each other

(2nd Set)

The drum is handed to the chief priest, & after a short prelude of drumming he becomes more & more inspired, & sings the following Midē song:

Let us be a spirit, let the spirit
come from the mouth

I own this lodge, through which I pass

Mother is having it over again

Friends I am afraid, I am afraid, friends, of
the spirits sitting around me

I am going with medicine bag to the
lodge

We are still sitting in a circle

Half the sky

The spirit has pity on me now

In my heart I have the spirit

I take the earth, friends

Let us get him to take this water

I take this rattle

See how I shine in making medicine

(3rd Set)

The candidate is then led around the interior of the inclosure, followed by all the others present, excepting the musicians. During the circuit, which is performed slowly, the chief Midē drums upon the Midē drum & chants.

A spirit, a spirit, you who sit there,
who sit there

The fog wind goes from place to place where
the wind blows

Rest

I who acknowledge you to be a spirit &
am dying

I am trying you who are the bear

The bird, the crow bird's skin is the reason
why I am a spirit

The sound of the thunder is the white bear of fire

(Ojibwa)

Ten Chippewa (Ojibwa) Songs

1

a loon
I thought it was
but it was
my love's
splashing oar

—Mary English

2

the blue, overhanging
sky
answers me back

—Wabezic

3

(a death song)

large bear
deceives me

—Gawitayac

4

the odor of death
I discern the odor of death
in front of my body

—Namebines

5

(a war song)

in the coming heat
of the day
I stood there

—*Memengwa*

6

is there anyone who
would weep for me?
my wife
would weep for me

—*Midewigijig*

7

(the deer's song)

my shining horns

—*Meckawigabau*

8

as my eyes
search
the prairie
I feel the summer in the spring

—*Ajidegijig*

9

(a death song)

whenever I pause
the noise
of the village

—*Kimiwun*

10

(song of the game of silence)

it is hanging
in the edge of sunshine
it is a pig   I see
with its double hoofs
it is a very fat pig
the people who live in a hollow tree
are fighting
they are fighting bloodily
he is rich
he will carry a pack toward the great water

—*John W. Carl* (*Mejakigijig*)

Five Teton Sioux Songs

1

owls
(were) hooting
in the passing of the night
owls
(were) hooting
                    —by *Brave Buffalo*

2

"where the wind is blowing"

where
the wind
is blowing
the wind
is roaring
I stand
westward
the wind
is blowing
the wind
is roaring
I stand
                    —by *Teal Duck*

3

someone
somewhere
is speaking
from the north
a sacred-stone nation
is speaking
you will hear
someone
somewhere
is speaking

—by *Bear Necklace*

4

from everywhere
they come
flying
(from) the north
the wind is blowing
to earth
rattling
flying
they come
they come
from everywhere
they come

—by *Bear Necklace*

5

today
is mine (I claimed)
(to) a man
a voice
I sent
you grant me
this day
is mine (I claimed)
(to) a man
a voice
I sent
now
here
(he) is

—by *Shell Necklace*

SONGS OF THE MASKED DANCERS

1

When the earth was made
when the sky was made
when my songs were first heard
the holy mountain was standing toward me with life.

At the center of the sky, the holy boy walks four ways with
 life.
My mountain became my own: standing toward me with life.
The dancers became: standing toward me with life.

When the sun goes down to the earth
where Mescal Mountain lies with its head toward the sunrise
black spruce became: standing up with me.

2

Right at the center of the sky the holy boy with life walks
 in four directions.
Lightning with life in four colors comes down four times.
The place called black spot with life,
the place called blue spot with life,
the place called yellow spot with life,
they have heard about me
the black dancers dance in four places.
The sun starts down toward the earth.

3

The living sky black-spotted
The living sky blue-spotted
The living sky yellow-spotted
The living sky white-spotted
The young spruce as girls stood up for their dance in the
    way of life.

When my songs first were, they made my songs with words
    of jet.
Earth when it was made
Sky when it was made
Earth to the end
Sky to the end
Black dancer, black thunder, when they came toward each
    other
All the bad things that used to be vanished.
The bad wishes that were in the world all vanished.
The lightning, the black thunder struck four times for them.
It struck four times for me.

4

When my songs first became
when the sky was made
when the earth was made
the breath of the dancers against me made only of down:
when they heard about my life
where they got their life
when they heard about me:
it stands.

(Apache)

SONGS IN THE GARDEN OF THE HOUSE GOD

Now in the east
the white bean
& the great corn-plant
are tied with white lightning.
Listen! rain's drawing near!
The voice of the bluebird is heard.

    Now in the east
    the white bean
    & the great squash
    are tied with the rainbow.
    Listen! the rain's drawing near!
    The voice of the bluebird is heard.

From the top of the great corn-plant the water foams, I hear
    it.
Around the roots the water foams, I hear it.
Around the roots of the plants it foams, I hear it.
From their tops the water foams, I hear it.

    The corn grows up. The waters of the dark clouds drop,
        drop.
    The rain comes down. The waters from the corn leaves
        drop, drop.
    The rain comes down. The waters from the plants drop,
        drop.
    The corn grows up. The waters of the dark mists drop,
        drop.

    Shall I cull this fruit of the great corn-plant?
Shall you break it?
    Shall I break it?
Shall I break it?
    Shall you break it?

Shall I?
    Shall you?
Shall I cull this fruit of the great squash vine?
    Shall you pick it up?
Shall I pick it up?
    Shall I pick it up?
Shall you pick it up?
    Shall I?
Shall you?

(Navaho)

A Song from "The Enemy Way"

(Chorus)

A nice one, a nice one, a nice one now gave a sound, a nice, a nice, a nice one now gave a sound, so it did.

1.

Now I am Changing Woman's child when a nice one gave its sound, so it did

In the center of the turquoise home a nice one gave its sound, so it did

On the very top of the soft goods floor a nice one gave its sound, so it did

It's the nice child of a dark water pot that just gave its sound, so it did

Its lid is a dark cloud when the nice one gave its sound, so it is

Sunray encircles it when the nice one gave its sound, so it does

Water's child is sprayed upon it when the nice one gave its sound, so it is

At its front it is pleasant when the nice one gave its sound, so it is

At its rear it is pleasant when the nice one gave its sound, so it is

It's the nice child of long life & happiness that just gave its sound, so it is.

(Chorus)

A nice, a nice one, a nice one now gave its sound, so it did.

2.

Now I am Changing Woman's grandchild when a nice one
   gave its sound, so it did
In the center of the white bead home a nice one gave its
   sound, so it did
On the very top of a jeweled floor a nice one gave its sound, so
   it did
It's the nice child of the blue water pot that just gave its sound,
   so it is
Blue cloud is its lid when a nice one gave its sound, so it is
Rainbow encircles it when a nice one gave its sound, so it does
Water's child is sprayed upon it when a nice one gave its sound,
   so it is
In its rear it is pleasant when a nice one gave its sound, so it is
At its front it is pleasant when a nice one gave its sound, so it is
It's the nice child of long life & happiness that just gave its
   sound, so it is

(Chorus)

A nice one, a nice one, a nice one just gave its sound, that's all!

(Navaho)

OLD SONG: FOR THE TALL ONE

1

I am in my house—a cave—alone.
Outside there is a great disturbance.
I want to know what is happening.
I hear a great noise of the thunder
& with my very long bow
I shoot an arrow at a giant cactus.
It blows up like lightning—
blows up & falls.

When I come outside I tell them
I cannot sleep. Only a woman can sleep.
The ants are biting me & keeping me awake
& I want quiet.
If I can't sleep I will take my weapons
& will go out to fight my enemies.
Therefore I go forth with my arms.
I hunt the trail of one who comes,
hidden by a dry giant cactus.

2

He comes with his head so high
it is in the sky.
His hat is so high
it is like a cloud.
His eyes are so high
that he cannot see me on earth.
He is angry when he cannot find me
& he pulls his mustache,
he is so angry
because he cannot find me.

His head is so high
that when he looks to the ground
he cannot see me.

The Tall One is so brave
& the Tall One is so strong
that I sit down in fear
behind a dry ironwood.
I load my medicine pipe
it is so very large;
& with a dry stick, twirling,
I make fire, to light my pipe.
And I quit smoking, afraid.
The tears run down my cheeks
because I am afraid.

3

I shoot an arrow through him
from side to side,
but he is not dead.
He says: 'Do not kill me—
I won't fight any more.'
I grab his great bow
& smash his head
but he is not dead.

I chop off his head
& make a hole in his cheek
& drag his great head
to the people who made so much noise
that I could not sleep.
They see I am very brave
& they dance for a long time
before my house.

(Seri)

A SONG OF THE WINDS
(by Santo Blanco)

Below the sea there is the mouth of a cave
In which all the winds are born.
He comes below the sea and mounts up
To where there is no sun.
But the cave is light, like the sun.

Another mouth is smooth & slippery
& hard, like ice.
He stands erect with his arms outstretched
& from each finger there comes a wind.

First he blows the White Wind
then he blows the Red Wind
then he blows the Blue Wind.
And from his little finger
he blows the Black Wind,
which is stronger than them all.

The White Wind comes from the north
& is very hot.
Blue comes from the south.
The Red Wind comes from the west
In the middle of the day, & is soft.
The Black Wind comes from beyond the mountains
& is strongest of them all.
The whirlwind comes from the east.

(Seri)

Six Seri Whale Songs
(by Santo Blanco)

1

The sea is calm
there is no wind.
In the warm sun
I play on the surface
with many companions.
In the air spout
many clouds of smoke
& all of them are happy.

2

The mother whale is happy.
She swims on the surface, very fast.
No shark is near
but she swims over many leagues
back & forth, very fast.
Then she sinks to the bottom
& four baby whales are born.

3

First one comes up to the surface
in front of her nose.
He jumps on the surface.
Then each of the other baby whales
jumps on the surface.

Then they go down
into the deep water to their mother
& stay there eight days
before they come up again.

4

The old, old whale has no children.
She does not swim far.
She floats near the shore & is sad.
She is so old & weak
she cannot feed like other whales.
With her mouth on the surface
she draws in her breath—hrrr—
& the smallest fish & the sea birds are swallowed up.

5

The whale coming to shore is sick
the sharks have eaten her bowels
& the meat of her body.
She travels slowly—her bowels are gone.
She is dead on the shore
& can travel no longer.

6

Fifty sharks surrounded her.
They came under her belly
& bit off her flesh & her bowels
& so she died. Because she had no teeth
to fight the sharks.

(Seri)

From INATOIPIPPILER

(by Akkantilele)

[*The Living Beings*]

Down below a way is being opened for them
Under the great waves the boys come to life again
In front of them a world of living beings is moving, living
   beings are swimming
In front of them living beings are wavering, living beings are
   making a noise
All like golden bells the living beings sound down below
All like golden guitars the living beings sound down below
All like golden watches the living beings sound down below
The living beings make a noise like panpipes and flutes
The living beings make a noise down below like the *kokke*-flute
The living beings are making a noise down below
The living beings make a noise like that of many different
   instruments
In front of them the living beings are making a noise like the
   suppe-flute
The living beings are making a noise down below
The living beings make a noise like the *tolo*-flute
The living beings are making a noise down below
The living beings make a noise like the *tae*-flute
The living beings are making a noise down below
The living beings make a noise like many different instruments

. . . .

The boys have come to life again: in front of them a world of
   living beings is teeming
In front of them the world is making a noise, living beings are
   fluttering

Uncle Oloyailer's river opens up
Uncle Oloyailer's river lies flaming
The boys stand regarding the place
The boys go forward into the empty space
The boys descend along the middle of the river
Uncle Oloyailer's river opens up
The river lies with bays and inlets as from big rocks
The river lies with bays and inlets as from seaweed
The wind of Uncle Oloyailer's river is blowing
The wind of the river is rippling the ground

[*The Boy Inatoipippiler*]

The boy Inatoipippiler stands looking around
The river of Kalututuli is rising, the river of Kalututuli is
    illuminating the place
Beside Kalututuli, beside the river bank, Uncle Nia's women
    are expecting them
The boy Inatoipippiler stands arranging his hair, he stands
    letting down his hair.
The boy Inatoipippiler stands taking off his shirt and pants
He stands taking off his white shirt
He descends into the middle of the river, he is bathing in the
    river
He is combing his noble hair, he is letting down his hair, his
    hair is reaching far down
Among the tufts of his hair the fish of the sea, the sardines
    are swimming
The boy Inatoipippiler climbs up on the river bank
He stands arranging his hair, he stands combing his hair
With the comb he stands loosening his hair
He stands spreading out his hair, he stands twisting his hair
He stands putting the comb into his hair
The boy Inatoipippiler stands putting on his shirt and pants
He stands putting on his white shirt
He stands tying his golden necktie for the sake of the feast

He stands putting on his golden coat, he stands putting on his
  golden chain
His golden chain hangs down eightfold as he stands
The golden chain glistens as he stands, the golden chain shines
  reaching down to his waist
The boy Inatoipippiler stands putting on his golden socks, he
  stands putting on his golden shoes
He stands putting on his golden hat, he stands with his golden
  hat shining
He stands with his golden hat glistening like the sun
He stands with his golden hat shining, he stands with his golden
  shoes creaking

(Cuna)

Three Nahuatl Poems

1

One by one I proclaim your songs:
  I bind them on gold crabs as if they were anklets:
  like emeralds I gather them.
Clothe yourself in them: they are your riches.
  Bathe in feathers of the quetzal,
your treasury of birds' plumes black and yellow,
the red feathers of the macaw
beat your drums about the world:
deck yourself out in them: they are your riches.

2

Where am I to go, whither?
  The road's there, the road to Two-Gods.
  Well, who checks men here,
here where all lack a body,
at the bottom of the sky?
Or, maybe, it is only on Earth
that we loose the body?
  Cleaned out, rid of it completely . . .
His House: there remains none on this earth!
Who is it that said:
Where find them? our friends no longer exist!

3

Will he return will Prince Cuautli ever return?
Will Ayocuan, the one who drove an arrow into the sky?
Shall these two yet gladden you?
  Events don't recur: we vanish once only.

Hence the cause of my weeping:
Prince Ayocuan, warrior chief
gouverned us harshly.
His pride waxed more, he grew haughty
here among men.
    But his time is finished . . .
he can no longer come to bow down before Father and
   Mother . . .
This is the reason for my weeping:
He has fled to the place where all lack a body!

                      (Aztec)

FOR TLACAHUEPAN

The field where the hero's
body was left in the sun
A sudden ringing of bells

And yellow flowers
to sweeten
the kingdom of death

They have hidden you here
in the seven caves

The acacia bursts, a
lost cry of the tiger
answers the eagle's call

O quechol-bird
color of fire
moving at night
through this field
in the kingdom of death

(Aztec)

The Return of the Warriors

The city endures
among emerald lilies
And Mexico under a green sun
bathing the land

When the princes
come home
a fog lined with flowers
rises around them

> For which we pray,
> saying:
> Oh giver of life, whose household this is, our
> father ruling among us: the song in your praise
> will be heard in Anáhuac, & the cup will run
> over

Shadows hide the
white willow, in the dust
of white sedge
Mexico rises again

Over my head
a blue heron
comes flying

The grace of those wings
spreading open
Sweep of the tail

> Oh rule now over your sons, oh rule in this land:
> never be gone from us, live here forever among us

Who can master the grief
of Motecuzoma, the sorrows of
Totoquihuatzin

The god who came here
holds heaven & earth
in his hand

The cry of the men
preparing for battle
rides the four winds
A soldier gives birth to the sun

And the chroniclers wrote:
. . . so things fell out in the city of Motecuzoma
called Tenochtitlan, as also in Acolhuacan, city
of Nezahualpilli

With fans of quetzal-bird
feathers the chiefs
returned to their city

Sighs of sadness
fill Tenochtitlan
As the god would have had it

(Aztec)

From THE POPOL VUH

The Tree / The Skull / The Blood / The Owls

This is the story of a maiden, the daughter of a lord named Cuchumaquic.

A maiden, then, daughter of a lord heard this story. The name of the father was Cuchumaquic and that of the maiden was Xquic. When she heard the story of the fruit of the tree which her father told, she was amazed to hear it.

"Why can I not go to see this tree which they tell about?" the girl exclaimed. "Surely the fruit of which I hear tell must be very good." Finally she went alone and arrived at the foot of the tree which was planted in Pucbal-Chah.

"Ah!" she exclaimed. "What fruit is this which this tree bears? Is it not wonderful to see how it is covered with fruit? Must I die, shall I be lost, if I pick one of this fruit?" said the maiden.

Then the skull which was among the branches of the tree spoke up and said: "What is it you wish? Those round objects which cover the branches of the trees are nothing but skulls." So spoke the head of Hun-Hunahpú turning to the maiden. "Do you, perchance, want them?" it added.

"Yes, I want them," the maiden answered.

"Very well," said the skull. "Stretch your right hand up here."

"Very well," said the maiden, and with her right hand reached toward the skull.

In that instant the skull let a few drops of spittle fall directly into the maiden's palm. She looked quickly and intently at the palm of her hand, but the spittle of the skull was not there.

"In my saliva and spittle I have given you my descendants," said the voice in the tree. "Now my head has nothing on it any more, it is nothing but a skull without flesh. So are the heads of the great princes, the flesh is all which gives them a handsome appearance. And when they die, men are frightened by their bones. So, too, is the nature of the sons, which are like saliva and spittle, they may be sons of a lord, of a wise man, or of an orator. They do not lose their substance when they go, but they bequeath it; the image of the lord, of the wise man, or of the orator does not disappear, nor is it lost, but he leaves it to the daughters and to the sons which he begets. I have done the same with you. Go up, then, to the surface of the earth, that you may not die. Believe in my words that it will be so," said the head of Hun-Hunahpú and of Vucub-Hunahpú. . . .

After all of the above talking, the maiden returned directly to her home, having immediately conceived the sons in her belly by virtue of the spittle only. And thus Hunahpú and Xbalanqué were begotten.

And so the girl returned home, and after six months had passed, her father, who was called Cuchumaquic, noticed her condition. At once the maiden's secret was discovered by her father when he observed that she was pregnant.

Then the lords, Hun-Camé and Vucub-Camé, held council with Cuchumaquic.

"My daughter is pregnant, Sirs; she has been disgraced," exclaimed Cuchumaquic when he appeared before the lords.

"Very well," they said. "Command her to tell the truth, and if she refuses to speak, punish her; let her be taken far from here and sacrifice her."

"Very well, Honorable Lords," he answered. Then he questioned his daughter:

"Whose are the children that you carry, my daughter?" And she answered. "I have no child, my father, for I have not yet known a youth."

"Very well," he replied. "You are really a whore. Take her and sacrifice her, Ahpop Achih; bring me her heart in a gourd and return this very day before the lords," he said to the two owls.

The four messengers took the gourd and set out carrying the young girl in their arms and also taking the knife of flint with which to sacrifice her.

And she said to them: "It cannot be that you will kill me, oh, messengers, because what I bear in my belly is no disgrace, but was begotten when I went to marvel at the head of Hun-Hunahpú which was in Pucbal-Chah. So, then, you must not sacrifice me, oh, messengers!" said the young girl, turning to them.

"And what shall we put in place of your heart? Your father told us: 'Bring the heart, return before the lords, do your duty, all working together, bring it in the gourd quickly, and put the heart in the bottom of the gourd.' Perchance, did he not speak to us so? What shall we put in the gourd? We wish too, that you should not die," said the messengers.

"Very well, but my heart does not belong to them. Neither is your home here, nor must you let them force you to kill men. Later, in truth, the real criminals will be at your mercy and I will overcome Hun-Camé and Vucub-Camé. So, then, the blood and only the blood shall be theirs and shall be given to them. Neither shall my heart be burned before them. Gather the product of this tree," said the maiden.

The red sap gushing forth from the tree fell in the gourd and with it they made a ball which glistened and took the shape of a heart. The tree gave forth sap similar to blood, with the appearance of real blood. Then the blood, or that is to say the sap of the red tree, clotted, and formed a very bright coating inside the gourd, like clotted blood; meanwhile the tree glowed at the work of the maiden. It was called the "red tree of cochineal," but [since then] it has taken the name of Blood Tree because its sap is called Blood.

"There on earth you shall be beloved and you shall have all that belongs to you," said the maiden to the owls.

"Very well, girl. We shall go there, we go up to serve you; you, continue on your way, while we go to present the sap, instead of your heart, to the lords," said the messengers.

When they arrived in the presence of the lords, all were waiting.

"You have finished?" asked Hun-Camé.

"All is finished, my lords. Here in the bottom of the gourd is the heart."

"Very well. Let us see," exclaimed Hun-Camé. And grasping it with his fingers he raised it, the shell broke and the blood flowed bright red in color.

"Stir up the fire and put it on the coals," said Hun-Camé.

As soon as they threw it on the fire, the men of Xibalba began to sniff and drawing near to it, they found the fragrance of the heart very sweet.

And as they sat deep in thought, the owls, the maiden's servants, left, and flew like a flock of birds from the abyss toward earth and the four became her servants.

(Quiché Maya)

From THE POPOL VUH

The House of Cold / The House of Jaguars / The House of Fire / The House of Bats

Afterward they entered the House of Cold. It is impossible to describe how cold it was. The house was full of hail; it was the mansion of cold. Soon, however, the cold was ended because with [a fire of] old logs the boys made the cold disappear.

That is why they did not die; they were still alive when it dawned. Surely what the Lords of Xibalba wanted was that they would die; but it was not thus, and when it dawned, they were still full of health, and they went out again, when the messengers came to get them.

"How is this? They are not dead yet?" said the Lords of Xibalba. They were amazed to see the deeds of Hunahpú and Xbalanqué.

Presently the [boys] entered the House of Jaguars. The house was full of jaguars. "Do not bite us! Here is what belongs to you," [the boys] said to the jaguars. And quickly they threw some bones to the animals, which pounced upon the bones.

"Now surely they are finished. Now already they have eaten their own entrails. At last they have given themselves up. Now their bones have been broken," so said the guards, all happy because of this.

But they [the boys] did not die. As usual, well and healthy, they came out of the House of Jaguars.

"What kind of people are they? Where did they come from?" said all the Lords of Xibalba.

Presently they [the boys] entered into the midst of fire in the House of Fire, inside which there was only fire; but they were not burned. Only the coals and the wood burned. And, as usual, they were well when it dawned. But what they [the Lords of Xibalba] wished was that [the boys] would die rapidly, where they had been. Nevertheless, it did not happen thus, which disheartened the Lords of Xibalba.

Then they put them into the House of Bats. There was nothing but bats inside this house, the house of Camazotz, a large animal, whose weapons for killing were like a dry point, and instantly those who came into their presence perished.

They [the boys] were in there, then, but they slept inside their blowguns. And they were not bitten by those who were in the house. Nevertheless, one of them had to give up because of another Camazotz that came from the sky, and made him come into sight.

The bats were assembled in council all night, and flew about: "*Quilitz, quilitz,*" they said: So they were saying all night. They stopped for a little while, however, and they did not move and were pressed against the end of one of the blowguns.

Then Xbalanqué said to Hunahpú: "Look you, has it begun already to get light?"

"Maybe so. I am going to see," [Hunahpú] answered.

And as he wished very much to look out of the mouth of the blowgun, and wished to see if it had dawned, instantly Camazotz cut off his head and the body of Hunahpú was decapitated.

Xbalanqué asked again: "Has it not yet dawned?" But Hunahpú did not move. "Where have you gone, Hunahpú? What have you done?" But he did not move, and remained silent.

Then Xbalanqué felt concerned and exclaimed: "Unfortunate are we. We are completely undone."

They went immediately to hang the head [of Hunahpú] in the ball-court by special order of Hun-Camé and Vucub-Camé, and all the people of Xibalba rejoiced for what had happened to the head of Hunahpú.

(Quiché Maya)

Bean Flower

Bean flower,
Black & white
Like the heart of that dark man
Who loves two women.

Long live the apple.
Its tears are sweet.
This world has reason
To be bitter.

Little star of heaven
Lend me your brightness,
For the life of this world
Is a dark night.

(Quechua)

Like a Feather in the Air

My mother gave me my being,
        Ay!
In the middle of a rain cloud,
        Ay!
So that I would weep like rain,
        Ay!
So that I would go round like a cloud,
        Ay!
Wandering from door to door
        Ay!
Like a feather in the air,
        Ay!

(Quechua)

From The Elegy for the Great Inca Atawallpa

. . . You all by yourself fulfilled
    Their malignant demands,
But your life was snuffed out
    In Cajamarca.

Already the blood has curdled
    In your veins,
And under your eyelids your sight
    Has withered.
Your glance is hiding in the brilliance
    Of some star.

Only your dove suffers and moans
    And drifts here and there.
Lost in sorrow, she weeps, who had her nest
    In your heart.

The heart, with the pain of this catastrophe,
    Shatters.
They have robbed you of your golden litter
    And your palace.
All of your treasures which they have found
    They have divided among them.

Condemned to perpetual suffering,
    And brought to ruin,
Muttering, with thoughts that are elusive
    And far away from this world,
Finding ourselves without refuge or help,
    We are weeping,

And not knowing to whom we can turn our eyes,
 We are lost.

Oh sovereign king,
 Will your heart permit us
To live scattered, far from each other,
 Drifting here and there,
Subject to an alien power,
 Trodden upon?

Discover to us your eyes which can wound
 Like a noble arrow;
Extend to us your hand which grants
 More than we ask,
And when we are comforted with this blessing
 Tell us to depart.

       (Quechua)

My Sun, the Golden Garden of Your Hair

My Sun, the golden garden of your hair
Has begun to flame
And the fire has spread over our corn-fields.

Already the green ears are parched
Pressed by the presence of your breath
And the last drop of their sweat is wrung from them.

Strike us with the rain of your arrows,
Open to us the door of your eyes,
Oh Sun, source of beneficent light.

(Quechua)

MY RAGGED SEA-LETTUCE

My ragged sea-lettuce,
Oh water-plant,
You, not sharing my torments,
Are not moved to weep,
You my beauty, you that are my queen,
That are my princess.
Abundance of tears flood me,
Abundant rain beats me down
At the sight of your shawl,
And when I see your skirt.
The day has not yet brightened;
When I wake from the night
The day is not yet to be seen.
Yet, since you are a queen
You would not spare me a thought
Though the puma and the fox were to devour me in this
    valley
Where for your sake I am thus
Imprisoned, my beauty.

(Quechua)

When I Come to Visit You

When I come to visit you,
Do not fling me from your house
In my misery.

Sun, my father, moon my mother,
You might look at my face
Where the tears of blood run down.

(Quechua)

THE BROKEN VASE

Beautiful princess
your brother
has broken
your vase,
& that is why
it thunders, why lightning flashes
& thunderbolts roll.
But you, princess
mistress of the rain
you will give us water
&, at other times
your hand will scatter hail,
or snow.
Pachacamac,
Creator of the world,
& our god Viracocha
have given you a soul
& a body
for this sole purpose.

(Quechua)

Words from Seven Magic Songs
(by Tatilgäk)

    inop   ihumanut   erinaliot
For a man's mind   a magic song
           Big man,

           Big man!

           aglgagjuarit
           Your big hands

           Your big feet,

           make them smooth
           And look far ahead!

           Big man,

           Big man!

Your thoughts   smooth out

           and look far ahead!

           Big man,
           Big man!
Your weapons   let them fall!

                (Copper Eskimo)

A Song of Men's Impotence
& the Beasts They Hunted

Well—it is no matter
Udinuligrarame
was full of dread
he sat with clenched
teeth
arnan ima akunane
yes, between women.
Well—it is no matter
Udinuligrarame
full of dread he was
(what was in a caribou stomach)
when he sat with clenched
teeth
his two eyes   those   there
were frightful
in loneliness there
aqara   inilughinartoq
my tongue   sings but one song

how far, how far   one becomes cold with dread
at having a mate   who like a human
never becomes full grown
no one wanted to imitate
Pamerfiugame   inugtutle
because he became full-grown like an ordinary man
like a busybody
Down here-yi-ya   one becomes cold with fear
havkua afufuaqpat
The beasts out there, those that usually flee.
The big black bears and the big musk-oxen

Down there-yi-ya   where to, I wonder?
havkua   anutighat havkua
Those down there, the beasts, those down there
Those that flee at nothing
The big caribou cows and the big bulls
The beasts down there, those that flee at nothing

(Copper Eskimo)

THE DEAD HUNTER SPEAKS THROUGH THE VOICE OF A SHAMAN

To be beyond you now, to feel
joy burning inside me when the sun
burns thru the terrible sky
To feel joy in the new sun, aie!
in the sky's curved belly

But restless more likely, restless
These flies swarm around me, dropping
eggs in the rotting collarbone,
into my eyes, their cold mouths moving
I choke on such horrors

& remembering the last fear, I remember
a dark rim of ocean, remembering
the last fear, the broken boat drifting,
drawing me into that darkness, aie!
Now the other side holds me

& I remember men's fear in the boats
I see the snow forced into my door, fear's
shadow over the hut, while my body
hung in the air, the door hidden, aie!
When I cried in fear of the snow

Horror stuck in my throat, the hut
walled me in, slowly the ice-floe broke
Horror choked me, the thin sky
quivered with sound, the voice
of the dark ice cracking, cold mornings

(Copper Eskimo)

Eskimo Prose Poems

The Splendor of the Heavens

Two men came to a hole in the sky. One asked the other to lift him up. If only he would do so, then he in turn would lend him a hand.

His companion lifted him up, but hardly was he up when he shouted aloud for joy, forgot his companion & ran into heaven.

The other could just manage to peep in over the edge of the hole; it was full of feathers inside. But so beautiful was it in heaven that a man who looked in over the edge forgot everything, forgot his companion whom he had promised to help up & simply ran off into all the splendor of heaven.

(Told by Inugpasugjuk)

A Mother & Child

A pregnant woman brought forth a child. The child was hardly born before it flung itself upon its mother & killed her, & began eating her.

Suddenly the infant cried:

My mother's little first finger stuck crosswise in my mouth, & I could hardly manage to get it out again.

And with these words, the infant killed itself, after first having murdered & eaten its mother.

(Told by Inugpasugjuk)

The Woman Who Took In a Larva To Nurse

There was once a barren woman, who could never have any children, at last she took in a larva & nursed it in her armpits, & it was not long before the larva began to grow up. But the more it grew the less blood the woman had for it to suck. Therefore she often went visiting the homes near by, to set the blood in motion, but she never stayed long away from home, for she was always thinking of her dear larva, & hurried back to it. So greatly did she long for it, so fond of it had she grown, that whenever she came to the entrance of her house, she would call out to it:

Oh, little one that can hiss, say 'te-e-e-e-E·r.'

And when she said that, the larva would say in answer: Te-e-e-e-E·r.

The woman then hurried into the house, took the larva on her lap & sang to it:

> Little one that will bring me snow
> when you grow up
> Little one that will find meat for me
> when you grow up!

And then she would bite it out of pure love.

The larva grew up & became a big thing. At last it began to move about the village among the houses, & the people were afraid of it & wanted to kill it, partly because they were afraid & partly because they thought it was a pity to let the woman go on growing paler & paler from loss of blood.

So one day when the woman was out visiting, they went into her house & threw the larva out into the passage. Then the dogs flung themselves on it & bit it to death. It was completely filled with blood, & the blood poured out of it.

The woman who had been out visiting came home all unsuspecting, & when she got to the entrance of her house, called out to the larva as she was wont to do. But no one answered, & the woman exclaimed:

Oh, they have thrown my dear child out of the house.

And she burst into tears & went into the house weeping.

(Told by Ivaluardjuk)

When Houses Were Alive

One night a house suddenly rose up from the ground and went floating through the air. It was dark, & it is said that a swishing, rushing noise was heard as it flew through the air. The house had not yet reached the end of its road when the people inside begged it to stop. So the house stopped.

They had no blubber when they stopped. So they took soft, freshly drifted snow & put it in their lamps, & it burned.

They had come down at a village. A man came to their house & said:

Look, they are burning snow in their lamps. Snow can burn.

But the moment these words were uttered, the lamp went out.

(Told by Inugpasugjuk)

ASIA

The Quest of Milarepa

I

When named I am the man apart;
I am the sage of Tibet;
I am Milarepa.
I hear little but counsel much;
I reflect little but persevere much;
I sleep little but endure in meditation much.
My narrow bed gives me ease to stretch & bend;
my thin clothing makes my body warm;
my scanty fare satisfies my belly.
Knowing one thing I have experience of all things;
knowing all things I comprehend them to be one.
I am the goal of every great meditator;
I am the meeting place of the faithful;
I am the coil of birth & death & decay.
I have no preference for any country;
I have no home in any place;
I have no store of provisions for my livelihood.
I have no fondness for material things;
I make no distinction between clean & unclean in food;
I have little torment of suffering.
I have little desire for self-esteem;
I have little attachment or bias;
I have found the freedom of Nirvana.
I am the comforter of the aged;
I am the madman who counts death happiness;
I am the playmate of children.

2

When the tiger-year was ending
& the hare-year beginning
on the sixth day of the month of the barking of the fox,
I grew weary of the things of this world;
& in my yearning for solitude
I came to the sanctuary wilderness, Mount Everest.
Then heaven & earth took counsel together
& sent forth the whirlwind as messenger.
The elements of wind & water seethed
& the dark clouds of the south rolled up in concert;
the sun & the moon were made prisoner
& the twenty-eight constellations of the moon were fastened
    together;
the eight planets in their courses were cast into chains
& the faint milky way was delivered into bondage;
the little stars were altogether shrouded in mist
& when all things were covered in the complexion of mist
for nine days & nine nights the snow fell,
steadily throughout the eighteen times of day & night it fell.
When it fell heavily the flakes were as big as the flock of
    wool,
& fell floating like feathered birds.
When the snow fell lightly the flakes were small as spindles,
& fell circling like bees.
Again, they were as small as peas or mustard-seed,
& fell turning like distaffs.
Moreover the snow surpassed measure in depth,
the peak of white snow above reached to the heavens
& the trees of the forest below were bowed down.
The dark hills were clad in white,
ice formed upon the billowing lakes
& the blue Tsangpo was constrained in its depths.

The earth became like a plain without hill or valley,
& in natural consequence of such a great fall
the lay folk were mewed up;
famine overtook the four-footed cattle,
& the small deer especially found no food;
the feathered birds above lacked nourishment,
& the marmots & field-mice below hid in their burrows;
the jaws of beasts of prey were stiffened together.
In such fearsome circumstances
this strange fate befell me, Milarepa.
There were these three: the snowstorm driving down from on
   high,
the icy blast of mid-winter,
& the cotton cloth which I, the sage Mila, wore;
& between them rose a contest on that white snow peak.
The falling snow melted into goodly water;
the wind, though rushing mightily, abated of itself,
& the cotton cloth blazed like fire.
Life & death wrestled there after the fashion of champions,
& swords crossed victorious blades.
That I won there the heroic fight
will be an example to all the faithful
& a true example to all great contemplatives;
more especially will it prove the greater excellence
of the single cotton cloth & the inner heat.

3

That the white ice-peak of Tisé, great in fame,
is just a mountain covered with snow,
proves the whiteness of Buddha's teaching.
That the turquoise lake of Mapang, great in fame,
is water through which water flows,
proves the dissolution of all created things.

That I, Milarepa, great in fame,
am an old & naked man,
proves that I have forsaken & set at nought self-interest.
That I am a singer of little songs,
proves that I have learned to read the world as a book.

(Tibet)

Keeping Still / The Mountain

The Judgment
KEEPING STILL. Keeping his back still
So that he no longer feels his body.
He goes into his courtyard
& does not see his people.
No blame.

1.

Mountains standing close together:
The image of KEEPING STILL.

2.

Keeping his toes still.
No blame.
Continued perseverance furthers.

3.

Keeping his calves still.
He cannot rescue him whom he follows.
His heart is not glad.

4.

Keeping his hips still.
Making his sacrum stiff.
Dangerous. The heart suffocates.

5.

Keeping his trunk still.
No blame.

6.

Keeping his jaws still.
The words have order.
Remorse disappears.

7.

Noblehearted keeping still.
Good fortune.

(China)

THE MARRYING MAIDEN

The Judgment

THE MARRYING MAIDEN
Undertakings bring misfortune.
Nothing that would further.

1.

Thunder over the lake:
The image of THE MARRYING MAIDEN.

2.

The marrying maiden as a concubine.
A lame man who is able to tread.
Undertakings bring good fortune.

3.

A one-eyed man who is able to see.
The perseverance of a solitary man furthers.

4.

The marrying maiden as a slave.
She marries as a concubine.

5.

The marrying maiden draws out the allotted time.
A late marriage comes in due course.

6.

The sovereign *I* gave his daughter in marriage.
The embroidered garments of the princess
Were not as gorgeous
As those of the servingmaid.
The moon that is nearly full
Brings good fortune.

7.

The woman holds the basket, but there are no fruits in it.
The man stabs the sheep, but no blood flows.
Nothing that acts to further.

(China)

Origin-Legend of the Chou Tribe

She who in the beginning gave birth to the people,
This was Chiang Yüan.
How did she give birth to the people?
She sacrificed and prayed
That she might no longer be childless.
She trod on the big toe of God's footprint,
Was accepted and got what she desired.
Then in reverence, then in awe
She gave birth, she nurtured;
And this was Hou Chi.

The mother had fulfilled her months,
And her first-born came like a lamb
With no bursting or rending,
With no hurt or harm.
To make manifest His magic power
God on high gave her ease.
So blessed were her sacrifice and prayer
That easily she bore her child.

They put it in a narrow lane;
But oxen and sheep tenderly cherished it.
They put it in a far-off wood;
But it chanced that woodcutters came to this wood.
They put it on the cold ice;
But the birds covered it with their wings.
The birds at last went away,
And Hou Chi began to wail.

Truly far and wide
His voice was very loud.
Then sure enough he began to crawl;
Well he straddled, well he reared,
To reach food for his mouth.
He planted large beans;
His beans grew fat and tall.
His paddy-lines were close set,
His hemp and wheat grew thick,
His young gourds teemed.

Truly Hou Chi's husbandry
Followed the way that had been shown.
He cleared away the thick grass,
He planted the yellow crop.
It failed nowhere, it grew thick,
It was heavy, it was tall,
It sprouted, it eared,
It was firm and good,
It nodded, it hung—
He made house and home in T'ai.

The lucky grains were sent down to us,
The black millet, the double-kernelled,
Millet pink-sprouted and white.
Far and wide the black and the double-kernelled
He reaped and acred;
Far and wide the millet pink and white
He carried in his arms, he bore on his back,
Brought them home, and created the sacrifice.

What are they, our sacrifices?
We pound the grain, we bale it out,
We sift, we tread,
We wash it—soak, soak;
We boil it all steamy.
Then with due care, due thought
We gather southernwood, make offering of fat,
Take lambs for the rite of expiation,
We roast, we broil,
To give a start to the coming year.
High we load the stands,
The stands of wood and of earthenware.
As soon as the smell rises
God on high is very pleased:
'What smell is this, so strong and good?'
Hou Chi founded the sacrifices,
And without blemish or flaw
They have gone on till now.

(China)

SONG OF THE DEAD, RELATING THE ORIGIN OF BITTERNESS	

(Set One)		
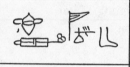		
To learn to do things here is bitterness	Ssu-ssa-zo of Shu-lo	when he was old but didn't know it

made a yellow wooden bowl	went to wash gold in it	Ssu-ssa-zo's shadow was projected on the water

he saw his shadow reflected on the water	his own shadow	that he saw reflected

he was old then & he knew it	on the horizon where the clouds touch heaven the old crane still didn't know that he was old	

(Set Two)		
How he was shaking his own body	his own white feathers dropping down before him	now that he knew that he was old
old tiger of the place called Such-&-Such	still didn't know that he was old	his long white fangs were falling down before him
& now he knew that he was old	At Such-&-Such-Another-Place	the white stag didn't know that he was old
now he was shaking his own body	his white antlers were falling down before him	then he knew that he was old

(Set Three)		
Now we will go with the dead & will suffer the bitterness of the dead	we will dance again & vanquish demons again	but if no one had told us where the dance began

we would never dare to speak about the dance	for unless one knows the origin of the dance	one cannot dance it

On top of Such-&-Such-a-Mountain	the yak said he would like to dance	but for the yak	there was no custom of the dance

no custom for the goat that followed	The sons of bitterness are here—they wear their hats

(Set Four)		
The yak will dance there, as the custom is	on top of Such-&-Such-a-Mountain	the stag said he would like to dance there
but for the stag	there was no custom of the dance	Shoes of elfskin & white toes
the sons of bitterness will wear them	the stag will dance there, as the custom is	& where the pinetrees grow the young deer try to dance
they beat their cloven hoofs in rhythm	swaying, dancing, as the custom is	& all the people of the village

(Set Five)	
& all the sons of bitterness	who have slim hips & sway in rhythm
who sway & dance again, as is the custom	we will follow the crane to his clouds
will go with the tiger to his high mountain	& with our ancestor into the sky
the crane wants to fly to the shining white gate in the clouds	all those born with wings
have followed the crane to his clouds	but his ability we do not allow to pass

(China: Na-Khi)

From THE NINE SONGS

Song V

The Big Lord of Lives

The gates of Heaven are open wide;
Off I ride, borne on a dark cloud!
May the gusty winds be my vanguard,
May sharp showers sprinkle the dust!
The Lord wheels in his flight, he is coming down;
I will cross K'ung-sang and attend upon you.
But all over the Nine Provinces there are people in throngs;
Why think that his task is among *us*?
High he flies, peacefully winging;
On pure air borne aloft he handles Yin and Yang.
I and the Lord, solemn and reverent,
On our way to God cross over the Nine Hills.
He trails his spirit-garment,
Dangles his girdle-gems.
One Yin for every Yang;
The crowd does not understand what we are doing.
I pluck the sparse-hemp's lovely flower,

Meaning to send it to him from whom I am separated.
Age creeps on apace, all will soon be over;
Not to draw nearer is to drift further apart.
He has driven his dragon chariot, loudly rumbling;
High up he gallops into Heaven.
Binding cassia-branches a long while I stay;
Ch'iang! The more I think of him, the sadder I grow,
The sadder I grow; but what does sadness help?
If only it could be forever as this time it was!
But man's fate is fixed;
From meetings and partings none can ever escape.

Song VI

The Little Lord of Lives

The autumn orchid and the deer-fodder
Grow thick under the hall,
From green leaves and white branches
Great gusts of scent assail me.
Among such people there are sure to be lovely young ones;
You have no need to be downcast and sad.
The autumn orchid is in its splendour;
Green its leaves, purple its stem.
The hall is full of lovely girls;
But suddenly it is me he eyes and me alone.

When he came in he said nothing, when he went out he said no
      word;
Riding on the whirlwind he carried a banner of cloud.
There is no sadness greater than that of a life-parting;
No joy greater than that of making new friends.
In coat of lotus-leaf, belt of basil
Suddenly he came, and as swiftly went.

At nightfall he is to lodge in the precincts of God.
Lord, for whom are you waiting, on the fringe of the clouds?
I bathed with you in the Pool of Heaven,
I dried your hair for you in a sunny fold of the hill.
I look towards my fair one; but he does not come.
With the wind on my face despairing I chant aloud.
Chariot-awning of peacock feathers, halcyon flags—
He mounts to the Nine Heavens, wields the Broom-star.
Lifts his long sword to succour young and old;
Yes, you alone are fit to deal out justice to the people.

Song VIII

The River God (Ho-po)

With you I wandered down the Nine Rivers;
A whirlwind rose and the waters barred us with their waves.
We rode in a water-chariot with awning of lotus-leaf
Drawn by two dragons, with griffins to pull at the sides.
I climb K'un-lun and look in all directions;
My heart rises all a-flutter, I am agitated and distraught.
Dusk is coming, but I am too sad to think of return.
Of the far shore only are my thoughts; I lie awake and yearn.

In his fish-scale house, dragon-scale hall,
Portico of purple-shell, in his red palace,
What is the Spirit doing, down in the water?
Riding a white turtle, followed by stripy fish
With you I wandered in the islands of the River.
The ice is on the move; soon the floods will be down.
You salute me with raised hands, then go towards the East.
I go with my lovely one as far as the southern shore.
The waves surge on surge come to meet him,
Fishes shoal after shoal escort me on my homeward way.

Song IX

The Mountain Spirit (Shan-kuei)

It seems there is someone over there, in that fold of the hill,
Clad in creepers, with a belt of mistletoe.
He is gazing at me, his lips parted in a smile;
'Have you taken a fancy to me? Do I please you with my lovely
    ways?'
Driving red leopards, followed by stripy civets,
Chariot of magnolia, banners of cassia,
Clad in stone-orchid, with belt of asarum,
I go gathering sweet herbs to give to the one I love.
I live in a dark bamboo grove, where I never see the sky;
The way was perilous and hard; that is why I am late for the
    tryst.

High on the top of the hill I stand all alone;
Below me the clouds sweep past in droves.
All is murk and gloom. *Ch'iang!* Darkness by day!
The east wind blows gust on gust, spreading magic rain.
Waiting for the Divine One I linger and forget to go back.
The year is drawing to its close; who will now beflower me?
I pluck the Thrice-blossoming amid the hills,
Among a welter of rocks and vine-creeper spreading between.
Wronged by my Lord I am too sad to think of going back.
You love me, I know it; nothing can come between us.
He of the hills is fragrant with the scent of galingale,
He drinks from a spring amid the rocks,
He shelters under cypress and pine.
You love me, I know it; despite all doubts that rise.
His chariot thunders, the air is dark with rain,
The monkeys twitter; again they cry all night.
The wind soughs and soughs, the trees rustle;
My love of my Lord has brought me only sorrow.

(China)

From CHAO HUN, OR THE SUMMONS OF THE SOUL

The Lord God said to Wu Yang:
   'There is a man on earth below whom I would help:
   'His soul has left him. Make divination for him.'
Wu Yang replied:
   'The Master of Dreams . . .
   'The Lord God's bidding is hard to follow.'
[The Lord God said:]
   'You must divine for him. I fear that if you any
   longer decline, it will be too late.'
Wu Yang therefore went down and summoned the soul, saying:
'O soul, come back! Why have you left your old abode and sped
   to the earth's far corners,
Deserting the place of your delight to meet all those things of
   evil omen?
O soul, come back! In the east you cannot abide.
There are giants there a thousand fathoms tall, who seek only
   for souls to catch,
And ten suns that come out together, melting metal, dissolving
   stone.
The folk that live there can bear it; but you, soul, would be
   consumed.
O soul, come back! In the east you cannot abide.
O soul, come back! In the south you cannot stay.
There the people have tattooed faces and blackened teeth;
They sacrifice flesh of men, and pound their bones to paste.
There are coiling snakes there, and the great fox that can run a
   hundred leagues,
And the great Nine-headed Serpent who darts swiftly this way
   and that,
And swallows men as a sweet relish.

O soul, come back! In the south you may not linger.

O soul, come back! For the west holds many perils:

The Moving Sands stretch on for a hundred leagues.

You will be swept into the Thunder's Chasm, and dashed in
    pieces, unable to help yourself;

And even should you escape from that, beyond is the empty
    desert,

And red ants as huge as elephants, and wasps as big as gourds.

The five grains do not grow there; dry stalks are the only food;

And the earth there scorches men up; there is nowhere to look
    for water.

And you will drift there for ever, with nowhere to go in that
    vastness.

O soul, come back! lest you bring on yourself perdition.

O soul, come back! In the north you may not stay.

There the layered ice rises high, and the snowflakes fly for a
    hundred leagues and more.

O soul, come back! You cannot long stay there.

O soul, come back! Climb not to the heaven above.

For tigers and leopards guard the gates, with jaws ever ready to
    rend up mortal men,

And one man with nine heads, that can pull up nine thousand
    trees,

And the slant-eyed jackal-wolves pad to and fro;

They hang out men for sport and drop them in the abyss,

And only at God's command may they ever rest or sleep.

O soul, come back! lest you fall into this danger.

O soul, come back! Go not down to the Land of Darkness,

Where the Earth God lies, nine-coiled, with dreadful horns on
    his forehead,

And a great humped back and bloody thumbs, pursuing men,
    swift-footed:

Three eyes he has in his tiger's head, and his body is like a
    bull's.

O soul, come back! lest you bring on yourself disaster.

O soul, come back! and enter the gate of the city.

The priests are there who call you, walking backwards to lead
   you in.
Ch'in basket-work, silk cords of Ch'i, and silken banners of
   Cheng . . .
High walls and deep chambers, with railings and tiered bal-
   conies;
Stepped terraces, storied pavilions, whose tops look on the high
   mountains;
Lattice doors with scarlet interstices, and carving on the square
   lintels;
Draughtless rooms for winter; galleries cool in summer;
Streams and gullies wind in and out, purling prettily;
A warm breeze bends the melilotus and sets the tall orchids
   swaying.
Crossing the hall into the apartments, the ceilings and floors are
   vermilion,
The chambers of polished stone, with kingfisher hangings on
   jasper hooks;
Bedspreads of kingfisher seeded with pearls, all dazzling in
   brightness;
Arras of fine silk covers the walls; damask canopies stretch
   overhead,
Braids and ribbons, brocades and satins, fastened with rings of
   precious stone. . . .
Bright candles of orchid-perfumed fat light up flower-like faces
   that await you . . .
Women with hair dressed finely in many fashions fill your
   apartments . . .
In your garden pavilion, by the long bed-curtains, they wait
   your royal pleasure . . .
The walls, red; vermilion the woodwork; jet inlay on the roof-
   beams;
Overhead you behold the carved rafters, painted with dragons
   and serpents;
Seated in the hall, leaning on the balustrade, you look down on
   a winding pool.

Its lotuses have just opened; among them grow water-chestnuts,

And purple-stemmed water-mallows enamel the green wave's surface.

Attendants quaintly costumed in spotted leopard skins wait on the sloping bank;

A light coach is tilted for you to ascend; footmen and riders wait in position.

An orchid carpet covers the ground; the hedge is of flowering hibiscus. . . .

Envoi

In the new year, as spring began, I set off for the south.

The green duckweed lay on the water, and the white flag flowered.

My road passed through Luchiang and to the right of Ch'ang-po.

I stood on the marsh's margin and looked far out on the distance.

My team was of four jet horses; we set out together a thousand chariots strong.

The beaters' fires flickered skyward, and the smoke rose like a pall.

I trotted to where the throng was, and galloped ahead to draw them;

Then reined as we sighted our quarry, and wheeled around to the right hand.

I raced with the King in the marshland to see which could go the faster.

The King himself shot the arrow, and the black ox dropped down dead.

'The darkness yields to daylight; we cannot stay much longer.

The marsh orchids cover the path here: this way must be too marshy.'

On, on the river's waters roll; above them grow woods of maple.

The eye travels on a thousand *li*, and the heart breaks for sorrow.

O soul, come back! Alas for the Southern Land!

(China)

What Was Said

Nine Tamil Love Poems from the Kuruntokai

1. *what the girl said:*

Once: if an owl hooted on the hill,
if a male ape leaped and loped
out there on the jackfruit bough in our yard
my poor heart would melt for fear. But now
in the difficult dark of night
nothing can stay its wandering
on the long sloping mountain-ways
of his coming.

by Kapilar
Kuruntokai 153

2. *what the lover said:*

If one can tell morning
from noon from listless evening,
townslept night from dawn, then one's love
is a lie.
If I should lose her
I could proclaim my misery in the streets
riding mock-horses on palmyra-stems in my wildness:
but that seems such a shame.
But then,
living away from her,
living seems such a shame.

by Allūr Nanmullaiyār
Kuruntokai 32

3. *what she said:*

They who know the way he went
say: where he goes now,
he crosses water-passes in the mountain
which are like passages in an ant-hill.
He has to climb rocks
hot as a blacksmith's anvil.
Where his road branches,
that's where the clansman
with the bent bow
whets the point of his arrow,
   But this loud-mouthed town
   knows nothing of my fears
   for the hardship of his ways,
   and taunts me
   for being lovesick.

                              Kuruntokai 12

4. *what he said:*

When love is ripe beyond bearing
and goes to seed,
men will ride even palmyra-stems
like horses; will wear on their heads
the reeking dense blossom of the erukkam
for emblems; will lie in streets
in the midst of onlookers' gossip;

and will do worse.

                              Kuruntokai 17

5. *what her friend said:*

The great city fell asleep
but we did not sleep.
Clearly we heard, all night
from the hillock next our house
the tender branches of the flower-clustered tree
with leaves like peacock-feet
let fall
its blue-sapphire flowers.

> by Kollan Alici
> Kuruntokai 138

6. *what he said:*

As a little white snake
with lovely stripes on its young body
troubles the jungle elephant,
     this slip of a girl,
     her teeth like sprouts of new rice,
     her wrists stacked with bangles,
     troubles me.

> by Catti Nātanār
> Kuruntokai 119

7. *what she said:*

Before I laughed with him

> nightly,
> the slow waves beating
> on his wide shores
> and the palmyra
> bringing forth heron-like flowers
> near the waters,

my eyes were like the lotus
my arms had the grace of the bamboo
my forehead was mistaken for the moon.

> But now

> by Maturai Eruttālan Cēntampūtan
> Kuruntokai 226

8. *what her girl-friend said to him* (when he wanted
   to come by night):

Man-eaters, male crocodiles with crooked legs,
cut off the traffic on these water-ways.
> But you,
in your love, will come to her swimming
through the shoals of fish in the black salt-marshes.
> And she,
she will suffer in her simpleness.
> And I,
what can I do but shudder in my heart
like a woman watching her poisoned twins?

> by Kavaimakan
> Kuruntokai 324

9. *what he said:*

Does that girl,
              eyes like flowers, gathering flowers
from pools for her garlands, driving away the parrots
from the millet-fields,

                  does that girl know at all
or doesn't she,
              that my heart is still there with her
              bellowing sighs
              like a drowsy midnight elephant

                    by Kapilar
                    Kuruntokai 142

                       (India)

THREE LOVE-CHARMS FROM CHHATTISGARH

1

Bagful of haldi-roots
Eye-girl lighting a lamp
Hold out their hands
The dark girls, the fair girls
Go my strong strong charm
Go my leaping charm
Awake love in this girl
Love in her walking feet
Love in the dust her feet stir
Love in her seeing eyes
Love in her moving eyelids
Love in her listening ears
Love in her speaking tongue
Love in her laughing teeth
Awake love, my charm
Love in the breasts ready to be fondled
Love in the vulva fit for love
Go my strong strong charm
Let the charm take this girl

2

As a net spreads across the river
May my love-charm fall upon her
In my net I bind the river-weed
In my net I bind the little fish
I bind as far as nine ploughs can go
I bind the spite of witches
I bind her house and door of victory
I bind the seats of four wise men

May my love-net fall upon her
To what village will you go?
Take the four-fingers-breadth of pleasure
Under the thighs is *jujuk-mujuk*
Inside is a well
The red-beaked parrot
Drinks the water of the cloud
May my love-net fall upon her

3

Almoha Jalmoha, may my love's enchantment
Take the water & the green scum on the water
& the water-girl at the time of fetching water
May my charm possess & madden
Her silver pitcher & its gold support
Her two-&-thirty teeth that shine like diamonds
Her speaking tongue, her smiling lips, her eyelids
May my love's enchantment madden
The vermilioned parting of her hair
Her bun of hair, the ribbon tying it
The *silver* in her ears, her nose-ring
The ten hundred rings upon her fingers
Her armlets & the bangles on her wrists
Her shining bangles & her sounding anklets
The ten hundred scorpion-rings upon her toes
Her spring-lovely sari twelve cubits long
The jacket tightening around her breasts
The fish that darts *chir-chir* in the stream
May my love's enchantment madden
This girl that pisses in the mortar
Her waist-belt, the cloth around her little sister
Go, go, my love-charm
Go eight hundred Mohani, nine hundred Chhittawar
Go fourteen hundred Singhi Tumi, go
Go by my Guru's word & by my word

To such & such a girl, enchant her with my love
Let her weep when she looks at other men
Let her laugh when she looks at me
Let her close her legs when other men approach her
Let her spread them wide, lying on her back, when I come near
Let her two-&-thirty teeth shine with the happiness of love
May my love's enchantment madden her
May the eight parts of her body tremble with desire
When she sees me, let her undo her cloth
When she does not see me, let her weep *dhar-dhar-dhar*
When she does not see me, let her breasts wobble
When she does not see me, let her vulva quiver
May my love's enchantment madden her
I will sacrifice a fresh black goat
& two young fowls
When I gain my desire

(India)

THE WITCH

1

I have cut the plantain grove
I have taken off my clothes
I have learnt from my mother-in-law
How to eat my husband
On the hills the wind blows
I have cut the thatching grass
I have grown weary
Weary of eating rice

2

The weapons are ready
The axe glitters
Over the smooth verandah
The wasps are swarming
O Bagru leave us
Kill the young servants
Kill the girls, kill the boys

(India: Santal)

MANTRA FOR BINDING A WITCH

1

I bind the sharp end of a knife
I bind the glow-worm in the forehead
I bind the magic of nine hundred guru
I bind the familiars of nine hundred witches
I bind the fairies of the sky

Let the sky turn upside down, let the earth be overturned, let
horns grow on horse & ass, let moustaches sprout on a young
girl, let the dry cow-dung sink & the stones float, but let
this charm not fail

2

I bind the glow-worm of a virgin
I bind every kind of Massan
The nail of bone
The lamp of flesh
Who binds the spirits?
The guru binds & I the guru's pupil
May the waters of the river flow uphill
May the dry cow-dung sink & stones float
But let my words not fail.

(India: Baiga)

THE PIG

1

Crushing the Pig

Ter na ni na O! Ter na ni na O!
Make a hole in the big gourd. I will go for water.
The old mother blows me out of the house.

O ter na ni na O!
The leaves of the parsa tree have long stalks.
You've been lying with your son.

I am going to cut my bewar.
You've been sleeping with your brother.
I am busy making rope.

You've been lying with your sister's son.
I am roasting gram.
I am lying with you, and your mother's watching us.

I am cutting wood for the fire.
You've been lying with a little boy.
Ter na ni na O! Ter na ni na O!

2

The Blood-Letting

Bring water, bring water! I'll wash his feet with water.
Bring oil, bring oil! I'll wash his feet with oil.
Bring milk, bring milk! I'll wash his feet with milk.

Teri na ho! Na na re na! Teri na na mor na na!
Today is Saturday, this is the night for the Laru!
We put the belwanti on the feet of the god.

I make a square of pearls.
O master, sit here on your throne.
Tare nake namare nana saheb! Tare nake namare nana!

3

The Coming of the Demon
Ter nana ke nano ho!

Where were you born? Where is your dwelling-place?
I was born down below. I live on the fence.
I am going to live with you.

Then I'll sleep with your sister.
O Phulera, dance and dance again.
Are you cooking in your kitchen?

May a cat dishonour you!
Don't have an old woman, she looks so very dirty.
By enjoying young girls, my life is satisfied.

Bring the root of adrak: may your father have you!
Where are you off to, girl?
May your brother dishonour you!

(India: Baiga)

AFTER THE HARVEST: A PRAYER

Then the fifth month harvest was over
we were ready to bring in the winter rice
to build up our dams & shut in the water
then the water would soon be getting in the rice-fields
& we waited for the fish in our ditches & dams
careful in our work
when no man worked for nothing
nor was used to coming home with nothing
then the buffalo went first
& worried that they'd twist their hindlegs
we walked behind them
or worried that they'd sprain their forelegs
or worried that things wouldn't work out well
or worried that the cattle weren't right
the bowl of water & the toothpicks for the god
& the plates of welldone meat, the skin & liver
Then we would bow a hundred times & make great greetings
so that my skin grows pale to think of it
& I would follow out the ritual of the months & years
not going till then, not meeting them till then
not being-at-their-service till then or bowing down
Then I would go to make a sign, would go
would ask my lord Ko'l Kwa to come
master of our ponds Ko'l Kwa master of our rice-fields
& others we would ask to bring it off
Mr Hin & Mrs Ho
the gang of mandarin lieutenants
Miss To Pa
& went as far as My Lord Cho
& My Lord Da
& went as far as My Lord You

Ko'l Kwa

I asked you to come see us, to come down to us
come eat the rice under our window
& drink the alcohol inside our house
all this so that the rice would work out well
so that the grain would grow real tight
& since I was a priest I rose
& standing, then & there, addressed you
rose up & being-in-your-service
then & there I stammered out my prayers
or standing on my feet I clasped my hands
& since I was a priest I had the rules by heart
the rules for measure & for order
for bowing crosswise, showing you my side & heart
what man speaks true?
whose heart is always righteous?
asks the priest
the head of me the priest
the doorway made of straw & flowers
my hand that holds a fan with sprigs of flowers
my loins beneath this cloth
my back that wears this sash with fringes
the priest who rising, here & now, addresses you
now when the bodies of dead children fill the earth
& the vanished people fill the villages & compounds
& the troops & officers are in our beds
& the sons of nobles & the high-born girls
ride by in carriages, returning to the throne
& though I was a priest I didn't ask them
on cloudy days I waited You were banned I asked You in
on sunny days Your name was interdicted
& only I knew what Your highest name was
only I knew all your names
so long ago, so many names & times
so many times I asked you to come down to us

master of our ponds Ko'l Kwa master of our rice-fields
come eat the rice under our window
& drink the alcohol inside our house
for I have followed out the ritual of the months & years
the ritual of the months & years

(Vietnam: The Muong)

THE SEVEN

They are 7 in number, just 7
In the terrible depths they are 7
Bow down, in the sky they are 7

In the terrible depths, the dark houses
They swell, they grow tall

They are neither female nor male
They are a silence heavy with seastorms
They bear off no women their loins are empty of children
They are strangers to pity, compassion is far from them
They are deaf to men's prayers, entreaties can't reach them
They are horses that grow to great size that feed on mountains
They are the enemies of our friends
They feed on the gods
They tear up the highways they spread out over the roads
They are the faces of evil they are the faces of evil

They are 7 they are 7 they are 7 times 7
In the name of Heaven let them be torn from our sight
In the name of the Earth let them be torn from our sight

(Sumerian)

ENKI & UTTU

The eye . . .

. . .

. . . Uttu, the fair lady *. . . ,*

. . . ,

. . . in his . . . ,

. . . heart *. . .*

Bring [the cucumbers in *their . . .*],

Bring [*the apples*] in their [*. . .*],

Bring the grapes in their *. . . ,*

In the house may he take hold of my leash,

May Enki there take hold of my leash."

A second time while he was filling with water,

He filled the dikes with water,

He filled the ditches with water,

He filled the uncultivated places with water.

The gardener *in the dust* in his joy *. . . ,*

He embrac[es] him.

"Who art thou who . . . [my] garden?"

Enki [answers] the gardener:

" *. . . ,*

[*Bring me the cucumbers in their . . .*],

[*Bring me the apples in their . . .*],

[*Bring me the grapes in their . . . .*]"

[He] *brought* him the cucumbers in *their . . . ,*

He *brought* him *the apples* in their *. . . ,*

He *brought* him the grapes in their *. . . ,* he heaped them
on his lap.

Enki, his face turned green, he gripped the staff,

To Uttu Enki directed his step.

"Who . . . st *in her house,* open."

"Thou, who art thou?"

"I, the gardener, would give thee cucumbers, *apples,* and
   grapes as a 'so be it.'"
Uttu with joyful heart opened the door of the house.
Enki to Uttu, the *fair lady,*
Gives the cucumbers in their . . . ,
Gives *the apples* in their . . . ,
Gives the grapes in their. . . .
Uttu, the fair lady . . . s the . . . for *him,* . . . s the . . .
   for *him*.
Enki took his joy of Uttu,
He embraced her, lay in her lap,
He . . . s the thighs, he touches the . . . ,
He embraced her, lay in her lap,
With the young one he cohabited, he kissed her.
Enki poured the semen into the womb,
She took the semen into the womb, the semen of Enki.
Uttu, the fair lady . . . ,
Ninhursag . . . d the *semen from the thighs*

(Sumerian)

Prayer to the Gods of the Night

They are lying down, the great ones.
The bolts are fallen; the fastenings are placed.
The crowds and people are quiet.
The open gates are (now) closed.
The gods of the land and the goddesses of the land,
Shamash, Sin, Adad, and Ishtar,
Have betaken themselves to sleep in heaven.
They are not pronouncing judgment;
They are not deciding things.
The night is veiled.
The temple and the most holy places are quiet and dark.
The traveler calls on (his) god;
And the litigant is tarrying in sleep.
The judge of truth, the father of the fatherless,
Shamash, has betaken himself to his chamber.
O great ones, gods of the night,
O bright one, Gibil, O warrior, Irra,
O bow (star) and yoke (star),
O Pleiades, Orion, and the dragon,
O Ursa major, goat (star), and the bison.
Stand by, and then,
In the divination which I am making,
In the lamb which I am offering,
Put truth for me.

(Sumero-Akkadian)

CHILD-BEARING TEXT

[. . .] her breast
[. . .] the beard
[. . .] the cheek of the man.
[. . .] & the raising
[. . .] of both eyes, the wife & her husband.
[Fourteen mother]-wombs were assembled
[Before] Nintu.
[At the ti]me of the new moon
[To the House] of Fates they called the *votaries*.
[*Enkidu* . . .] came &
[*Kneel*]*ed down,* opening the womb.
[. . .] . . . and happy was his countenance.
[. . . bent] the knees [. . .],
[. . .] made an opening,
She brought forth her issue,
Praying.
Fashion a clay brick into a core,
Make . . . stone in the midst of [. . .];
Let the vexed rejoice in the house of the one in childbirth!
As the Bearer gives birth,
May the mo[ther of the ch]ild bring forth by herself!

(Old Babylonian)

THE GODDESS

[. . .] . . .
Henna of seven maids,
  Smell of coriander and *ambergris.*
She *locked the gates* of Anath's house
  And met the picked fighters in . . .
Now Anath doth battle in the plain,
  Fighting between the two towns;
Smiting the *Westland's* peoples,
  Smashing the folk of the Sunrise.
Under her, *hea*[*ds*] like *sheaves;*
  Over her, *hands* like locusts,
  Like a grassho[*pper*]-mass heroes' hands.
She binds the *heads* to her back,
  Fastens the hands in her girdle.
She p[lunges] knee-deep in knights' blood,
  Hip-deep in the gore of heroes.
With darts she drives . . . ,
  With the . . . of her bow . . .
Now Anath goes to her house,
  The goddess proceeds to her palace.
Not sated with battling in the plain,
  With her fighting between the two towns,
She *pictures* the chairs as heroes,
  Pretending a table is warriors,
  And that the footstools are troops.
Much battle she does and beholds,
  Her fighting contemplates Anath:
Her liver *swells* with laughter,
  Her heart fills up with joy,
  Anath's liver *exults;*

For she plunges knee-deep in knights' blood,
    Hip-deep in the gore of heroes.
Then, sated with battling in the house,
    Fighting between the two tables,
. . . [. . .]s the knights' blood,
    Pours the fatness of [de]w in a bowl.
Ma[id]en Anath washes her hands,
    Yabamat Liimmim her fingers;
[She w]ashes her hands of knights' blood,
    Her [fi]ngers of gore of heroes.
[. . .] . . . to chairs,
    Table also to table;
    Footstools *turn back* into footstools.
[She] draws some water and bathes;
    Sky-[d]ew, fatness of earth,
    Spray of the Rider of Clouds;
Dew that the heavens do shed,
    [Spray] that is shed by the stars.
She rubs herself in with *ambergris*
    [*From a sperm-whale*] *whose home's* in the sea.
[. . .] . . .

(Canaanite)

HEBREW VISIONS

1

And Jacob went out from Beersheba & went toward Haran.

And he lighted upon a certain place, & tarried there all night, because the sun was set: & he took hold of the stones of that place, & put them for pillows, & lay down in that place to sleep.

And he dreamed, & behold, a ladder set up on the earth, & the top of it reached to heaven: & behold, the angels of God ascending & descending on it.

And behold, the Lord stood above it, & said, I am the Lord God of Abraham thy father, & the God of Isaac: the land whereon thou liest, to thee will I give it, & to thy seed.

And thy seed shall be as the dust of the earth; & thou shall spread abroad to the west, & to the east, & to the north, & to the south: & in thee & in thy seed shall all the families of the earth be blessed.

2

The burden of the desert of the sea. As whirlwinds in the south pass through; so it cometh from the desert from a terrible land.

A grievous vision is declared unto me; The treacherous dealer dealeth treacherously, & the spoiler spoileth. Go up, O Elam: besiege, O Media; all the sighing thereof have I made to cease.

Therefore are my loins filled with pain: pangs have taken hold upon me, as the pangs of a woman that travaileth: I was bowed down at the hearing of it; I was dismayed at the seeing of it.

My heart panted, fearfulness affrighted me: the night of my pleasure hath he turned into fear unto me.

Prepare the table, watch in the watchtower, eat, drink; arise, ye princes, & anoint the shield.

For thus hath the Lord said unto me, Go, set a watchman, let him declare what he seeth.

And he saw a chariot with a couple of horsemen, a chariot of asses, & a chariot of camels; & he hearkened diligently with much heed:

& he cried, A lion: My lord, I stand continually upon the watchtower in the day time, & I am set in my ward whole nights.

And behold, here cometh a chariot of men, with a couple of horsemen. And he answered & said, Babylon is fallen, is fallen; & all the graven images of her gods he hath broken unto the ground.

O my threshing, & the corn of my floor: that which I have heard of the Lord of hosts, the God of Israel, have I declared unto you.

The burden of Dumah. He calleth to me out of Seir, Watchman, what of the night? Watchman, what of the night?

The watchman said, The morning cometh, & also the night: if ye will inquire, inquire ye: return, come.

The burden of the valley of vision. What aileth thee now, that thou art wholly gone up to the house-tops?

Thou that art full of stirs, a tumultuous city, a joyous city: thy slain men are not slain with the sword, nor dead in battle.

All thy rulers are fled together, they are bound by the archers: all that are found in thee are bound together, which have fled from far.

3

And I looked, &, behold, a whirlwind came out of the north, a great cloud, & a fire infolding itself, & a brightness was about it, & out of the midst thereof as the color of amber, out of the midst of the fire.

Also out of the midst thereof came the likeness of four living creatures. And this was their appearance; they had the likeness of a man.

And every one had four faces, and every one had four wings.

And their feet were straight feet; & the sole of their feet was like the sole of a calf's foot; & they sparkled like the color of burnished brass.

And they had the hands of a man under their wings on their four sides; & they four had their faces & their wings.

Their wings were joined one to another; they turned not when they went; they went every one straight forward.

As for the likeness of their faces, they four had the face of a man, & the face of a lion, on the right side: & they four had the face of an ox on the left side; they four also had the face of an eagle.

Thus were their faces: & their wings were stretched upward; two wings of every one were joined one to another, & two covered their bodies.

And they went every one straight forward: whither the spirit was to go, they went; & they turned not when they went.

As for the likeness of the living creatures, their appearance was like burning coals of fire, & like the appearance of lamps: it went up & down among the living creatures; & the fire was bright, & out of the fire went forth lightning.

And the living creatures ran & returned as the appearance of a flash of lightning.

Now as I beheld the living creatures, behold one wheel upon the earth by the living creatures, with his four faces.

The appearance of the wheels & their work was like unto the color of a beryl: & they four had one likeness: & their appearance & their work was as it were a wheel in the middle of a wheel.

When they went, they went upon their four sides: & they turned not when they went.

As for their rings, they were so high that they were dreadful; & their rings were full of eyes round about them four.

And when the living creatures went, the wheels went by them: & when the living creatures were lifted up from the earth, the wheels were lifted up.

4

And there appeared a great wonder in heaven; a woman clothed with the sun, & the moon under her feet, & upon her head a crown of twelve stars:

And she being with child cried, travailing in birth, & pained to be delivered.

And there appeared another wonder in heaven; & behold a great red dragon, having seven heads & ten horns, & seven crowns upon his heads.

And his tail drew the third part of the stars of heaven, & did cast them to the earth: & the dragon stood before the woman which was ready to be delivered, for to devour her child as soon as it was born.

And she brought forth a man child, who was to rule all nations with a rod of iron: & her child was caught up unto God, & to his throne.

And the woman fled into the wilderness, where she hath a place prepared of God, that they should feed her there a thousand two hundred & three score days.

And there was a war in heaven: Michael & his angels fought against the dragon; & the dragon fought & his angels,

& prevailed not; neither was their place found any more in heaven.

. . . .

And when the dragon saw that he was cast unto the earth, he
persecuted the woman which brought forth the man child.

And to the woman were given two wings of a great eagle, that
she might fly into the wilderness, into her place, where she
is nourished for a time, & times, & half a time, from the face
of the serpent.

And the serpent cast out of his mouth water as a flood after the
woman, that he might cause her to be carried away of the
flood.

And the earth helped the woman, & the earth opened her
mouth, & swallowed up the flood which the dragon cast out of
his mouth.

OCEANIA

Twelve Kura Songs from Tikopia

1

o kume kume of the falling rain
kume to draw near
& to ask after kume

& One-Before-Us to draw near

to do something to enter, o
to do something to turn to us

2

stand firm, my housepost
& stand firm for me, my housepost
rata was dancing in front
he had followed me

he had followed me, o
he had followed me here like the iron tree
he had followed me, o

3

& knock away the rear of the hermit crab, o
my maleness had long been prepared
now was ready

now that you've turned on your back
& sleep snoring

4

your pit, your cherry
is concealed & must stay hidden

must not spread your legs apart
but hide what smells there

5

take it
& keep on scorching it
& turn it over nicely
with legs apart

& call the long one penis
to turn it over nicely
& desire it

6

he is like a spider, he shits
& comes on as a tree trunk

& shits, o he shits on that road
all men reach for

7

& is red as rata

& as all this land

& its mountains

8

asking my wife to come near
to hold up my penis
& say:
you are penis

like the cunt of an unmarried woman
his penis is dark

9

the woman you found on the road
who stayed on the road
& brought the men to fulfillment

whose buttocks are black as an oven

10

leave me only
the lips of my throat
o my belly is hungry

o this bright red flower
you carried away
& my fear you would drop it

11

the bright red flower of that road
adorned by woman

you came walking down that road
your body glowing

12

your penis, penis of the hot cordyline root
your fruit-dark penis

that looks dark, looks dark to me
in front of you
& darker, like a cowry shell
for darkness

(British Solomon Islands)

The Gumagabu Song

(by Tomakam)

I

The stranger of Gumagabu sits on the top of the mountain.
'Go on top of the mountain, the towering mountain . . .'
——They cry for Toraya. . . .——
The stranger of Gumagabu sits on the slope of the mountain.
——The fringe of small clouds lifts above Boyowa;
The mother cries for Toraya——
'I shall take my revenge.'
The mother cries for Toraya.

II

Our mother, Dibwaruna, dreams on the mat.
She dreams about the killing.
'Revenge the wailing;
Anchor; hit the Gabu strangers!'
——The stranger comes out;
The chief gives him the *pari;*
'I shall give you the *doga;*
Bring me things from the mountain to the canoe!'

III

We exchange our *vaygu'a;*
The rumour of my arrival spreads through the Koya
We talk and talk.
He bends and is killed.

His companions run away;
His body is thrown into the sea;
The companions of the stranger run away,
We sail home.

IV

Next day, the sea foams up,
The chief's canoe stops on the reef;
The storm approaches;
The chief is afraid of drowning.
The conch shell is blown:
It sounds in the mountain.
They all weep on the reef.

V

They paddle in the chief's canoe;
They circle round the point of Bewara.
'I have hung my basket.
I have met him.'
So cries the chief,
So cries repeatedly the chief.

VI

Women in festive decoration
Walk on the beach.
Nawaruva puts on her turtle rings;
She puts on her *luluga'u* skirt.
In the village of my fathers, in Burakwa.
There is plenty of food;
Plenty is brought in for distribution.

(New Guinea: Trobriand Islands)

The Poetics of Hunger

I

Trumpet shell, restore, restore
The hunger-swollen belly, trumpet shell, restore, restore
The hunger exhaustion, trumpet shell, restore, restore
The hunger faintness, trumpet shell, restore, restore
The hunger prostration, trumpet shell, restore, restore
The hunger depression, trumpet shell, restore, restore
The hunger drooping, trumpet shell, restore, restore
The hunger famine, trumpet shell, restore, restore
The utter famine, trumpet shell, restore, restore
The drooping famine, trumpet shell, restore, restore
Round the house, trumpet shell, restore, restore
Round the earth oven, trumpet shell, restore, restore
Round the hearth-stones, trumpet shell, restore, restore
Round the foundation-beams, trumpet shell, restore, restore
Round the rafters, trumpet shell, restore, restore
Round the ridge pole, trumpet shell, restore, restore
Round the front frame of my thatch, trumpet shell, restore, re-
store
Round the shelves of my house, trumpet shell, restore, restore
Round the threshold boards of my house, trumpet shell, restore,
restore
Round the ground fronting my house, trumpet shell, restore,
restore
Round the central place, trumpet shell, restore, restore
Round the beaten soil, trumpet shell, restore, restore
Round where the road starts, trumpet shell, restore, restore
Round the roads themselves, trumpet shell, restore, restore
Round the sea shore, trumpet shell, restore, restore

Round the low-water mark, trumpet shell, restore, restore
Round the shallow water, trumpet shell, restore, restore
Restore this way, restore that way

2

This is not thy wind, O hunger, thy wind is from the north-west
This is not thy sea-passage, the sea-passage of Kadinaka is thy
    sea-passage
This is not thy mountain, the hill in Wawela is thy mountain
This is not thy promontory, the promontory of Silawotu is thy
    promontory
This is not thy channel, the channel in Kalubaku is thy channel
This is not thy sea-arm, the passage of Kaulokoki is thy sea-arm
Get thee to the passage between Tuma & Buriwada
Get thee to Tuma
Disperse, begone
Get old, begone
Disappear, begone
Die away, begone
Die for good & all, begone
I sweep thee, O belly of my village
The belly of my village boils up
The belly of my village is darkened with plenty
The belly of my village is full of strong beams
The belly of my village streams with sweat
The belly of my village is drenched with sweat

(New Guinea: Trobriand Islands)

The Daybreak

Day breaks: the first rays of the rising Sun,
    stretching her arms.
Daylight breaking, as the Sun rises to her feet.
Sun rising, scattering the darkness;
    lighting up the land . . .
With disc shining, bringing daylight,
    as the birds whistle and call . . .
People are moving about, talking, feeling the warmth.
Burning through the Gorge, she rises,
    walking westwards,
Wearing her waist-band of human hair.
She shines on the blossoming coolibah tree,
    with its sprawling roots,
Its shady branches spreading . . .

                    (Australia: Mudbara)

The Waves

Waves coming up: high waves coming up
   against the rocks,
Breaking, shi! shi!
When the moon is high with light upon the
   waters:
Spring tide; tide flowing to the grass,
Breaking, shi! shi!
In its rough waters, the young girls bathe.
Hear the sound they make with their hands
   as they play!

(Australia: Laragia)

The Lightning Snakes

(A Love Poem)

The tongues of the Lightning Snakes flicker and twist, one to the
other . . .
They flash across the foliage of the cabbage palms . . .
Lightning flashes through the clouds, with the flickering tongue
of the Snake . . .
It is always there, at the wide expanse of water, at the place of
the sacred tree . . .
All over the sky, their tongues flicker: above the place of the
Rising Clouds, the place of the Standing Clouds . . .
All over the sky, tongues flickering and twisting . . .
They are always there, at the camp by the wide expanse of
water . . .
All over the sky, their tongues flicker: at the place of the Two
Sisters, the place of the Wauwalak . . .
Lightning flashes through the clouds, flash of the Lightning
Snake . . .
Its blinding flash lights up the cabbage palm foliage . . .
Gleams on the cabbage palms and on the shining leaves . . .

(Australia: Arnhem Land)

SIGHTINGS: KUNAPIPI

(1st Set)

1   The musk of her
         red-walled vagina
      inviting coitus

2   Her skin soft like fur

3   She is shy at first, but soon
      they laugh together

4   Laughing-together
      Clitoris
      Soft-inside-of-the-vagina

5   Removing her pubic cloth
         opening
               her legs
         lying between them &
      coming

6   And copulating for a child

7   Fire   Fire
      Flame   Ashes

8   fire sticks &
      flames are
      flaring
      sparks
      are flying

9   Urination
      Testes
      Urination

10 Loincloth
    (red)
    Loincloth
    (white)
    Loincloth
    (black)

                    (*2nd Set*)

1   "penis"   incisure   incisure
    penis   penis   semen

2   Semen white like the mist

3   with penis erect
    the kangaroo
    moves its buttocks

4   step by step
    (she) walks away from coitus
    her back to them

5   the catfish swimming
    & singing

6   the bullroarer's string

7   The nipples of the young girl's breasts
        protrude—
    & the musk of her vagina—

8   creek
    moving

    "creek"

9   mist covering
    the river

10 cypress branches
    cypress cone
    seeds of the cone

                (Australia: Arnhem Land)

From THE DJANGGAWUL SONG CYCLE

Song 157

What is that crying? It is a parakeet nestling crying softly, upon
   the *djuda:*
Crying softly, as it saw the warm rays of the sun in the west, at
   Djurabula.
Crying as it saw the sun, the long cry of the parakeet:
Drying its feathers in the rising heat of the sun . . .
Drying its red breast feathers, its nestlings. 'Ah, my children!
   (says the parakeet). My downy feathers!'
It clasps the tree, as feathered strings cling to the sacred
   rangga . . .
Clasping the *djuda* with its claws, moving along . . .
It saw the sun's rays and the red glow of the sunset:
'You, red clouds! You I saw reflected in the sacred *nara* shade,
   spreading from Milngurmuru, from Milngaidja.'
Crying, the birds vanish within the peak of the mat, and are
   covered up . . .

Song 158

Go, carefully flatten the mat and its transverse fibre; spread it
   firmly out on the ground, opening it wide . . .
Yes, go quickly, get a stone knife.
Where is the transverse fibre of the mat?
Lie down carefully, quietly, in the *nara* shade, resting your head
   as if in sleep on the *rangga* emblems:
In the sacred shade where we have made country, building the
   sandhill mound:
Go, carefully lie there with legs apart!
I shall cut the clitoris, and put more *rangga* people:
Is it done? Yes, come close to me for coitus!

What is that there, blocking me? There is something within the
vagina; I must go carefully!

Yes, go, cut the clitoris . . .

Ah, go carefully! Be gentle!

The sound of my cry flies over to Dulmulwondeinbi. Be gentle!

Shall this one sound go over to Dambala?

Carefully they are dancing towards the sacred well, at Jiganjindu, Bulbulmara, Marabai:

For within the well we shall cover up the sacred severed clitoris,
within the well at Jiganjindu.

Covered up, from within the mat, its transverse fibre, its inner
peak . . .

Thus, turn over, into the warm caressing rays of the sun . . .

Open your legs to the healing warmth of the sun, labia minora
glowing with redness, with blood, like the breast feathers of
the parakeet!

We take hot coals from the wood of the claypan tree, heating a
stone to dry the blood from the cut clitoris.

Covering up that clitoris within the mat, with its transverse fibre,
making it like a younger sibling:

Reverently put it within the *ngainmara,* covering it up for
sleeping.

For the *mauwulan* has been plunged in, all the way, dragging
along; so carefully, dry the smell . . .

Song 159

Go, take that hot stone, and heat it near her clitoris:

For the severed part is a sacred *djuda rangga.* Covering up the
clitoris within the mat, within its transverse fibre, within its
mouth, its inner peak . . .

Go, the people are dancing there, like *djuda* roots, like spray,
moving their bodies, shaking their hair!

Carefully they beat their clapping sticks on the *mauwulan*
point . . .

Go, stand up! See the clansfolk beyond the transverse fibre of the
mat!

They come from the Sister's womb, lifting aside the clitoris, coming out like *djuda* roots . . .

Into the sacred shade, the *rangga* folk come dancing from the inner peak of the mat . . .

Only a few people will be left here: some we shall put into the coarse grass.

We are putting the *rangga* clansfolk . . .

Song 160

Go, put out the *rangga,* making it big: open your legs, for you look nice!

Yes, take Miralaidj, my Sister. Yes, the mouth of the mat is closed.

Yes, go, rest there quietly, for the vagina is sacred, and the *rangga* are hidden there, like younger siblings, covered up so no one may see.

Thus, climb up, put it into the mouth of the mat!

What is this, blocking my penis? I rest above her, chest on her breasts!

Do not push hard! The sound of her cry echoes.

Covered up, so no one may see, like a younger sibling . . .

Do not move what is within, for it is sacred!

For it rests there within, like the transverse fibre of the mat.

Blood running, sacredly running!

Yes, they, the *rangga* clansfolk, are coming out like *djuda* roots, like spray . . .

Go, digging within, causing the blood to flow, sacred blood from the red vagina, that no one may see!

Very sacred stands the *rangga* penis!

Song 161

Hit your loins, so that blood flows into the mouth of the sacred shade:

Yes, go, cover up the blood which has fallen!

For yes, go, let the *rangga* people come out . . .

Put your foot on the navel, releasing the blood, pushing strongly
   and breaking up the clot, to let it flow . . .
Go, put your foot on the navel, carefully, so that the sacred
   blood may flow . . .
It is done. Yes, go, cover the fallen blood in here, dragging the
   mud in the well to cover it up . . .
Is it done? Yes, put her into the mouth of the shade, beneath the
   transverse fibre of the mat: she is tabu, like a younger sibling.
   Let her sleep there within, quietly, shining, like a younger
   sibling . . .
The sound of clapping sticks, tapping against the *rangga!*
She lies there quietly, moving her shoulders to the rhythm, lying
   in sacred tabu-ness . . .
The sound of the clapping sticks echoes within, the sound of
   singing . . .
For she is within the inner peak of the mat, the sacred shade!

(Australia: Arnhem Land)

THE MOON-BONE CYCLE

I

The people are making a camp of branches in that country at
    Arnhem Bay:
With the forked stick, the rail for the whole camp, the
    'Mandʒikai people are making it.
Branches and leaves are about the mouth of the hut: the middle
    is clear within.
They are thinking of rain, and of storing their clubs in case of a
    quarrel,
In the country of the Dugong, towards the wide clay pans made
    by the Moonlight.
Thinking of rain, and of storing the fighting sticks.
They put up the rafters of arm-band-tree wood, put the branches
    on to the camp, at Arnhem Bay, in that place of the Du-
    gong . . .
And they block up the back of the hut with branches.
Carefully place the branches, for this is the camp of the Morn-
    ing-Pigeon man,
And of the Middle-of-the-Camp man; of the Mangrove-Fish
    man; of two other head-men,
And of the Clay Pan man; of the *'Baijini*-Anchor man, and of
    the Arnhem Bay country man;
Of the Whale man and of another head-man; of the Arnhem
    Bay Creek man;
Of the Scales-of-the-Rock-Cod man; of the Rock Cod man, and
    of the Place-of-the-Water man.

2.

They are sitting about in the camp, among the branches, along
    the back of the camp:

Sitting along in lines in the camp, there in the shade of the
 paperbark trees:
Sitting along in a line, like the new white spreading clouds:
In the shade of the paperbarks, they are sitting resting like clouds.
People of the clouds, living there like the mist; like the mist sit-
 ting resting with arms on knees,
In here towards the shade, in this Place, in the shadow of paper-
 barks.
Sitting there in rows, those *'Wɔnguri-'Mandʒikai* people, pa-
 perbarks along like a cloud.
Living on cycad-nut bread; sitting there with white-stained fin-
 gers,
Sitting in there resting, those people of the Sandfly clan . . .
Sitting there like mist, at that place of the Dugong . . . and of
 the Dugong's Entrails . . .
Sitting resting there in the place of the Dugong . . .
In that place of the Moonlight Clay Pan, and at the place of
 the Dugong . . .
There at that Dugong place they are sitting all along.

3.

Wake up from sleeping! Come, we go to see the clay pan, at the
 place of the Dugong . . .
Walking along, stepping along, straightening up after resting:
Walking along, looking as we go down on to the clay pan.
Looking for lily plants as we go . . . and looking for lily foli-
 age . . .
Circling around, searching towards the middle of the lily leaves
 to reach the rounded roots.
At that place of the Dugong . . .
At that place of the Dugong's Tail . . .
At that place of the Dugong; looking for food with stalks,
For lily foliage, and for the round-nut roots of the lily plant.

4.

The birds saw the people walking along.

Crying, the white cockatoos flew over the clay pan of the Moon-light;

From the place of the Dugong they flew, looking for lily-root food; pushing the foliage down and eating the soft roots.

Crying, the birds flew down and along the clay pan, at that place of the Dugong . . .

Crying, flying down there along the clay pan . . .

At the place of the Dugong, of the Tree-Limbs-Rubbing-Together, and of the Evening Star.

Where the lily-root clay pan is . . .

Where the cockatoos play, at that place of the Dugong . . .

Flapping their wings they flew down, crying, "We saw the people!"

There they are always living, those clans of the white cockatoo . . .

And there is the Shag woman, and there her clan:

Birds, trampling the lily foliage, eating the soft round roots!

5.

An animal track is running along: it is the track of the rat . . .

Of the male rat, and the female rat, and the young that hang to her teats as she runs,

The male rat hopping along, and the female rat, leaving paw-marks as a sign . . .

On the clay pans of the Dugong, and in the shade of the trees,

At the Dugong's place, and at the place of her Tail . . .

Thus, they spread paw-mark messages all along their tracks,

In that place of the Evening Star, in the place of the Du-gong . . .

Among the lily plants and into the mist, into the Dugong place, and into the place of her Entrails.

Backwards and forwards the rats run, always hopping along . . .

Carrying swamp-grass for nesting, over the little tracks, leaving their signs.

Backwards and forwards they run on the clay pan, around the place of the Dugong.

Men saw their tracks at the Dugong's place, in the shade of the trees, on the white clay;

Roads of the rats, paw-marks everywhere, running into the mist.

All around are their signs; and there men saw them down on the clay pan, at the place of the Dugong.

6.

A duck comes swooping down to the Moonlight Clay Pan, there at the place of the Dugong . . .

From far away. "I saw her flying over, in here at the clay pan . . ."

Floating along, pushing the pool into ripples and preening her feathers.

"I carried these eggs from a long way off, from inland to Arnhem Bay . . ."

Eggs, eggs, eggs; eggs she is carrying, swimming along.

She preens her feathers, and pulls at the lily foliage,

Drags at the lily leaves with her claws for food.

Swimming along, rippling the water among the lotus plants . . .

Backwards and forwards: she pulls at the foliage, swimming along, floating and eating.

This bird is taking her food, the lotus food in the clay pan,

At the place of the Dugong there, at the place of the Dugong's Tail . . .

Swimming along for food, floating, and rippling the water, there at the place of the Lilies.

Taking the lotus, the rounded roots and stalks of the lily; searching and eating there as she ripples the water.

"Because I have eggs, I give to my young the sound of the water."

Splashing and preening herself, she ripples the water, among the lotus . . .

Backwards and forwards, swimming along, rippling the water,

Floating along on the clay pan, at the place of the Dugong.

7.

People were diving here at the place of the Dugong . . .

Here they were digging all around, following up the lily stalks,

Digging into the mud for the rounded roots of the lily,

Digging them out at that place of the Dugong, and of the Evening Star,

Pushing aside the water while digging, and smearing themselves with mud . . .

Piling up the mud as they dug, and washing the roots clean.

They saw arm after arm there digging: people thick like the mist . . .

The Shag woman too was there, following up the lily stalks.

There they saw arm after arm of the 'Mandʒikai Sandfly clan,

Following the stalks along, searching and digging for food:

Always there together, those 'Mandʒikai Sandfly people.

They follow the stalks of the lotus and lily, looking for food.

The lilies that always grow there at the place of the Dugong . . .

At that clay pan, at the place of the Dugong, at the place of the lilies.

8.

Now the leech is swimming along . . . It always lives there in the water . . .

It takes hold of the leaves of the lily and pods of the lotus, and climbs up on to their stalks.

Swimming along and grasping hold of the leaves with its head . . .

It always lives there in the water, and climbs up on to the people.

Always there, that leech, together with all its clan . . .

Swimming along towards the trees, it climbs up and waits for people.

Hear it swimming along through the water, its head out ready to grasp us . . .

Always living here and swimming along.

Because that leech is always there, for us, however it came there:

The leech that catches hold of those *'Mandʒikai* Sandfly people . . .

9.

The prawn is there, at the place of the Dugong, digging out mud with its claws . . .

The hard-shelled prawn living there in the water, making soft little noises.

It burrows into the mud and casts it aside, among the lilies . . .

Throwing aside the mud, with soft little noises . . .

Digging out mud with its claws at the place of the Dugong, the place of the Dugong's Tail . . .

Calling the bone *'bukəlili,* the catfish *'bukəlili,* the frog *'bukəlili,* the sacred tree *'bukəlili* . . .

The prawn is burrowing, coming up, throwing aside the mud, and digging . . .

Climbing up on to the lotus plants and on to their pods . . .

10.

Swimming along under the water, as bubbles rise to the surface, the tortoise moves in the swamp grass.

Swimming among the lily leaves and the grasses, catching them as she moves . . .

Pushing them with her short arms. Her shell is marked with designs,

This tortoise carrying her young, in the clay pan, at the place of
the Dugong . . .
The short-armed *'Mararlpa* tortoise, with special arm-bands,
here at the place of the Dugong . . .
Backwards and forwards she swims, the short-armed one of the
'Mararlpa, and the *'Dalwɔŋu.*
Carrying eggs about, in the clay pan, at the place of the Du-
gong . . .
Her entrails twisting with eggs . . .
Swimming along through the grass, and moving her patterned
shell.
The tortoise with her young, and her special arm-bands,
Swimming along, moving her shell, with bubbles rising;
Throwing out her arms towards the place of the Dugong . . .
This creature with the short arms, swimming and moving her
shell;
This tortoise, swimming along with the drift of the water . . .
Swimming with her short arms, at the place of the Dugong . . .

II.

Wild-grape vines are floating there in the billabong:
Their branches, joint by joint, spreading over the water.
Their branches move as they lie, backwards and forwards,
In the wind and the waves, at the Moonlight Clay Pan, at the
place of the Dugong . . .
Men see them lying there on the clay pan pool, in the shade of
the paperbarks:
Their spreading limbs shift with the wind and the water:
Grape vines with their berries . . .
Blown backwards and forwards as they lie, there at the place of
the Dugong.
Always there, with their hanging grapes, in the clay pan of the
Moonlight . . .
Vine plants and roots and jointed limbs, with berry food, spread-
ing over the water.

12.

Now the New Moon is hanging, having cast away his bone:
Gradually he grows larger, taking on new bone and flesh.
Over there, far away, he has shed his bone: he shines on the
    place of the Lotus Root, and the place of the Dugong,
On the place of the Evening Star, of the Dugong's Tail, of the
    Moonlight Clay Pan . . .
His old bone gone, now the New Moon grows larger;
Gradually growing, his new bone growing as well.
Over there, the horns of the old receding Moon bent down,
    sank into the place of the Dugong:
His horns were pointing towards the place of the Dugong.
Now the New Moon swells to fullness, his bone grown larger.
He looks on the water, hanging above it, at the place of the
    Lotus.
There he comes into sight, hanging above the sea, growing
    larger and older . . .
There far away he has come back, hanging over the clans near
    Milingimbi . . .
Hanging there in the sky, above those clans . . .
"Now I'm becoming a big moon, slowly regaining my round-
    ness . . ."
In the far distance the horns of the Moon bend down, above
    Milingimbi,
Hanging a long way off, above Milingimbi Creek . . .
Slowly the Moon-Bone is growing, hanging there far away.
The bone is shining, the horns of the Moon bend down.
First the sickle Moon on the old Moon's shadow; slowly he
    grows,
And shining he hangs there at the place of the Evening Star . . .
Then far away he goes sinking down, to lose his bone in the sea;
Diving towards the water, he sinks down out of sight.
The old Moon dies to grow new again, to rise up out of the sea.
Up and up soars the Evening Star, hanging there in the sky.

Men watch it, at the place of the Dugong and of the Clouds, and of the Evening Star,

A long way off, at the place of Mist, of Lilies and of the Dugong.

The Lotus, the Evening Star, hangs there on its long stalk, held by the Spirits.

It shines on that place of the Shade, on the Dugong place, and on to the Moonlight Clay Pan . . .

The Evening Star is shining, back towards Milingimbi, and over the 'Wu:lamba people . . .

Hanging there in the distance, towards the place of the Dugong,

The place of the Eggs, of the Tree-Limbs-Rubbing-Together, and of the Moonlight Clay Pan . . .

Shining on its short stalk, the Evening Star, always there at the clay pan, at the place of the Dugong . . .

There, far away, the long string hangs at the place of the Evening Star, the place of Lilies.

Away there at Milingimbi . . . at the place of the Full Moon,

Hanging above the head of that 'Wɔnguri tribesman:

The Evening Star goes down across the camp, among the white gum trees . . .

Far away, in those places near Milingimbi . . .

Goes down among the 'ŋurulwulu people, towards the camp and the gum trees,

At the place of the Crocodiles, and of the Evening Star, away towards Milingimbi . . .

The Evening Star is going down, the Lotus Flower on its stalk . . .

Going down among all those western clans . . .

It brushes the heads of the uncircumcised people . . .

Sinking down in the sky, that Evening Star, the Lotus . . .

Shining on to the foreheads of all those headmen . . .

On to the heads of all those Sandfly people . . .

It sinks there into the place of the white gum trees, at Milingimbi.

(Australia: Arnhem Land)

A Dream of the Afterlife

Since she died
I have counted the days:
Fifteen days until full moon.
She went away
& walked around in the sky
in the bright moonlight.

"I am afraid of a ghost,
that old husband of mine:
if he comes he will seize me
& throw me into Rourou."
He saw her & rubbed his hands together in glee.
But the ghost of her brother called out a warning.

Many demons seized upon her,
but seeing her brother she was not afraid.
"Come down here, away from those demons."
But the ghost of her husband said,
"Don't look around; follow me!"

They came to that dread lake
where people never come up alive
but are cast into Piseram.
People said, *She will never return*,
but her brother had saved her from the demon.
He gave her a heavenly flower for protection,
a flower of the *geran*, the *warung*.
She took it back to earth with her
& showed it to the people.

She wanted many men to sleep with her
but people said, *She nearly died*,

she is between dead & alive
like the black tern, the urugao.
So the men she wanted for lovers would not come to her.

One man, though, was unafraid:
in spite of the malicious talk
he stood up & saw her
where she loomed like a cloud
& glowed like a flame.

A demon's hand laid hold of her.
"Yuk! What are you doing to me?"
With a rope he tied their bodies together.
Her brother called out, "Don't go with him!"
He looked around, but she was gone.
"Come away from that demon!"
The demon sounded his hunting cry.
Another hid behind a tree to put sickness upon her;
but her brother gave her heavenly medicine,
perfume of the gods to save her.
She smelled it & did not die.
He gave her face-paint from Yap & Truk,
repeatedly sprinkled her with the perfume,
reached her his walking stick:
"Catch hold of that & you will not die!"
She arose from her sickbed
& pointed the stick toward home.
"As you go you will see a golden plover,
he will be close beside your home."
When the plover saw her he nodded,
beckoned her with his wing:
"Come quick so the demons won't catch you.
Come to the *warung* tree that the gods love.
Come make a wreath of its flowers."
She made the wreath & put it on her head.

"I won't talk about your coming back from the dead—
if they gossip about me & you, never mind them.

Ordinary people won't come to see you, but I searched you out."
Thus spoke the god Alumaseragu.

But the demon Rangewau came in between them;
many demons seized upon her;
she was surrounded by them.
They frolicked around her
like boys playing with a toy canoe,
darted about her like surgeonfish.

Her husband saw her: "Are you waiting here too?
After tomorrow we'll stay together."
So after two days he went out,
left the heat of the house behind
& went in the woods, where they used to go.
He found a secluded place
where people hardly ever go.
They lay down—but she kept away from him.
"Why can't it be like the last time?
Are you afraid of me, that you keep away?"
Then they both fell asleep.
Lying side by side.

He made a light so they could smoke,
striking stone on steel.
He made a coconut-leaf torch, so he could see her body.
"If you keep away from me tonight, I'll never come again.
For a long time I could not see you; now I want you.
What has come over you?
A month has gone down into the sea since we were together.
Come to me now & be my sweetheart!"

He caught at her genitals; she was afraid.
His penis was erect with passion.
She was afraid; it was too big.
Afraid that if he lay with her she would die.

She talked to him as he had to her:
"I think before you loved me;
now you don't any more;
I think you are lying to me now."

She went back into the sky, leaving him disconsolate.
He took no interest in food; would not bathe or anoint himself,
would not put on the turmeric face-paint.
Last night he saw her in a dream.
"Now I know that you truly love me," she said.
"You were telling the truth; you can come to me now."
But he answered: "What is this you say?
You are not human. You are a demon!
I'll do with you as I please;
your mouth is like a big devil."
He turned over & snored.

(Micronesia: Ifaluk Atoll)

From THE LEGEND OF SAVEASI'ULEO

Ulufanuasesee. Why do you want to
eat me, brother?

Saveasi'uleo. Can't you see I'm
a sea-monster?

U. Slippery as you are, an
eel, I can slip through
your fingers.

S. You don't stand a chance
against me, I've already eaten
your four older brothers.

U. But, brother, why eat
your brothers? Aren't we
born of the same father?

S. I didn't choose to be
born a monster. It was
Father who screwed me up.

U. Here I stand on this flat
rock. See if you can
get closer.

S. It will be too late to
tell Muli, your father and
your mother, by the time you're
squirming in my stomach.

U. But I'm not weak like
my older brothers. I can
swim against the tides
in shark-filled waters.

S. I'm Saveasi'uleo, the sea
eel, who makes even
the sharks quiver.

U. I can catch you by your
tail and dash you
against the rocks.

S. How I would love to get
at you, brother! Your boast
whets my appetite for blood.

U. Come, if you like,
let's wrestle. I'll
give you such a hold
you'll be crushed.

S. Oh, you make my mouth
water. Your hairless legs
are fine to start with.

U. A kick in your middle
and you'll split.

S. Oh, let me slip up
your legs, wrap around
your thighs, and enter.

U. Ha, ha, keep your
itch to yourself. I don't
care for a slimey eel's touch.

S. Let my body move against
yours all over. Your body
is more muscular than your
brothers'.

U. That's why I can swim
faster and better. And I
conquer the waves
when I surf.

S. Your tempting body and words
    are hard to resist. Let me
    work on you this instance.

U. So you still want me,
    water-monster. Then, come
    up and eat your youngest
    brother. Come on! Eat me!

(*Ulufanuasesee beats on his chest.*)

S. Your courage has moved me,
    brother. Though I won't
    eat you until later, the
    taste of your words I shall
    savor. Let us make
    a pact: Our children shall
    be united.

U. I shall swim to Faletatai
    in Upolu. When I have
    a daughter, she shall be
    yours.

S. Brother, let us pledge our
    kinship. On this rock
    let us lean wet and naked
    and press our bodies
    against each other's.

                    (Samoa)

NIGHT BIRTHS

(from *The Kumulipo* by Keaulumoku)

•

At the time when the earth became hot
At the time when the heavens turned about
At the time when the sun was darkened
To cause the moon to shine
The time of the rise of the Pleiades
The slime, this was the source of the earth
The source of the darkness that made darkness
The source of the night that made night
The intense darkness, the deep darkness
Darkness of the sun, darkness of the night
  Nothing but night

I

The train of walruses passing by
Milling about in the depths of the sea
The long lines of opule fish
The sea is thick with them
Crabs and hardshelled creatures
They go swallowing on the way
Rising and diving under swiftly and silently
Pimoe lurks behind the horizon
On the long waves, the crested waves
Innumerable the coral ridges
Low, heaped-up, jagged
The little ones seek the dark places
Very dark is the ocean and obscure

A sea of coral like the green heights of Paliuli
The land disappears into them
Covered by the darkness of night
  Still it is night

2

With a dancing motion they go creeping and crawling
The tail swinging its length
Sullenly, sullenly
They go poking about the dunghill
Filth is their food, they devour it
Eat and rest, eat and belch it up
Eating like common people
Distressful is their eating
They move about and become heated
Act as if exhausted
They stagger as they go
Go in the land of crawlers
The family of crawlers born in the night
  Still it is night

3

The parent rats dwell in holes
The little rats huddle together
Those who mark the seasons
Little tolls from the land
Little tolls from the water courses
Trace of the nibblings of these brown-coated ones
With whiskers upstanding
They hide here and there
A rat in the upland, a rat by the sea
A rat running beside the wave
Born to the two, child of the Night-falling-away
Born to the two, child of the Night-creeping-away

The little child creeps as it moves
The little child moves with a spring
Pilfering at the rind
Rind of the 'ohi'a fruit, not a fruit of the upland
A tiny child born as the darkness falls away
A springing child born as the darkness creeps away
Child of the dark and child in the night now here
  Still it is night

4

Fear falls upon me on the mountain top
Fear of the passing night
Fear of the night approaching
Fear of the pregnant night
Fear of the breach of the law
Dread of the place of offering and the narrow trail
Dread of the food and the waste part remaining
Dread of the receding night
Awe of the night approaching
Awe of the dog child of the Night-creeping-away
A dog child of the Night-creeping-hither
A dark red dog, a brindled dog
A hairless dog of the hairless ones
A dog as an offering for the oven
Palatable is the sacrifice for supplication
Pitiful in the cold without covering
Pitiful in the heat without a garment
He goes naked on the way to Malama
Where the night ends for the children of night
From the growth and the parching
From the cutting off and the quiet
The driving Hula wind his companion
Younger brother of the naked ones, the 'Olohe
Out from the slime come rootlets
Out from the slime comes young growth

Out from the slime come branching leaves
Out from the slime comes outgrowth
Born in the time when men came from afar
  Still it is night

(Polynesia: Hawaii)

THE BODY-SONG OF KIO
(by Ruea-a-raka)

Then Kio again spoke to Oatea, saying:

Take	hold	of	my	flattened-crown
"	"	"	"	wrinkled-brow
"	"	"	"	observing-eye
"	"	"	"	obstructed-nose
"	"	"	"	conversing-mouth
"	"	"	"	chattering-lips
"	"	"	"	flower-decked-ears
"	"	"	"	distorted-chin
"	"	"	"	descending-saliva
"	"	"	"	crooked-neck
"	"	"	"	broad-chest
"	"	"	"	contracted-hands
"	"	"	"	grasping-fingers
"	"	"	"	pinching-nails
"	"	"	"	flexed-side
"	"	"	"	bulging-ribs
"	"	"	"	inset-navel
"	"	"	"	princely-belly
"	"	"	"	small-of-the-back
"	"	"	"	swollen-penis
"	"	"	"	tightly-drawn-testicles
"	"	"	"	evacuating-rectum
"	"	"	"	twisted-knee
"	"	"	"	splay-foot
"	"	"	"	given-over-body

(Polynesia: Tuamotua)

FUNERAL EVA
(by Koroneu)

(Solo)   Oh, Priest Pangeivi, you let go
my son, the canoe of his life
is dashed and sunk.

(Chorus)   O Tane, you could have saved him,
made him return, a
sapling among our aging forest.
But he died, woman-like, wet
on his pillow, far from the
crash of spears and adzes. You could have
done better than god Turanga, a bag
of lies not worth our prayers.

Your belly full, you can't be bothered.
Let shitballs be thrown at you,
Let you be smeared all over,
Let piss and shit dribble down your
fat cheeks, you bum god. Any man
can do better.

(Solo)   Fart, O Tiki, let your wind go.
Fart on this phoney god not worth
our curses.

(Chorus)   Fart, fart, fart.
Swallow the wind, O Pangeivi.
Having eaten my son, you
shall eat our feces.

(Polynesia: Mangaian)

THE LOVERS I
(by Tomoki)

The woman went searching inland, for what?
    May the hermit crab enter
Only this: I was up at the north here,
Spread my knees until the thing was very thick.
Floated to you at the edge of the pool, landed.
(You said) "Haul up my fat fish that I am starving for."
I then eat the part between the two ventral fins.
(You said) "Float to my mouth."
You separated, separated from me.
The hermit crab which came, cast down its eyes.

            (Polynesia: Kapingamarangi)

The Lovers II
(by Tomoki)

Carrying his coarse mat under his arms he unrolls & spreads it
beneath his pandanus tree where a space has been cleared—then
   gropes
for his sea-urchin pencil spines, lined with ridges like the *waka
   mara*—
with these he pulls out her pubic hairs—& they pop
like the splitting of leaves *hakapaki eitu*
Only some short ones are left
                inside the vagina
                        (he asks):
Where are they?

        At the end of the space
        between the buttocks, accustomed
        place for the grinning of
        the teeth of my lover
        who rules it.
        If you were going to eat it
        the thing isn't clean

(He says)
Your eyes are red with hard crying.

(She says) I am carried up to the skies
my toes spread apart with the thrill of it   I put
my feet at their place
               around your neck.

(He says)   I land my might—
gather to push open
that mouth.
Not yet soft. I
look along her belly.
She lies flat.

(She says)   Why're you
lying down
Stand
up, the rain
is coming seaward of
Hukuniu Island.
The island is buried, the rain
moves eastward
see what its nature is.

(He says)   It will pass us, it blocks
to the east of us.

(She says)   Lie
on your bed, come
back
to the swollen thing—
crawl here!

(Polynesia: Kapingamarangi)

Flight of the Chiefs: Song V

(by Daubitu Velema)

I was sweating: then I hurdled the threshold.
Then I came outside; then I circled about.
I broke off the dangling uci shrub
And I inserted it above my ear.
When the dangling *uci* shrub is bruised,
It quivers like the tail feathers of the cock.
And now Lady Song-of-Tonga speaks:
    "Why is the dangling *uci* broken?"
And now The-Eldest answers:
    "Leaves for garlands have no worth as food;
    I am using it just as an ornament."
I descended down to the shore.
I leapt into the bow of my canoe;
Its timbers were felled at The-Task-is-Complete;
The artist, Flaming-Moon, felled them;
Its name was The-Turmeric-of-the-Mother-and-Child.
And shells concealed the tying of its sennit.
The walls of the chief's house were hung with barkcloth.
And a large dentalium adorned the chief's house.
And there were four figureheads together.
And Lady Song-of-Tonga is weaving her fishnet.
And Fruit-of-the-Distant-Sleep crawls to her.
And she grasped the weaving hook from my hand.
I struck her with the handle of the net.
And the child is smothered black from weeping.
And now The-Eldest speaks:
    "Lady Song-of-Tonga, what evil have you done?
    You strike a helpless creature."
And I grasped the forearm of the child.

Then I slung her to my back and carried her.
And now The-Eldest speaks:
    "O my child, for what blossom are you weeping?
    Are you crying for the red *leba?*
    Look there at the ripe ones on the branch."
I grasped the handle of my ray-spined spear.
Reaching upward I tapped a fruit in the cluster.
It fell and I halved it straightway.
And the red *leba* speaks in his hand:
    "Why am I broken in half?"
And now The-Eldest answers:
    "You are halved to no purpose."
Fruit-of-the-Distant-Sleep is weeping.
She sees, and now her thoughts are soothed.
Then I threaded the leba on a girdle cord.
And dangled it there before her.
And now the child is angry and refuses to look.
And she leaps down and scratches the earth;
And she scoops up a handful and casts it on her back.
And I grasped the forearm of the child.
And I slung her to my back and carried her.
    "O my child, for what blossom are you weeping?"
And The-Eldest is looking about.
And my glance fell upon Clapping-Out-of-Time;
I saw him; then I shouted calling.
And now Clapping-Out-of-Time speaks:
    "The-Eldest, why am I called?"
And now The-Eldest speaks:
    "You are called for no purpose.
    Fruit-of-the-Distant-Sleep is weeping.
    Come dance to see if you can please her."

Leap to the mote on the landward side.
Leap to the mote on the seaward side.
And he twists bending in the dance and stands again.
Saliva drips forth from his mouth.
       "Come, watch, Fruit-of-the-Distant-Sleep."
She looks but asks no questions.
And the child is smothered black from weeping.
And I grasped the forearm of the child
And I slung her to my back and carried her.
And Sailing-the-Ocean is sorrowful.
Returning I carried Fruit-of-the-Distant-Sleep;
Went to enter The-Grass-Strewn-Floor.

                                                        (Fiji)

THE SOARING-DART

I.

I am wandering at the *karasiga* tree
And the wind from Tokalau blows quietly;
Its waves blossom against the shore.
I begin the forms of the dance.
The scent of the *makita* rises.
You cast down the short coconuts,
They fall to earth and you spin them.
Call your child to pick them up.
I grasp a nut and tear off the husk.
Let us return again to the rear,
To enter into the woven house
And offer up The Soaring-Dart.
Let the noise of the clapping resound.

II.

Sleep there at the Koro-Bugale.
The morning springs forth and the beach lies wide.
And I draw forth my small fishing net
And I tie it there to its frame.
I scoop with it through the flooding water.
I twist the net and the fish are enmeshed.
I cast my eyes about on the shore.
Roko Seruvati appears.
And there with my arm I shake out the net.
    "Come down; let us converse.
    Sir, I am a woman who marries.
    Your wife, Yadi, is not dead.

She stands here and touches the sky . . .
    It is finished; let us separate."
I enter inside and stay in the house.
My stomach is strangely sick.
I try to swallow and my throat is hesitant.
The pain lies in my stomach's lining,
As though I had drunk kava without eating afterwards,
As though my mother had died.
I descended and I spoke with Yadi:
    "You, Yadi, are only chattering;
    You credit the speech of fun-making,
    You plot against me so that I die."
The sun sinks and the hurricane blows.

III.

House for beating barkcloth,
I leap and I am there above its foundation.
I try to anoint my head with ash-lime.
I dip my head and there is but fresh water;
And I stir to make it cloudy.
And I shake down the ripe fruit of the red *leba*.
And I cast away the seeds separately.
And the scent of garlands rises.
The children are crying, and they mourn.
    "Crying, you go to your father, your mother."
A sacred fish basks through the blossoming hedges,
Eats shoals of fish in the sea weed.
And I draw forth my pointed spear;
I stand outside, and dragging it I go.
At the point of the rock I hurl it;
I thrust it and the fish jump clear.
I retire again to fresh water.
And offer up The Soaring-Dart,
And let its clapping leap outwards.

It is not a dance to learn at Island.
It is our dance for love-making.
Clap for the dance and make them speechless.

IV.

Half-waking the red fowl cries.
And I wander around the outer wall
And I thrust at the face of the land.
There at Nasoga there is a mist.
And at Kavewa; and Double-Canoe is floating.
The headland at Double-Barkcloth lies clear;
The Ruarua is lying clear.

And the sacred fish ripples the water.
Spears for it, I raise up both of them.
I implant them at Peninsula.
I descend to the fish, and I wade.
The spears I raise in one arm.
And I thrust at the fish who leap separately.
And my thrusting strikes a single one.
It is dead and I drag it to the shore.
And I go to draw out my spear;
It shatters like the petals of spent blossoms.
And two persons are begging for the fish.
    "*Isa,* Sir, You have given it away.
    They beg for your fish while I weep for it.
    You throw it away to them."
    "Yadi, your mother is growing large.
    Your child cries and you do not give it breast.
    It cries for milk, that you let it drink.
    And it cries for you to fill its mouth.
    You carry it on your back, and together you stay outside.
    Wants conflict inside you, Yadi:
    You credit the words of our ancestors;

While the words of fun-making stand just beyond.
If you refuse, you shall be strangled."
Today the moon sinks unexpectedly.

V.

And sweating I am watching at The-Door.
And the young men are preparing to sail.
They are rigging the mast of our canoe.
Now Anoints-With-Red-Paint calls,
Prays to the Ancestors of The-Door;
   "Let a wind come for us."
There is wind from the southwest, and the waves shimmer.
And they are sailing beyond Mali.
The point at Udu lies clear in view.
We reach Nasoga when it is evening.
We descend to the land to wander about.
And there we beg for a dance.
We beg a dance and are refused.
It is calm and there is fair weather.
And we are desolate there on the shore.
My mother, perhaps, is sick from crying;
She thinks, perhaps, that I am dead.
And blossoms are strewn under the *tiale* tree.
Singly, I pick them up and carry them into the house.
I fasten them into garlands
For the dance of the young men,
Garlands for the dance in the evening.
The sun sinks close to Namatari.

                       (Fiji)

ANIMAL STORY X
(by Wiliami Naura)

Let it be told, *iya, iya, iya*
Vuai na dri, vuai na dra,
Source of the blossoms of the Malay apple.
Crane falls; Goose awakes;
Rail knocks,
Knocks at the village of The-Strong,
Cock crows, crows in the village,
Crows there in the branch of the black tree,
The rotten core of the branched taro,
And the eggs of the chicken hatch,
And the hatchlings flap their wings.
And the eggs of the rail hatch,
And the hatchlings kick their feet.
Crane flies down,
Snaps the anus of Parrot.
Defecate what? Defecate brown.
Brown woman is born therefrom.
Who is to place a name upon her?
Woman, *soqiri;* woman, *soqara.*
What ship is approaching there near Kana?
The ship of the Roko, it chugs like a steamer.
It chugs upon me, I recognize one;
It chugs upon me, I recognize two.
A Fireman is Red Rail; always knows the firewoods.
The branch of hibiscus is beating,
And there is a heap of *molau.*
One piece of *basina* is long;
It is bad, the path to River's-Mouth.
Return the song, all you young people.

One piece of *basina* is short;
It is bad, the path to Nakavakea.
Return the song, all you women.
One piece of *basina* is fine, is fine.
Mynah makes merry.
The eyes are blind, missing.
O-i! A fine village.

(Fiji)

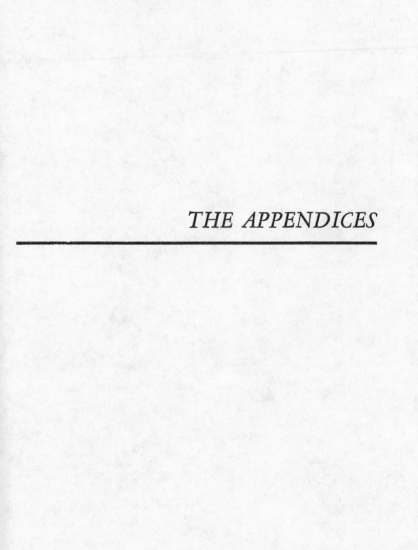

THE APPENDICES

APPENDIX A: STATEMENTS ON POETRY

(1)

This ceremony molded me. I paid the most careful attention to it. I worshiped it as best I knew how. . . . The members of the Medicine Rite told me that if, properly & reverently, I obeyed all the things the ceremony enjoined, I would return to Earth-maker. I was considerate to everyone & everyone loved me. This ritual was made with love!

> (Statement by Warudjaxega, "Crashing-Thunder," Winnebago Indian)

(2)

The mind, *nanola,* by which term intelligence, power of discrimination, capacity for learning magical formulae, & all forms of non-manual skill are described, as well as moral qualities, resides somewhere in the larynx. . . . The memory, however, the store of formulae & traditions learned by heart, resides deeper, in the belly. . . . The force of magic, crystallized in the magical formulae, is carried by men of the present generation in their bodies. . . . The force of magic does not reside in the things; it resides within man & can escape only through his voice.

> (Trobriands, New Guinea)

(3)

Songs are thoughts, sung out with the breath when people are moved by great forces & ordinary speech no longer suffices. Man is moved just like the ice floe sailing here & there in the current. His thoughts are driven by a flowing force when he feels joy, when he feels fear, when he feels sorrow. Thoughts can wash over him like a flood, making his breath come in gasps & his heart throb. Something like an abatement in the weather will keep him thawed up. And then it will happen that we, who always think we are small, will feel still smaller. And we will fear to use words. But it will happen that the words we need will come of themselves. When the words we want to use shoot up of themselves—we get a new song.

(Statement by Orpingalik, Netsilik Eskimo)

(4)

I must first sit a little, cooling my arms; that the fatigue may go out of them; because I sit. I do merely listen, watching for a story, which I want to hear; while I sit waiting for it; that it may float into my ear. These are those to which I am listening with all my ears; while I feel that I sit silent. I must wait listening behind me, while I listen along the road; while I feel that my name floats along the road; they (my three names) float along to my place; I will go to sit at it; that I may listening turn backwards (with my ears) to my feet's heels, on which I went; while I feel that a story is the wind. It, the story, is wont to float along to another place. Then our names do pass through those people; while they do not perceive our bodies go along. For our names are those which, floating, reach a different place. The mountains lie between the two different roads. A man's name passes behind the mountains' back; those names with which returning he goes along.

(Statement by ‖kábbo, African Bushman)

(5)

The artist: disciple, abundant, multiple, restless.
The true artist: capable, practicing, skillful;
maintains dialogue with his heart, meets things with his mind.
The true artist: draws out all from his heart,
works with delight, makes things with calm, with sagacity,
works like a true Toltec, composes his objects, works dexterously,
    invents;
arranges materials, adorns them, makes them adjust.

The carrion artist: works at random, sneers at the people,
makes things opaque, brushes across the surface of the face of
    things,
works without care, defrauds people, is a thief.

(Aztec)

(6)

My young men shall never work. Men who work cannot
dream, & wisdom comes in dreams.

You ask me to plow the ground. Shall I take a knife & tear
my mother's breast? Then when I die she will not take me to her
bosom to rest.

You ask me to dig for stone. Shall I dig under her skin for
bones? Then when I die I cannot enter her body to be born
again.

You ask me to cut grass & make hay & sell it, & be rich like
white men. But how dare I cut off my mother's hair?

It is a bad law, & my people cannot obey it. I want my people
to stay with me here. All the dead men will come to life again.
We must wait here in the house of our fathers & be ready to
meet them in the body of our mother.

(Statement by Smohalla, Nez Percé Indian)

(7)

And I, Daniel, alone saw the vision: for the men that were with me saw not the vision; but a great quaking fell upon them, so that they fled to hide themselves.

Therefore I was left alone, & saw this great vision, & there remained no strength in me: for my comeliness was turned in me into corruption, & I retained no strength.

Yet heard I the voice of his words: & when I heard the voice of his words, then was I in a deep sleep on my face, & my face toward the ground.

(Hebrew)

APPENDIX B: *From* KUNAPIPI
(original texts with literal & free translations)

From R. M. Berndt, *Kunapipi* (1951), pp. 121–31. A selection from these songs has been presented above, pages 316–17, & the commentary on pages 507–9 explains the actual context.

SONG 91.

maladada	*djililma*	*dju:kwu:wa'wondi:nga*
a	coitus	b

Notes: a Red colouring inside vagina.

    b The smell of a woman's vaginal juices, prior to coitus.

General Translation:

    The musk of her red-walled vagina, inviting coitus. . . .

Comments:

  Referring to the period of ceremonial copulation on the Kunapipi ground. The energetic opossum dancing of the women prior to intercourse, and its erotic content, cause juices to collect in the vagina, emitting a musk said to be attractive to men.

SONG 92.

djali:ma	*ru:wa:ra*	*miru:min'djuralji*
woman's arm band	worn loosely	inside of arm band

nainbak

its "outside" name

General Translation:

    Her arm band is loose. . . .

Comments:

  As the woman holds the man during coitus, he can feel the looseness of her arm band.

SONG 93.

wu:lanbulga	*wu:lanbulga*	*wu:lanmari'wu:lanmari*
fur	fur	"you can take that fur"

General Translation:

    Her skin is soft like fur. . . .

Comments:

  This song refers not only to the opossum, but to a girl's soft skin, which is likened to fur.

SONG 94.

ngapa:ma	*d'ramad'r*	*pi:tjama'pi:tjama*
her back	walking step by step	that way

d'ramad'r
walking step by step
General Translation:

> Step by step she walks back to her husband;
> she is shy and turns her back. . . .

Comments:

The young woman returns to the main camp after having had coitus with her Kunapipi partner, in this case her *gurung* (of the same moiety). She walks slowly, step by step, shyly because she sees her real husband; she is so shy that she turns her back on him and edges away.

SONG 95.

go:ra'ngelmingelmi	*dji:da'wurumburu*
shy/meet and sit down	laughing together

General Translation:

> She is shy at first, but soon they laugh together.

Comments:

The young girl shyly meets her husband, on her return from the Kunapipi ground, and they sit down; as soon as they meet, they look at each other and begin to laugh. For the husband has sanctioned his wife's behavior, and they find the situation amusing.

SONG 96.

dji:da'wurumburu	*kandi*	*ngalanggu'ngalanggu*
laughing together	clitoris[a]	soft inside of the vagina

Note: a Or *ki:ndi.*
General Translation:

> They are copulating and laughing together. . . .

Comments:

On her return from the Kunapipi, husband and wife laugh together and retire to their camp or the bush for coitus. As they play together, they laugh over their Kunapipi coitus and tell each other of their previous partners. When they are thoroughly stimulated, and the woman's clitoris is erect her husband copulates with her.

SONG 97.

ngu:lpambi:ng'ngu:lpambi:ng	balalwara	limbinja'limbinja
removing woman's pubic covering	small pubic cloth	opening her legs
ngu:lpambi:ng'ngu:lpambi:ng	djangu:lpa'mila	
removing woman's pubic covering	place legs between hers/semen	

General Translation:

Removing her pubic cloth, opening her legs, lying between them and ejaculating. . . .

Comments:

Referring to the husband copulating with his wife on her return from the Kunapipi. Two types of female pubic coverings are mentioned; the first is in the form of a narrow strip of cloth suspended from a cord tied around the waist, and the smaller one is a strip of cloth extending from the waist-cord in front between the legs and attached to the cord at the back; this latter, called in pidgin English a "G-string," is usually worn by very young girls.

SONG 98

didji'barangala	ju:walanbani
copulating for a child	"singing" name for latter
walman'barangala	
"singing" name for latter	

General Translation:

And copulating for a child. . . .

Comments:

It is considered particularly auspicious for a husband and wife to have sexual relations after the ceremonial copulation of the Kunapipi in order to obtain a child. This aspect brings into perspective the general purpose of the Kunapipi ceremony, whose intent is primarily one of fertility. Women who have immediate relations with their own husbands, after having had ceremonial intercourse, are believed to conceive at once.

SONG 99.

manangeijalpijalpi	*ngaindja*	*ngu:ri*
spear-thrower	its hook	"inside" name of latter

jama:lana
"head" (handle) of spear-thrower
General Translation:
The spear-thrower there with its hook. . . .
Comments:
The Wauwalak are said to have possessed a spear-thrower which they brought to Muruwul.

SONG 100.

kanggarara	*dji:nbili:nbili*	*kanggarara*
fire	flame	fire

dju:ndju:nlangu
ashes
General Translation:
There are the fire and it ashes. . . .
Comments:
This refers to the fire-throwing ritual which is part of the Kunapipi. This is the core of the *djamala* ceremony: see also the two following songs.

SONG 101.

go:ngwanduwandu	*reidji:gai'gandi:nja*
flame	sparks flying out

djeiamili
the flare
General Translation:
Fire sticks and flames are flaring, sparks are flying. . . .
Comments:
This song refers to the *djamala* fire-throwing ritual. As the postulants dance before the novices, they hit fire-sticks together so that the sparks fly out and across the young boys.

SONG 102.

kanggarara	gurawanduwandu	reidji:gai'gandi:nja
fire[a]	singeing hair	sparks flying out

Note: a "Put fire into the young boy": that is, throw it across the crescent trench in which the novices lie: after the throwing they are ready to "come outside."

General Translation:

Fire singes their hair, and sparks are flying.

Comments:

This song also refers to the throwing of fire-sticks in the *djamala* ceremony: sparks singe the hair of novices.

SONG 103.

kanangaka	wararindji	kanangakana
urination[a]	testes	urination

djirimba:lji
"inside" name for testes

Note: a Of the Snake, Julunggul.

General Translation:

There is the Snake urinating, there are his testes. . . .

Comments:

The significance of this song was not known.

SONG 104.

nganman	djaridjari	nganman	gudilagudila
jiritja	red	loin cloth	white cloth
loin cloth			

nganman	djara:wondi:nja
loin cloth	black

General Translation:

There are the men with red and black and white loin cloths. . . .

Comments:

This song is of comparatively modern inclusion, and comes from the Roper River Mission station where aboriginal men wear loin cloths.

SONG 105.

djapi:dja	*dankilikilikil*	*muditjbawona*
tobacco	smoke coming out	inside of the long pipe

wu:kalji
tobacco burning while being smoked

General Translation:

There they are smoking their long pipes. . . .

Comments:

The long-barrelled carved pipe was introduced into north-eastern Arnhem Land by early Macassan voyagers, and is now in general use. The song refers to men smoking and resting between rituals outside the sacred Kunapipi ground.

SONG 106.

djani	*gurlga*	*balang*	*gurlga*	*balang*
penis aperture[a]	penis	incisure	penis	incisure

niminijani
semen[b]

Notes: a This is the "inside" term

b Semen: the "old" name (still in general use) is *ju:tu,* which literally means "child." Also called *buktunura* and *burlktun. Niminijani* is probably derived from *ni-minimi,* to copulate, and its further meaning is "projected by or arising from the act of coitus."

General Translation:

Those people with subincised penes ejaculate semen. . . .

Comments:

The people referred to are those further south, from whom the Yirrkalla version of the Kunapipi was obtained. The song relates to ceremonial intercourse in this region, where subincision is practiced, and offspring resulting from the projection of the men's semen during coitus.

SONG 107.

wuna:ri	*bulganbulgan*	*jalmanila*	*kandju:lbre*
semen[a]	semen	coming out	coming out[b]

Notes: *a*   Translated as *ju:tu* (see Note *b*, Song 106).
      b   Meaning of these words uncertain.

General Translation:
   Semen ejaculating. . . .

Comments:
   Reference similar to that in Song 106.

SONG 108.

di:tji	*manggarumanggaru*	*kana*
[a]	mist	semen[b]

Notes: *a*   Unable to see the countryside for mist.
      b   The semen is likened to mist.

General Translation:
   Semen white like the mist. . . .

Comments:
   Reference similar to that of Songs 106 and 107.

SONG 109.

mula:ritj	*banga:la*	*djudju*
"inside" name for cypress	tree	bark

General Translation:
   There stands the cypress tree with its bark.

Comments:
   Referring to the tree from which bullroarers for the Kunapipi are made.

SONG 110.

jo:ro	*binamuna*	*kangakangabunja*
core of the cypress tree	pieces chipped off	"inside" name for pieces

General Translation:
   Cutting and shaping the wood for a bullroarer.

Comments:
   Referring to the making of the Kunapipi bullroarers.

SONG 111.

warambala	*nandja*	*d'rumbilbi:ala*
headband[a]	its "inside"	band
	singing name	

minjikala:rakala:ra	*walu:wakla:ra*
white paint on it	shining like the sun

Note: a Commonly called *marapipi;* this is the narrow band
worn by men in the Kunapipi.

General Translation:

Wearing white forehead bands, that shine like the sun. . . .

Comments:

Both men and women wear these headbands.

SONG 112.

djunbitj	*nganangana'mula:wa*	*wodjindji*[a]
kangaroo's	penis protruding	erect penis
rump		("inside" term)

Note: a Or *wondjiwondji.*

General Translation:

With penis erect the kangaroo moves its buttocks.

Comments:

Reference is made to ceremonial intercourse, stressing the main
theme of fertility.

SONG 113.

dunga:pa	*wiri:awiri:a*	*ngapalaubalan*
shoulders	step by step	walking away from

General Translation:

Step by step she walks away from coitus, her back to them.

Comments:

The song refers to coitus with a Kunapipi partner.

SONG 114.

djirindjiri:la	lindjaringa	walmanbari
excreta[a]	"inside" name for latter	anus

djinda:ra
"singing" name for latter

Note: a Of the Julunggul Snake.

General Translation:

Excreta are there, from the Snake's anus. . . .

Comments:

The Snake excretes as it crawls around Muruwul (name of the place where its water hole was located).

SONG 115.

kananakanana	ngo:ri	jarama:lana
excreta	a	a

jadbiridaïjadbiridai
a

Note: a Meanings unknown to informants.

Comments:

The meaning of songs of this type, which have come up from another region, is not always known to informants.

SONG 116.

doitjpajaridoitjpa	banambana:pa	djamala
dua catfish	swimming along	djamala singing

General Translation:

There the catfish swimming along and singing.

Comments:

The reason for the inclusion of the word *djamala* in this song is unknown.

SONG 117.

ngukaija	*juraru*	*linbanana*	*ngukaija*
bullroarer's string	string	swinging the cord	string

General Translation:

There the bullroarer's string. . . .

Comments:

This song is sung in both the *djamala* and Kudjiga ceremonies.

SONG 118.

baladada	*ngulpinngulpin*	*manggwoiulamanggwoi'a*
a	step by step	sit down

Note: *a* "Singing" term for the *bulan* subsection, *jiritja* moiety.

General Translation:

Step by step the *bulan* men walk along, and sit down.

Comments:

This song refers to the *bulan* subsection men who travel with the Ka'lerika'lering (performance name for the Wauwalak Sisters).

SONG 119.

djangu:lpam	*mila'jurarari*	*warambala*
string for headband	string for headband	headband

General Translation:

Their headbands are tied with string. . . .

Comments:

These headbands consist of narrow strips of cloth, woven pandanus, human hair or opossum fur, or paperbark, and are attached to fiber at each end. The headband itself when worn is tied and knotted at the back of the head. In this case they are worn by the *bulan* men (*vide* Song 118). See also Song 111.

SONG 120.

kana	*ngali:ndjiri*	*ngu:lbambi:n'ngu:lbambi:n*
spear	spear end	its stone blade

General Translation:

Carrying stone-tipped spears. . . .

Comments:

This song also refers to the *bulan* men.

SONG 121.

bulga'kalabulga	ngaijadi:nja	wolumiri
opossum fur string	fur	day time (sun up)

General Translation:

Their string of opossum fur shines in the sun.

Comment:

Opossum fur string is made by the *jiritja* people.

SONG 122.

di:tjakanabula:ri	manamana	bula:ri	manauwara
nipple*a*/semen/musk	breasts	musk	vagina

Note a Referring to the nipples of a young girl (called a *wirlkul*).

General Translation:

The nipples of the young *wirlkul*'s breasts protrude; and the musk of her vagina. . . .

Comments:

Among the *jiritja* men are young *jiritja* girls.

SONG 123.

di:ntju:lba'nani:nja	japa'ngalangala
emus	sisters walk along

General Translation:

Two emu sisters walk along.

Comments:

The two female emus symbolize the Wauwalak Sisters.

SONG 124.

maiamaiala	djunbilidjunbili	maijang
creek*a*	moving*b*	creek

Notes: a Maijang refers to a creek bed, which may be dry or full.
     b In this case, the word means the movement of running water.

General Translation:

Beside the running water of the creek.

Comments:

This refers to the water running into Muruwul, the Julunggul Snake's water hole.

SONG 125.

bulu'djiridjirila	jalinmara	gulangu
jiṟitja crocodile/lying on back	head	tail[a]

Note: a   This crocodile is lying in its nest.

General Translation:

Close to the nesting crocodile.

Comments:

Crocodiles are nesting on the banks of the running creek.

SONG 126.

ji:wali	manggaru	ngi:galan
mist	mist	covering up

General Translation:

Mist covering the river.

Comments:

This song refers to mist rising from the creek and covering the adjacent country. Vide Song 108.

SONG 127.

lukambagamba	mirigala:ra	lukambagamba
white clay shining like mist	headband tied	white clay shining like mist

General Translation:

The white headband blinding the eyes like mist.

Comments:

Referring to the white coloring of the headband. Vide Songs 111 and 119.

SONG 128.

gunggu	wilu:ma	mandani	maraula'kitjani
vein	running	coming quickly	coming out

General Translation:

Arm blood flowing. . . .

Comments:

Arm blood is obtained for decoration purposes during the Kunapipi.

SONG 129.

| *dju:dadum* | *la:rdi:nja* | *kanggaralbunja* |
| cypress branches | cypress cone | seeds of the cone |

General Translation:

Cypress branches, with cones full of seeds.

Comments:

Vide Songs 109 and 110.

[The selected series of songs given here belong to the ceremonies called the Djamala. Hundreds of others are sung during the performance of the Kunapipi. The subject matter of the Djamala and the related Kudjiga is similar; both deal with the great Julunggul Snake, the sacred billabong of Muruwul, and the adventures of the Wauwalak. The great majority of songs concerns the natural species, which are represented also in ceremonial dancing, for the Kunapipi ensures their increase. This aspect is also apparent in the constant reference to the mateship of animals and birds, their nesting, and production of eggs and young; while an undercurrent of eroticism runs through the Kunapipi cycle. The latter is centered on ceremonial copulation, since that aspect crystallizes the ritual intent and expresses the fundamental issues of Kunapipi doctrine.]

APPENDIX C: "Doings" & "Happenings"

Notes on a performance of the Seneca Eagle Dance along with the scenario for Gift Event III, based on its orders

by Jerome Rothenberg

> *& if you love me take with both hands*
> (R. Kelly)

JANUARY 21ST 1967. NOTES TAKEN AT A PERFORMANCE OF THE EAGLE DANCE. COLDSPRING LONGHOUSE. STEAMBURG, NEW YORK. AN EVENT FOR ORATORS, DANCERS, MUSICIANS & PEOPLE. BLESSING & CURING. A PART OF THE WINTER "DOINGS."

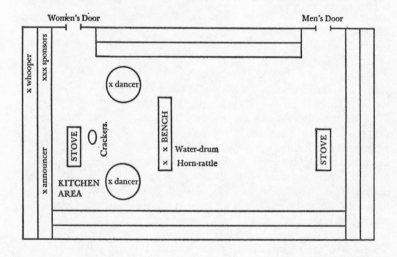

Musicians (water-drum & horn-rattle) move to places on bench. Two gourd-rattles, two feather-sticks passed around to two boy-dancers.

Rapping of long (orator's) stick (branch) to announce each new speaker.
Whoop precedes start of music.
Music stops.
Stick raps.
Orator speaks. (Thanking & prayer to begin it.)
Old man (Ed Currey), third to speak, puts tub (wash-basin) of saltine crackers near stove. Empty cracker boxes or paper bags are placed near participants & recipients (sponsors) for deposit of crackers. Music up. Two boys dance out to center, crouching, shake feather-sticks & rattles, bob heads towards each other & in sidewise motion. Return to their stools. The music stops. New speaker "orates," then takes handfuls of crackers & distributes several to each participant, the (three) sponsors, & a few others (named by the sponsors?)
Whoop. Music. Dance. (Each dance ends with a sound: hmmmmmmmm or whheeeeeee.) New speaker. Raps with the stick before speaking. More crackers. Deposit or mouthing of crackers. *Whoop. Music. Dance. Rap. Speaker.* Etc. This is the over-all pattern, never rigid—toward an actual openness, prescribed as well? Ways of handling the stick vary. Speaker raps for his own oration; sometimes (properly?) slides stick at next speaker; sometimes "announcer" (m.c.) brings it around; shorter & longer orations; hard raps, light raps, staccato, etc. Laughter, etc. At one point new crackers are added to basin; they overflow as next speaker passes them out; they fall on the floor. Occasional punctuation of speeches by light drum-tap. Often at end. Distribution (except for main participants) seems erratic. A speaker forgets to pass crackers. Reminded with laughter. Boy-dancers walk out during one oration. Buzzing of voices, etc. Some joking about deposit of crackers into boxes. Dancers, seated & facing, hold a mute conversation. (Feather-stick in front of face like boy with the flamenco fan in Cordoba.) Two men enter with large cauldron of water for women preparing (corn) soup at the side. People drifting in & out. Time passes. Sounds of Seneca I cannot understand. Three teen-aged girls are laughing in the back. Nobody rushes. Everyone will speak.
After the first woman orator distributes the last of the crackers, the empty tub is turned over in front of the stove. A male speaker

(who may have opened things to start with, i.e., the one I'm calling the "announcer") speaks without preliminary dancing— followed by music, dance, etc. New speaker (woman) raps. Speaks. (Some participants now drinking coffee.) She finishes, distributes something small to the three "sponsors." Music, etc. New woman speaker. Avery Jimerson (horn-rattle) goes out, Dick Johnny John (drum) walks to side for cigarette. Speaker distributes fruit (apples) to the three sponsors. New woman speaker without music (Salina Johnny John)—distributes bananas. Still no music. New woman speaker. Gives coins to the dancers, the musicians, the "announcer," the whooper.

Ed Currey raps, speaks. Distributes packs of cigarettes. Whoop. Music. Dance. Sticks & gourds are set down on the floor. The "announcer" collects them. Ed Currey speaks again. Voice moving as in prayer. Announcer distributes pinches from tobacco bowl to various participants & individuals around the room who accept it or refuse.

GIFT EVENT III: A CELEBRATION FOR POETS, MUSICIANS & DANCERS, BASED ON THE ORDERS OF THE SENECA INDIAN EAGLE DANCE & PERFORMED AT THE JUDSON DANCE THEATER, JUDSON MEMORIAL CHURCH, NEW YORK CITY, MARCH 21ST & 22ND 1967. A PART OF THE SPRING "HAPPENINGS."

Adaptation by Jerome Rothenberg
Choreography by Carol Ritter
Music by Philip Corner

Jackson Mac Low
Dick Higgins
Susan Sherman
Clayton Eshleman
Robert David Cohen
Hannah Weiner
Carol Bergé
George Kimball
Eleanor Antin
David Antin
Paul Blackburn
Jerome Rothenberg (poets)

Christopher Beck
Nannette Sievert
Bernard Spriggs
Margaret Williams (dancers)

Ferdinando Buonanno
Billy Fisher
Cyrelle Forman
Bill Friedman
Edward Goldstein
Malcolm Goldstein
Maud Haimson
Susan Hartung
Alison Knowles
Carol Marcy
Max Neuhaus
Carol Reck
David Reck
Steve Reich
Carolee Schneemann
James Tenney (musicians)

STAGE AND ALTAR

P — poets
M — musicians   position freely taken;
D — dancers   movement at will

1. As the audience is taking seats, "poor man music"* is performed. This is the music throughout.

2. The first poet (who thereafter acts as m.c.) raps for silence with a sounding-stick.† The music stops. He reads a greeting-poem. The music starts again, & he empties several boxes of crackers‡ into a large wash-basin at center of the performance area & arranges simple gifts on the stage-apron for later distribution. Empty boxes or paper bags are given to the dancers for deposit of crackers & gifts.

3. The second poet (Jackson Mac Low) receives the sounding-stick from the m.c. & raps for silence. He reads a (thanking) poem of his own.** The music starts up again as he distributes crackers to the dancers & any other performers he can reach. (Distribution may also be extended to the audience.)†† After the distribution, the dancers perform an extended piece to the "poor man music."

---

* ["Poor man" because the sounds are those a man can make with his own body or simple extensions thereof. In Corner's words]:
> "The simplest materials
>   and the things your own body is
>   and does
> —claps, slaps, stamps. rubbing and scratching: body—all
>   parts, and clothing if any
> voices. and all the sounds your voice and breath and
>   throat may make
>   /except words."

[The rhythms follow the pulsebeat, faster or slower but with its regularity—beats within the group, starting apart, meeting, changing, entering & re-entering, meeting elsewhere, etc.]

† In this case, a broomstick (red) was used. (The Senecas use a broom-handle to announce entry of the "husk-face" masked dancers in another winter event.) The wash-basin was also a red plastic.

‡ The saltine crackers of the Seneca source were almost unanimously overridden in favor of graham crackers (Nabisco).

** The first three poems were designated by the adapter; the rest were of each poet's own choice.

†† The act of finding-each-other (between participants & audience) was the principal departure from the Seneca source. The event continued to change under this impulse, from a situation where community is taken for granted to one where the activity may finally create it.

4. When the first dance is over, the m.c. hands the stick to the third poet (Dick Higgins), & the same series of actions (*rapping-for-silence, reading, music up, distribution of crackers, dance,* etc.) is repeated. This goes on (with the dance segments getting successively shorter) through the dance that follows the reading by the fifth poet (Clayton Eshleman)—by which time the basin should be empty of crackers. Before handing the stick to the sixth poet, the m.c. turns the basin over.

5. From the sixth poet on, gifts are distributed in place of crackers, but there is no dancing. The music continues as before, except when poets have rapped for silence & are reading. This goes on until the next-to-the-last reader (Paul Blackburn), whose gift distribution is followed by a brief dance segment.

6. The m.c. now raps for silence & reads a poem of his own choice. To accompaniment of the "poor man music" he distributes the final gifts,* after which all performers do their pieces simultaneously.† As soon as each poet or dancer finishes, he leaves the performance area. When all the poets & dancers have left, the music stops.

Sequence of poems (except for the first piece, which is the introductory poem to this volume as well, there was no attempt to be Indian or to read poems on Indian themes; indeed, the point of the event, as it related to its source, was that the carry-over was not in content or in costume but in structure: a way of being heard):

1. Greeting-poem, read by J.R.; 2. *First Friendship Poem* by Jackson Mac Low; 3. Selection from *Six Considerations of the Angel* by Dick Higgins; 4. *The Meeting* by Susan Sherman; 5. *Walk I* (1st night), *Walk III* (2nd night) by Clayton Eshleman; 6. *Lines Written in Dejection* by Robert David Cohen; 7. *Persons indicated present their compliments to* by Hannah Weiner; 8. *Song for Beginning* by Carol Bergé; 9. *Poem* (untitled) by George

---

* In the actual performance the other poets joined the m.c. in the final act-of-giving. On the second night toy flutes & other sound-producing articles were included among the gifts, to give the audience a further means of participation.

† Simultaneities turn up, e.g., in the Eskimo "Going-Around Event," p. 112, above. There is no Seneca precedent in the Eagle Dance, but the husk-face ceremonies often involve several simultaneous dances by the masked beggar-clowns—usually while a round-dance is also in progress. The device has developed independently in modern "happenings" or in the poetry, e.g., of Jackson Mac Low & others.

Kimball; 10. *Poem for My Mother* by Eleanor Antin; 11. *Poem for Eleanor* (1st night), *4 Games for Eleanor* (2nd night) by David Antin; 12. *Het up, & take yr teeth with you* by Paul Blackburn; 13. *The Orators II* by Jerome Rothenberg.

. . . .

Be me who
Blesses.

Suffer. Destroy.

Be certain.

Merge a particular picture
Blossom. & open
This surface to clouds.

Be orators.

(j.r.)

THE COMMENTARIES

Come, Ascend the Ladder, p. 3

Invocation to the *U'wannami* (rainmakers) from Matilda Coxe Stevenson, *The Zuni Indians* (Bureau of American Ethnology, Annual Report No. 23 [1905]), pp. 175–76.

(1) Sprinkling water, pollen, meal, to accompany the invocation.

(2) Striking stones together, rolling them along the ground to make thunder.

(3) Flute playing, shell rattling, as the rainmakers (i.e., "ghosts of dead rain priests") move up the lines of pollen & meal.

Genesis I, p. 7

Condensed from Pliny Earle Goddard, *Kato Texts* (University of California Publications in American Archaeology & Ethnology [Berkeley, 1909]), Vol. 5, No. 3, pp. 71–74.

What's of interest here isn't the matter of the myth but the power of repetition & naming (monotony too) to establish the presence of a situation in-its-entirety. This involves the acceptance (by poet & hearers) of an indefinite extension of narrative time, & the belief that language (i.e., poetry) can make-things-present by naming them. The means employed include the obvious pile-up of nouns (until everything is named) & the use of "they say" repeated for each utterance. In Kato, this last is a quotative [*yaɛnɪ*], made from the root *-nɪ-n*, "to speak," & the plural prefix *yaɛ*. (Cp. use of Japanese particle *-to*.) While *yaɛnɪ* is undoubtedly less conspicuous in Kato than "they say" in English, it still gives the sense of a special (narrative or mythic) context. The editor's use of Goddard's literal over his free translation is based on such considerations; also from a feeling that "they say" plus other repetitions add something special to the English &/or American tongues. In brief: there's something going on here.

Summary & Addenda. Repetition & monotony are powers to be reckoned with; or, as the lady said to M. Junod after having heard the tale of Nabandji, the toad-eating girl, "I should never have thought there could be so much charm in monotony."

Charm, in the old sense.

Sounds, p. 8

(1) "Rain-chant" quoted by Baldwin Spencer in *Native Tribes of the Northern Territory of Australia* (London, 1904).

(2) A Navaho "coyote song" from Berard Haile, *Origin Legend of the Navaho Enemy Way* (Yale University Publications in Anthropology, No. 17 [1938]), p. 265.

> "The words have no meaning, but the song means, 'Take it, I give it to you.'"
> —A Navaho informant speaking to Father Berard

Sounds only. No meaning, they say, in the words, or no meaning you can get at by translation into-other-words; & yet it functions; the meaning contained then in how it's made to function. So here the key is in the "spell" & in the belief behind the "spell"—or in a whole system of beliefs, in magic, in the power of sound & breath & ritual to move an object toward ends determined by the poet-magus.

Magic, then, is the first key & from this the idea of a special language or series of languages, extraordinary in their nature & effect, & uniting the user (through what Malinowski calls "the coefficient of weirdness") with the beings & things he's trying to influence or connect-with for a sharing of power, participation in a life beyond his own, beyond the human, etc.

Such special languages—meaningless &/or mysterious—are a small but nearly universal aspect of "primitive-&-archaic" poetry. They may involve (1) purely invented, meaningless sounds, (2) distortion of ordinary words & syntax, (3) ancient words emptied of their (long since forgotten) meanings, (4) words borrowed from other languages & likewise emptied. And all these may, in addition, be explained as (1) spirit language, (2) animal language, (3) ancestral language—distinctions between them often being blurred.

C. M. Bowra, in his book on "primitive song," wrongly views sound-poems like these as truly rudimentary, a kind of rock-bottom poetics. He writes that "since such (meaningless) sounds are easier to fit to music than intelligible sounds are . . . (they) look as if they were the earliest kind of song practiced by man." And yet this mantric use of sound is as close to (say) the Hindu *om*—for which, see below—as to "purely" emotive sounds of the ay-ay-ay & yah-yah-yah variety. One could as well argue—at least where song is magic—that the use of words-emptied-of-meaning is a *late* development, even as geometric (abstract) art follows the naturalistic cows & bulls in the caves of Europe. The reappearance of the sound-poem among some twentieth-century poets (see below) is a further reminder that chronology isn't the question.

Addenda. (1) "Magic words, magic songs or magic prayers are fragments of old songs, handed down from earlier generations. . . . They may also be apparently meaningless sentences heard once in the days when the animals could talk, & remembered ever since through being handed down from one generation to another. Sometimes also a seemingly senseless jumble of words may derive force by a mystic inspiration which first gave them utterance. On the day when a man seeks aid in magic words, he must not eat of the entrails of any beast, & a man when uttering such words must have his head covered with a hood; a woman must have the whole spread of the hood behind thrown over her face." (K. Rasmussen, *Intellectual Culture of the Hudson Bay Eskimos,* p. 157.)

(2) "Take the principal spell of Omarakana garden magic, which begins with the word *vatuvi* . . . (a magical form that has no grammatical setting & is a root never met with in common speech). . . . The magician, after certain preparations & under the observance of certain rules & taboos, collects herbs & makes of them a magical mixture. . . . After ritually & with an incantation offering some . . . fish to the ancestral spirits, (he) recites the main spell, *vatuvi,* over the magical mixture. (In doing this) he prepares a sort of large receptacle for his voice—a voice-trap we might call it. He lays the mixture on a mat & covers this with another mat so that his voice may be caught & imprisoned between them. During the recitation he holds his head close to the aperture & carefully sees to it that no portion of the herbs shall remain unaffected by the breath of his voice. He moves his mouth from one end of the aperture to the other, turns his head, repeating the words over & over again, rubbing them, so to speak, into the substance. When you watch the magician at work & note the meticulous care with which he applies this most effective & most important verbal action to the substance . . . then you relize how serious is the belief that the magic is in the breath & the breath is the magic." (B. Malinowski, *Coral Gardens & Their Magic,* pp. 215–16, 260.)

(3) "The Moon thus says to the little Hare, that the little Hare is a little fool. Therefore his ears are red, because of the foolish things. He is not clever.

"The Moon speaks with the side of his tongue, because his tongue is upon his palate. Therefore he speaks with his tongue's tip because he feels he is the moon who tells his story, & he does so, because he feels that he is the Moon he is not a person, who will speak nicely, for he is the Moon. Therefore he tells the Moon's story, he does not tell a person's story, for he thus speaks, he thus tells the Moon's stories.

"Therefore he speaks turning up the other part of his tongue, for he feels that he is a shoe. Therefore he tells the shoe's stories, for he feels that he is not a man, but is the Moon. He is the Mantis' foot's shoe, & he feels that it was the Mantis who called his name, he will act like a shoe.

"Therefore he speaks like this, for he feels that he speaks like the Hare, he speaks in this manner, for he feels that he merely speaks with his tongue, he merely speaks like the Hare. The Hare speaks the Hare's language, he speaks like this. The Hare does like this the Hare talks. The Hare talks like his mother, he tells his mother's stories, his mother's stories as she tells them. And the little Hare listens to his mother's speech; he talks just like his mother, because he feels that his father talks like his mother, his father talks like this, for he feels that he speaks like his wife, he does like this, he speaks; they all tell one story for they feel that they talk their own language, they do not talk the people's language, for they tell their own stories, as they feel that another story is not there, that they may tell. For they tell one story, they do not tell the people's stories; for they speak like baboons, for they feel that baboons talk in this manner." (D. F. Bleek, "Speech of Animals & Moon Used by the |xam Bushmen," *Bantu Studies*, X, [1936], 187–89.)

(4) "It is noteworthy & perhaps to be interpreted as a general tendency in Hindu culture to *raise certain aspects of the subliminal to consciousness,* that Hinduism in general & the Tantric sects in particular make extensive use in ritual & religious practice generally, not only of the intrinsically meaningless gestures (of the dance & iconography), but also of *intrinsically meaningless vocables.* For example, the famous *om* & *hum* & the not so famous *hrim, hrām, phat,* & many others, are meaningless, religious noises in origin, whatever symbolic meanings are given

to them by the developed dogma." (M. B. Emenau in a review of La Meri's *The Gesture Language of the Hindu Dance*, in the *Journal of the American Oriental Society*, LXII [1942], 149.)

(5) "I invented," circa 1915, "a new species of verse, 'verse without words,' or sound poems, in which the balancing of vowels is gauged & distributed only to the value of the initial line. The first of these I recited tonight. I had a special costume designed for it. My legs were covered with a cothurnus of luminous blue cardboard, which reached up to my hips so that I looked like an obelisk. Above that I wore a huge cardboard collar that was scarlet inside & gold outside. This was fastened at the throat in such a way that I was able to move it like wings by raising & dropping my elbows. In addition I wore a high top hat striped with blue & white. I recited the following:

> *gadji beri bimba*
> *glandridi lauli lonni cadori*
> *gadjama bim beri glassala*
> *glandridi glassala tuffm i zimbrabim*
> *blassa galassasa tuffm i zimbrabim*

. . . I now noticed that my voice, which seemed to have no other choice, had assumed the age-old cadence of the sacerdotal lamentation. . . . The electric light went out, as I had intended, & I was carried, moist with perspiration, like a magical bishop, into the abyss. . . ." (Hugo Ball, quoted in *The Dada Painters & Poets*, ed. Robert Motherwell [George Wittenborn Publishers, New York, 1951], p. xix; tr. Eugene Jolas.)

[N.B. How different is Ball's dada-show from the Kirgiz-Tatar poet (shaman) who "runs around the tent, springing, roaring, leaping; he barks like a dog, sniffs at the audience, lows like an ox, bellows, cries, bleats like a lamb, grunts like a pig, whinnies, coos, imitating with remarkable accuracy the cries of animals, the songs of birds, the sound of their flight, & so on, all of which greatly impresses the audience." (M. Eliade, *Shamanism*, p. 97.) It is part of a world with Artaud's cries in *Pour en finir avec le jugement de Dieu* & McClure's poems, like the following, in "beast language." But there are plenty of less dramatic examples also.]

(6) Michael McClure

GHOST TANTRA ＃1 (1964)

GOOOOOOR! GOOOOOOOOOOO!
GOOOOOOOOOOR!
GRAHHH! GRAHH! GRAHH!
Grah gooooor! Ghahh! Graaarr! Greeeeer! Grayowhr!
Greeeeee
GRAHHRR! RAHHR! GRAGHHRR! RAHR!
RAHR! RAHHR! GRAHHHR! GAHHR! HRAHR!
BE NOT SUGAR BUT BE LOVE
looking for sugar!
GAHHHHHHHH!
ROWRR!
GROOOOOOOOOOH!

. . . .

＃49

SILENCE THE EYES! BECALM THE SENSES!
Drive drooor from the fresh repugnance, thou whole,
thou living creature. Live not for others but affect thyself
from thy enhanced interior—believing what thou carry.
Thy trillionic multitude of grahh, vhooshes, and silences.
Oh you are heavier and dimmer than you knew
and more solid and full of pleasure.
Grahhr! Grahhhr! Ghrahhhrrr! Ghrahhr. Grahhrrr.
Grahhrr-grahhhhrr! Grahhr. Gahrahhrr Ghrahhhrrrr.
Ghrarrrr. Ghrahhr! Ghrarrrrr. Gharrrr. Ghrahhhrr.
Ghrahhrr. Ghrahr. Grahhr. Grahharrr. Grahhrr.
Grahhhhr. Grahhhr. Gahar. Ghrahhr. Grahhr. Grahhr.
Ghrahhr. Grahhhr. Grahhr. Gratharrr! Grahhr.
Ghrahrr. Ghraaaaaaahrr. Grhar. Ghhrarrr! Grahhrr.
Ghrahrr. Gharr! Ghrahhhhr. Grahhrr. Ghraherrr.

. . . .

#51

I LOVE TO THINK OF THE RED PURPLE ROSE
IN THE DARKNESS COOLED BY THE NIGHT.
We are served by machines making satins
of sounds.
Each blot of sound is a bud or a stahr.
Body eats bouquets of the ear's vista.
Gahhhrrr boody eers noze eyes deem thou.
NOH. NAH-OHH
hrooor. VOOOR-NAH! GAHROOOOO ME.
Nah droooooh seerch. NAH THEE!
The machines are too dull when we
are lion-poems that move & breathe.
WHAN WE GROOOOOOOOOOOOOOOOR
hann dree myketoth sharoo sreee thah noh deeeeeemed ez.
Whan eeeethoooze hrohh.

["These are spontaneous stanzas published in the order and with
the natural sounds in which they were first written. If there is an
OOOOOOOOOOOOOOOH, simply say a long loud 'oooh.' If
there is a 'gahr' simply say gar and put an h in.

"Look at stanza 51. It begins in English and turns into beast
language—star becomes stahr. Body becomes boody. Nose becomes
noze. Everybody knows how to pronounce NOH or VOOR-NAH
or GAHROOOOO ME."

—Michael McClure]

Genesis II, p. 9

T. G. H. Strehlow, *Aranda Traditions* (Melbourne University
Press, 1947), pp. 7–8 (abridged).

A heavy ripeness, the swelling & bursting of a teeming life-
source, colors Australian views of the creation. The bandicoot-
father, fullness of the new light, sweet dark juice of honeysuckle
buds, a swarming sense of life—not two-by-two, in pairs, but
swarming—was turned-from in the West, reduced to images of
evil. Spenser's *Error* breeds "a thousand yong ones, which she
dayly fed, / Sucking upon her poisonous dugs"; & Milton's *Sin* is

the Prolific raped by her son into the production of "those yelling monsters, that with ceaseless cry / Surround me, as thou sawest, hourly conceived / And hourly born, with sorrow infinite," etc. But Blake renamed these "the Prolific" & marked a turning in man's relation to his "sensual existence."

Egyptian God Names, p. 10

Alexandre Piankoff, *The Shrines of Tut-Ankh-Amon* (Pantheon Books, New York, 1955), *passim.*

Poetry is I say essentially a vocabulary just as prose is essentially not.

And what is the vocabulary of which poetry absolutely is. It is a vocabulary based on the noun as prose is essentially and determinately and vigorously not based on the noun.

Poetry is concerned with using with abusing, with losing with wanting, with denying with avoiding with adoring with replacing the noun. It is doing that always doing that, doing that and doing nothing but that. Poetry is doing nothing but using losing refusing and pleasing and betraying and caressing nouns.

. . . So that is poetry really loving the name of anything and that is not prose.

—G. Stein, *Lectures in America,* pp. 231–32

But the physicality of her description sticks: how she points to a material condition of poetry prior to verse or sequence, a way of thinking & feeling that treats words—all words—as substantive, measurable, having each a certain weight & extension, roots of words holding them firmly to earth, which the man cuts loose at will to let float up, then take root again so that their weights are again felt. And since the words are "real" (being measurable by weight & extension), they may be called-forth again or withheld, & being called-forth are the things called-forth? This is what the man believed once who made magic—"spells" & "charms" (*carmina*) being words in search of things. Measurable words as real as measurable things where both words & things are present in the naming. And the same tangible quality of words was felt whether they were spoken (again that breath-entering-the-object Malinowski wrote of) or written or pictured or drummed. Something like that sensed then & there—rediscovered here & now.

Addenda. (1) Egyptian poetry, where it names & creates its gods, is at least as concerned with their energy as their dignity—is in fact rich in matter that Rundle Clark calls "obscene, brutal & inconsequential" & that "shows the Egyptians lived much closer to the dark powers of the unconscious than we realize." The same force turns up in other god-namings & god-poems, as when the Polynesians call Kiho:

First-Urge
Phallus
Rising-Sap
Tumidity   (J. Frank Stimson, *The Cult of Kiho-Timu*
The Denudation   [Bishop Museum, Honolulu, 1933],
etc.   pp. 20–21.)

& there too the translation muffles the force.

(2) Among the Navaho a list of god-names became the song, called *The Twelve-Word Song of Blessing*, "a combination of names" writes Reichard "(of) tremendous power":

TWELVE-WORD SONG
Earth
Sky
Mountain Woman
Water Woman
Talking God
xactceoγan
Boy-carrying-single-corn-kernel
Girl-carrying-single-turquoise
White-corn-boy
Yellow-corn-girl
Pollen Boy
Cornbeetle Girl

                    (G. Reichard, *Navaho Religion* [Pantheon,
                    New York, 1950], Vol. One, p. 273.)

Consider also the Polynesian genealogical poem (below, p. 394) & African praise-names & praise-poems (below, p. 418).

(3) "Victory will be above all / To see truly into the distance / To see everything / Up close / So that everything can have a new name."—Guillaume Apollinaire.

Genesis III, p. 13

Richard A. Taylor, *Te Ika a Maui: New Zealand & Its Inhabitants* (William Macintosh, London, 1870), pp. 109–10.

The coming of light as pivotal moment in the world's awakening gets a very lovely, very complex handling in Polynesian poetry. What's less apparent is that these light-poems (night-poems too) are in fact genealogical tables tracing the rulers' descents from the gods, the gods from the cosmic circumstances of the beginning. Night (*Te Po*) is both a name & a period of time, a force & a god: & the language holds it in delicate balance between concrete & abstract thought; so also for Conception, Increase, Great-Night, Nothing, Midday, etc. A similar chant turns up in a version by J. C. Anderson (1907), there as pure genealogy. The reciter is Mumuhu:

THE GENEALOGY OF THE GODS
FROM PRIMAL NOTHINGNESS:

1.	Te Kore	(the void)
2.	Te Kore-tua-tahi	(the first void)
3.	Te Kore-tua-rua	(the second void)
4.	Te Kore-nui	(the vast void)
5.	Te Kore-roa	(the far-extending void)
6.	Te Kore-para	(the sere void)
7.	Te Kore-whiwhia	(the unpossessing void)
8.	Te Kore-rawea	(the delightful void)
9.	Te Kore-te-tamaua	(the void fast bound)
10.	Te Po	(the Night)
11.	Te Po-teki	(the hanging Night)
12.	Te Po-terea	(the drifting Night)
13.	Te Po-wha-wha	(the moaning Night)
14.	Hine-ruaki-moe	(daughter of troubled sleep)
15.	Te Po	(the Night)
16.	Te Ata	(the Morning)
17.	Te Ao-to-roa	(the abiding Day)
18.	Te Ao-marama	(the bright Day)
19.	Whai-tua	(Space)

"(And) in *whai-tua* two existences formed without shape: *Maku* (moisture), a male, & *Mahora-nui-a-rangi* (the great expanse of heaven), a female; from whom sprang *Toko-mua*, Toko-roto & *Toko-pa*, parents of wind, of clouds, of mists, & fourth in birth, *Rangi-potiki*, who taking to wife *Papa*, produced the gods." (Johannes C. Anderson, *Maori Life in Ao-Tea*, p. 127.)

Addenda. (1) Paul Radin's reading (*Primitive Man as Philosopher*, pp. 292 ff.) suggests a high degree of systematization: that the first section describes the development of consciousness; the second predicates a mediating principle, the *word;* the third gives a genealogical history of matter; the fourth shows the birth of light itself. Even so there are many holes, many different texts & distributions of the ages. Signifying what? Either that a closed system had come apart, or that the Polynesian mind was in constant movement toward the making of a shifting series of possibilities. (See also the Hawaiian *Kumulipo*, p. 338, above; commentary, p. 513, below.)

(2) Greek cosmogonies like that (say) in Hesiod are the best Western tries at this sort of thing the editor knows of—but the blocks to feeling the concrete force of the namings, etc., are very great.

(3) Jackson Mac Low

> *1st Light Poem: for Iris—10 June 1962*
>
> The light of a student-lamp
> sapphire light
> shimmer
> the light of a smoking-lamp
>
> Light from the Magellanic Clouds
> the light of a Nernst lamp
> the light of a naphtha-lamp
> light from meteorites
>
> Evanescent light
> ether
> the light of an electric lamp
> extra light

Citrine light
kineographic light
the light of a Kitson lamp
kindly light

Ice light
irradiation
ignition
altar light

The light of a spotlight
a sunbeam
sunrise
solar light

Mustard-oil light
Maroon light
the light of a magnesium flare
light from a meteor

Evanescent light
ether
light from an electric lamp
an extra light

Light from a student-lamp
sapphire light
a shimmer
smoking-lamp light

Ordinary light
orgone lumination
light from a lamp burning olive oil
opal light

Actinism
atom-bomb light
the light of an alcohol lamp
the light of a lamp burning anda-oil

Images, p. 15

(1) *Report of the Canadian Arctic Expedition, 1913–1918:* to make the sun come out by assertion of its presence; (2) H. Vedder, *Die Bergdama,* tr. into English by C. M. Bowra, *Primitive Song:* sung to a bow made of *ha-*wood; (3) Bleek & Lloyd, *Specimens of Bushman Folklore:* in the jackal's language, i.e., with a special "click" not otherwise used; (4) Knud Rasmussen, as quoted in Caillois & Lambert, *Trésor de la poésie universelle* & there titled *Contre la mort;* (5) H. R. Schoolcraft, *Historical & Statistical Information Respecting the History, Condition & Prospects of the Indian Tribes of the United States, 1851–1857:* medicine song of the Chippewa (Ojibwa) Midēwiwin Society (see below, p. 472), drawing power from identification with totemic animal; (6) Bleek & Lloyd, *Specimens:* a hunting charm, power from description of the quarry; (7) F. Densmore, *The American Indians & Their Music:* more power from description—or simply the words as "given" to the vision-seeker.

Single-line poems, presented as such—in contrast to some of the longer works that follow & involve a linking of lines & images to make poems of greater complexity, showing development by image cluster, gaps in sequence, etc.

The poetry here is in song & image & word-play, but only the image comes near to translating, itself enough to make a poem, or so the argument would go. What's happened, simply, is that something has been sighted & stated & set apart (by name or by description); given its own tune, too, to make it special; fixed, held fast in all this vanishing experience. It is this double sense of sighted/sited that represents the basic poetic function (a setting-apart-by-the-creation-of-special-circumstances that the editor calls "sacralism") from which the rest follows—toward the building of more complicated structures & visions. But even here there is nothing naïve or minimal about the "sightings," save their clarity & the sense that, starting now, the plot (as Cage would say) is-going-to-thicken. Thickens, in fact, while we're watching; for the "single perception" of an image like *a splinter of stone/which is white* can as easily be sensed as two perceptions, & placed against the subject *(blue crane)* as two or three. But the decision has been made to voice it as a single line or musical phrase, & that decision itself is a statement about how we know things—& a choice.

Addenda. (1) The typical "primitive" song practice is to repeat (often also to distort) the one line indefinitely—or as long as the dance & ritual demand—then go on to a second song in the (ritual) sequence, a third, a fourth, etc. A turn in the ritual or dance would then represent something roughly equivalent to a strophe break, where a first series of single-line poems ends & a new, but related, series begins. This is utilized by the translators of works like *Djanggawul, Moon-Bone,* the African "praise-poems," etc., who follow the "orders" of the ritual in their arrangement of single-line works into larger structures. Lines & series will often seem disconnected except that they're performed & happen together. The impact of this for our own time can't be ignored.

(2) "Nothing of that, only an image—
    nothing else, utter oblivion—
    slanting through the words come vestiges of light!"
    —Franz Kafka

(3) Ian Hamilton Finlay

OCEAN STRIPE SERIES 2

~~— the little sail of your name —~~
the little sail of your name
~~— the little sail of your name —~~

[*Note.* Each element in Finlay's poem appears on a separate page, broken lines in blue, words in red; thus color & the page boundary function with relation to his "single-image" as music does elsewhere. Thus, too, the further you get into it the less sense it makes to speak of a single-line poem—as in the "primitive" poems where any change in the music, even if the words remain unchanged, will alter the entire piece.

Another poem of Finlay's reduces the verbal element to a single word:

        patch   patch   patch
        patch   patch-patch
        patch-patch-patch
                    (from *6 Small Songs in 3's*)

with which compare the Australian:

blue-tongue- lizard's-teeth (one word)	"singing name" for its teeth	blue-tongue- lizard's-teeth (one word)

& other songs in the literal section of the texts from the *Kunapipi* ceremonies (see above, p. 363).]

Bantu Combinations, p. 17

Henri A. Junod, *Life of a South African Tribe* (Macmillan & Co., 1912, 1927), *passim.*

Examples of plot-thickening in the area of "image": a conscious placing of image against image as though to see-what-happens. Apart from its presence in song, this juxtaposing of images turns up all over in the art, say, of the riddle—of which several of these "combinations" are, in fact, examples. Poem as opposition or balance of two or more images is also the basis of the haiku, less clearly of the sonnet. In all these the interest increases as the connection between the A & B sections becomes more & more strained, barely definable. Junod sensed this when he wrote:

> What makes a Bantu address especially interesting is . . . the *power of comparison* exhibited by Bantu speakers. . . . Sometimes the imagination is so subtle that the result is almost incoherent. They are satisfied even if the point which the two things compared have in common . . . is almost infinitesimal.

Not subtlety, though, but *energy:* the power of word & image. For it's right here that the light breaks through most clearly; not the light of logic & simile, not even the flashing of a single image or name, but what feels "deeper" because further into it by now in the process of boxing myself into some corner, & to which (for the first time) the word "vision" might be said to apply.

Addenda. (1) Now I a fourfold vision see
And a fourfold vision is given to me
Tis fourfold in my supreme delight
And three fold in soft Beulahs night
And twofold Always. May God us keep
From Single vision & Newtons sleep
—William Blake (1802)

(2) "The image cannot spring from any comparison but from the bringing together of two more or less remote realities. . . .

"The more distant and legitimate the relation between the two realities brought together, the stronger the image will be . . . the more emotive power and poetic reality it will possess."

—Pierre Reverdy

(3) Robert Kelly

NEW MOON OVER WHALEBACK

this new moon low down
a plain sky
holding it in place
/
I can't find the moon
where is it
a black face in black sky
/
her hands are fire-red
& hold me
it is just one hand
/
red bark the spring moon
going down
earth licks its fat lips
/
this is night's red eye
red-rimmed from
someone else's sun
/
the last days like this
a red stone
all we know of fire

(from *Lunes,* Hawk's Well Press, 1965)

Correspondences, p. 18

Selected from *The I Ching or Book of Changes,* translated from Chinese into German by Richard Wilhelm and rendered into English by Cary F. Baynes (Bollingen Series XIX, Pantheon Books, New York, 1950), pp. 295–99.

The *I Ching,* which some have dated as far back as 2000 B.C. (& if not that old is, anyway, very ancient), is the basis in China for the kind of thought that sees life & development as a working-out or constant reshuffling of contrary forces; or, as Blake had it

> without contraries is no progression;
> reason & energy, love & hate, good & evil,
> are all necessary to human existence.

While the "practical" side of the *I Ching* deals with divination by yarrow sticks, etc., some sections, like the one given here, show a developed ability to think-in-images, to place name against name, quality against quality, while retaining that passion for the names of things that Gertrude Stein saw as the basis of all poetry. Partly it's a question of resemblances & analogy, but at this point in where "we" are, what's of still greater importance is the possibility of a kind of tension, energy, etc., generated by the joining of disparate, even arbitrary, images. *Observation:* Every new correspondence acts on its subject, which it changes, & on the entire field; every change a measurable burst of energy. *Questions:* Is the correspondence *there,* is it imposed, & does it finally matter? If the common term "hot" or "dry" links "fire" with "the sun, the lightning, the upper part of the trunk," what links it with "big-bellied" or "lances & weapons"? What common quality "justifies" the linking of nouns in the "keeping still" series, & if you find one (Confucius did!) are you gaining consistency through a loss of power? The editor can only witness to his sense of this series of "correspondences" being a handy ancient manual of poetic process (of *all* those levels of vision Blake spoke of)—& values it as such.

Addenda. (1) For further selections from, comments on the *I Ching,* see above, p. 255, below, p. 489.

(2) André Breton

FREE UNION (1931)

My wife whose hair is a brush fire
Whose thoughts are summer lightning
Whose waist is an hourglass
Whose waist is the waist of an otter caught in the teeth of a tiger
Whose mouth is a bright cockade with the fragrance of a star of
the first magnitude
Whose teeth leave prints like the tracks of white mice over snow
Whose tongue is made out of amber and polished glass
Whose tongue is a stabbed wafer
The tongue of a doll with eyes that open and shut
Whose tongue is incredible stone
My wife whose eyelashes are strokes in the handwriting of a child
Whose eyebrows are nests of swallows
My wife whose temples are the slate of greenhouse roofs
With steam on the windows
My wife whose shoulders are champagne
Are fountains that curl from the heads of dolphins over the ice
My wife whose wrists are matches
Whose fingers are raffles holding the ace of hearts
Whose fingers are fresh cut hay
My wife with the armpits of martens and beech fruit
And Midsummer Night
That are hedges of privet and nesting places for sea snails
Whose arms are of sea foam and a land locked sea
And a fusion of wheat and a mill
Whose legs are spindles
In the delicate movements of watches and despair
My wife whose calves are sweet with the sap of elders
Whose feet are carved initials
Keyrings and the feet of steeplejacks who drink

My wife whose neck is fine milled barley
Whose throat contains the Valley of Gold
And encounters in the bed of the maelstrom
My wife whose breasts are of the night
And are undersea molehills
And crucibles of rubies
My wife whose breasts are haunted by the ghosts of dew-moistened
  roses
Whose belly is a fan unfolded in the sunlight
Is a giant talon
My wife with the back of a bird in vertical flight
With a back of quicksilver
And bright lights
My wife whose nape is of smooth worn stone and wet chalk
And of a glass slipped through the fingers of someone who has just
  drunk
My wife with the thighs of a skiff
That are lustrous and feathered like arrows
Stemmed with the light tailbones of a white peacock
And imperceptible balance
My wife whose rump is sandstone and flax
Whose rump is the back of a swan and the spring
My wife with the sex of an iris
A mine and a platypus
With the sex of an algae and old fashioned candles
My wife with the sex of a mirror
My wife with eyes full of tears
With eyes that are purple armor and a magnetized needle
With eyes of savannahs
With eyes full of water to drink in prisons
My wife with eyes that are forests forever under the axe
My wife with eyes that are the equal of water and air and earth
  and fire

(translation by David Antin)

Genesis IV, p. 20

Adapted from "The Secrets of Enoch," chapters XXV & XXVI, in *The Lost Books of the Bible & the Forgotten Books of Eden,* reprinted by World Publishing Co. (Cleveland, 1963), p. 90.

God's sexuality—lonely, hermaphroditic—is another, very natural way of imagining the creation. The most famous such account in the Near East was the Egyptian masturbation genesis:

> Heaven had not been created . . .
> The earth had not been created . . .
> I formed a spell in my heart . . .
> I made forms of every kind . . .
> I thrust my cock into my closed hand . . .
> I made my seed to enter my hand . . .
> I poured it into my mouth . . .
> I broke wind under the form of SHU . . .
> I passed water under the form of TEFNUT . . .

But even the priestly Genesis (Hebrew) couldn't unhook the mind from its old imaginings, hypotheses, etc.; *vide* the section collaged into the beginning of the fifth chapter:

> This is the book of the generations of Adam. In the day that
>   God created man, *in the likeness of God* made he him;
> *Male & female* created he them; & blessed them, & *called
>   their name Adam.*

But the idea—re-explored in the medieval *Zohar*—was already very old.

Aztec Definitions, p. 21

Bernardino de Sahagún, *Florentine Codex: General History of the Things of New Spain,* translated by Charles E. Dibble & Arthur J. O. Anderson (University of Utah Press, 1963), Vol. XII, *passim.*

Fray Bernardino de Sahagún, a Franciscan monk, began in 1547—only twenty-six years after the fall of Mexico-Tenochtitlan —to compile documents in Nahuatl from Indian elders who repeated what they had learned by memory in their schools, the *Calmécac* & the *Telpochcalli.* These Nahuatl texts have been preserved in three codices, two in Madrid & one in Florence. In the eleventh book of the Florentine codex—a kind of glossary of "earthly things"—the elders' minds & words are drawn toward definitions of the most ordinary debris of their lives.

Addenda. (1) "Everything goes but the words: the fragments of speech of a people who had learned that the mind's grain is our final clue to the real. He led them to a reconsideration, to an assemblage of 'the things of New Spain'—of their gods, their days, their signs & omens, their sacrifices, their songs, their defeats. . . . But . . . more astonishing than all that is how the habit of their minds begins to play among the everyday debris. . . . Here the mind finds release in a strange new encounter; free of ritual & myth [The-System]; it approaches its objects as if for the first time testing their existence. IT IS DARK, IT IS LIGHT: IT IS WIDE-MOUTHED, IT IS NARROW-MOUTHED: all of this said with no apparent sense of contradiction, as if, among these objects, the old pattern holds: of preparing chaos for the birth of something real.

"Having come to this for ourselves, we can draw close to them, can hear in these 'definitions' the sound of a poetry, a measure-by-placement-&-displacement not far from our own. . . . For surely it should be clear by now that poetry is less literature than a process of thought & feeling & the arrangement of that into affective utterances. The conditions these definitions meet are the conditions of poetry." (J.R., from "Introduction to Aztec Definitions," *Some/Thing* [Spring 1965], p. 2.)

(2) Gary Snyder

SAND (1966)

from the desert?
            —when will be sand again.

blowing sand   drifting sand-
      dunes at Bandon
      Oregon   sheltering in a shed of
driftwood, naked,   kelp whip
            "driving sand sends swallows flying—"

shirakawa. "white river" sand.
            what they rake out at Ryōan-ji;
clean crumbled creek-washed rotted granite
            quartz & feldspar   sand.

—I went there once to check the prices
bulk white sand to buy
black burnt workers spade it thru a flume

the sands of the Ganges
"all the grains of the sands of the sea"

blowing sand / running water
I slept up on your body;
walkt your valleys and your hills;

sandbox
sandpaper
sandy.

Genesis V, p. 27

Margot Astrov's translation from K. T. Preuss, *Die Religion und Mythologie der Uitoto* (1921), in *The Winged Serpent: An Anthology of American Indian Prose & Poetry* (The John Day Company, New York, 1946), pp. 325–26.

Creation by word & thought, but more particularly the recognition of "dream" as model for the creative process: a "reality" of a different order, of new combinations of objects: "thought" running ahead of "thinker," toward the making of a "world."

"Word" & "origin" & "father" immediately suggest St. John (result of Preuss' German?)—though there the Word didn't *make,* rather *was-with* & *was,* the father. And Aristotle had taught too that the origin of the gods was in men's dreamings, "for when the soul is alone in sleep, then it takes its real nature." In Australia the mythic period of the creative-beings was called the Dream-Time or The-Dreaming, which also included such latterday phenomena as participated in the sacred. Siberian & North American shamans received word & song in dreams, as did the Jewish prophets & certain Christian saints & poets.

In the early XXth century, dream (like drugs today) was turned-to to sanction the use of alternative, "non-logical" thought-processes in poetry, painting, etc., until some realized that no such sanction was needed. But dreaming remains everyone's chance for exposure to the possibilities of poetic process: of making the unknown known.

The Pictures, p. 28

Garrick Mallery, *Picture-Writing of the American Indians* (Bureau of American Ethnology, tenth Annual Report [1888–89]), pp. 472, 498, 167, 499, 526, 170.

Here & elsewhere in the anthology (see above, pp. 160, 195, & 262) are examples of visual poetry, i.e., non-verbal &/or pictorial structures with a language function analogous to but not (necessarily) identical with that of the poem. Workings of this kind are surprisingly widespread among non-literate peoples: most only a step away from writing, some having surely crossed the line. In Japanese the verb *kaku* means both to-write & to-draw: & in these examples too it is hard to keep the functions separate. Arts merge, then, & boundaries shift, & what started as an aid to memory develops as a distinct (but never isolated) activity; or later, where it becomes a system of writing, develops also into the art of calligraphy.

. . . .

1. Depiction of "the Giant Bird Kaloo . . . most terrible of all creatures . . . who caught the [Badger-Trickster] in his claws & . . . let him drop, & he fell from dawn to sunset."
2. Presentation of a shaman cure (*tamahnous*), which the artist (unnamed) describes as: "(Top left) shows the first sickness which Dr. Charley (the shaman) took. It has tails, which, when they come close to the sick person, make him worse. (Bottom left) is the way it goes when it kills a person & stays in his home. (Top right) is the second one & is hanging over (the sick person, center right). (Bottom right) is another sickness which is in him." Abstract forms to depict the unknown.
3. The chart accompanies a tradition chanted by the members of a secret society of the Osage tribe. It was drawn by an Osage, Red Corn, & images the world & early man's emergence. Tree of life & river at the top; sun, moon & stars beneath; four heavens or upper worlds at center, through which the ancestors passed before coming to this earth, etc. The pictographs are (mnemonic) clues to songs but the whole pictorial device is more-than-that (see description of the Midē songs, below, p. 472).

4. Pictographs in sequence (incised on an ivory bow) show hunter & shaman in postures of supplication & divination amid scenes of trees, dwellings, animals, etc., & (lower left) "a demon sent out by the shaman to drive the game in the way of the hunter." Pictured to the demon's left are his assistants.

5. Random distribution of images on "a kind of screen with mortuary or exorcistic use": sun, moon, stars, fish, lizard, pigs, ladder, axe, spear, palm tree, etc. The creation of a field.

6. Easter Island *rongorongo* writing: drawn on tablets called "singing wood" or "wood with hymns for recitation": thus (apparently) a system of writing for the transmission of (sacred) song. More recent workers have come up with tentative readings of the poems, e.g., Werner Wolff in *The Journal of the Polynesian Society,* 54 (1945), 1–38.

. . . .

Addenda. (1) "The word & the image are one. Painting & composing poetry belong together. Christ is image & word. The word & the image are crucified. . . ."—Hugo Ball, 1916, quoted in *The Dada Painters & Poets,* ed. Robert Motherwell, p. 52.

(2) "Christ, these hieroglyphs. Here is the most abstract & formal deal of all the things this people dealt out—and yet, to my taste, it is precisely as intimate as verse is. Is, in fact, verse. Is their verse. And comes into existence, obeys the same laws that, the coming into existence, the persisting of verse, does."—Charles Olson, *The Mayan Letters.*

(3) Some "modern" examples, out of many, follow; others appear, below, pages 464 & 465, & the reader can also check more immediate analogues in, e.g., Emmett Williams' *Anthology of Concrete Poetry* (Something Else Press, 1967).

BEHEMOTH & LEVIATHAN (1825)

William Blake

Can any understand the spreadings of the Clouds the noise of his Tabernacle

Also by watering he wearieth the thick cloud He scattereth the bright cloud also it is turned about by his counsels

Of Behemoth he saith, He is the chief of the ways of God Of Leviathan he saith, He is King over all the Children of Pride

Behold now Behemoth which I made with thee

W Blake invenit & sculpt

MADELEINE (1917)
Guillaume Apollinaire

MADELEINE

Dans le village   arabe

Photographie
tant attendue

CARNIVAL LATE AT NIGHT

Kenneth Patchen

Jess Collins

POEM & COLLAGE (1960)

) *imagine a margin an engine of genesis* (sea and land (and air, with fire understood far below and above) meeting in a shore/the margin of a book whose story and outside abyss are interchangeably land and sea. And on, yet merging into the shore a child makes castles/*comments* or peering at shells/*concretions* and crisp black seaweed. The *story/* land-sea is known by air or Another, its *genius is/genesis.* However no story unfolds to dreamer while pages turn as the air stirs and the child falls open to different ages inconsecutiv/unsequentially. Is the child now ancient mariner ¿Aphrodite? ¿old man of the sea? ¿sandpiper? ¿me for an instant? The child is on/*in* the margin, so linkd to unknown story as to be unfearing at bookedge, in contemplation on it. When the sea is out/a sandcastle, when inland out/a *conch*-creation . . . . and . . . . a shore breeze coolly there. Until the poem gets lost in a twister tearing the house down, dreamer me in a basement & the fire dept comes, , , , , , , , , Awake ¿at sea? now where is my margin of error?

The Girl of the Early Race Who Made the Stars, p. 34

Wilhelm H. I. Bleek & Lucy C. Lloyd, *Specimens of Bushman Folklore* (George Allen & Co., London, 1911), p. 72.

The Bleek-Lloyd workings—the English was apparently Lucy Lloyd's—are the best examples the editor knows of how a "literal" translation, when handled with respect for the intelligence & sense-of-form of the original maker, can point to the possibility of new uses in the translator's own language. Wilhelm H. I. Bleek, German-born philologist & collector, died in 1875, so that his contributions to the *Specimens* are from before that date & those of his sister-in-law not much later. This makes their very modern sound all the more astonishing—as close to the language, say, of Gertrude Stein (see below) as the form of an African mask to the paintings of Picasso or Modigliani.

"The Girl of the Early Race" was narrated by ‖kábbo (lit. "Dream") as told him by his mother !kwi-an. He was also the maker or transmitter of the Jackal's song (above, p. 15) & the account of the "floating names" that appears in Appendix A of the present volume.

Addenda. (1) Another characteristic of the Bleek-Lloyd translations is that they call into question the distinction (still strong among us) between poetry & prose, thus more faithful to the primitive situation; or, as Boas noted:

> The form of (our) prose is largely determined by the fact that it is read, not spoken, while primitive prose is based on the art of oral delivery & is, therefore, more closely related to modern oratory than to the printed literary style. . . . In other cases [the prose passages] are of rhythmic form & must be considered poetry or chants rather than prose.
>
> (*Race, Language & Culture,* p. 491)

Today too poetry & prose are coming to a place-of-meeting in the spoken language—& the distinctions made by previous centuries have come to mean much less.

(2) Gertrude Stein

from LISTEN TO ME (A Play, 1936)

Act III
Scene II
The moon

No dog barks at the moon.
The moon shines and no dog barks
No not anywhere on this earth.
Because everywhere anywhere there are lights many lights and
so no dog knows that the moon is there
And so no dog barks at the moon now no not
anywhere.
And the moon makes no one crazy no not now
anywhere.
Because there are so many lights anywhere.
That the light the moon makes is no matter.
And so no one is crazy now anywhere.
Because there are so many lights anywhere.
That the light the moon makes is no matter.
And no one is crazy now anywhere.
Because there are so many lights anywhere.
And so then there it does not matter
The sun yes the sun yes does matter
But the moon the moon does not matter
Because there are so many lights everywhere that any dog
knows that lights any night are anywhere.
And so no dog bays at the moon anywhere.
This is so
This we know
Because we wondered why,
Why did the dogs not bay at the
moon.
They did not but why
But of course why
Because there are lights everywhere
anywhere.
And that is what they meant by never
yesterday.

[*Note.* The editor has chosen to present the preceding as a running piece, though in the original the lines are spoken by five characters.]

The Fragments, p. 36

(1), (2), & (3) from Samuel A. B. Mercer, *The Pyramid Texts* (see note, p. 432), Utterances 561, 501, 502; (4) from S. Langdon, *Babylonian Penitential Psalms* (Librairie Orientaliste Paul Geuthner, Paris, 1927), p. 21.

Time & chance have worked on the materials, not only to corrode but to create new structures: as if "process" itself had turned poet, to leave its imprints on the work. This explains the gaps, the holes-punched-out-by-time. But the workers who pieced these together have left their marks too: of dots & brackets, parentheses & numbers & open spaces. So something else appears: a value, a new form to attract the mind: as a Greek statue that has lost its colors, tempts the sculptor into the sight of marble: something tough as rock.

See also the more complicatedly pieced-together fragments on page 291 & following.

Addenda. (1) Ezra Pound

PAPYRUS
Spring . . .
Too long . . .
Gongola . . .

(from *Lustra,* 1916)

(2) Armand Schwerner
from THE TABLETS (1966)

the calyx, the calyx, someone has ripped it
it will not make loam, it will crumble
the pig (god?) has pulled life off++++++++++++++++
the pig (god?) is stronger than a thoughtless child
my chest empties.........................my chest
I can no longer stand in the middle of the field and++++++++
I am missing, my chest has no food for the maggots
there is no place for the pollen, there is only a hole in the flower

the hummingbird............pus...............nectar
the field is a hole without pattern (shoes?)
there are no eyes in back of the wisent's sockets
the urus eats her own teats and her..............
the urus lies in milk and blood
the urus is a hole in the middle of the field
[testicles]......................for the ground
"with grey horses" drinks urine
"having fine green oxen" looks for salt
let us hold.................the long man upside down
let us look into his mouth..............selfish saliva
let us pluck+++++++++++++++++++++++for brother tree
let us kiss the long man, let us carry the long man
let us kiss the long man, let us fondle the long man
let us carry the long man as the ground sucks his drippings
let us feel the drippings from his open groin
let us kiss the hot wound, the wet wound...........nectar
let us wait until he is white and dry.............my chest
let us look into his dry evil mouth, let us fondle the long man
let us bypass the wisent on the river-road pintrpnit
let us avoid the urus on the river-road pintrpnit
let us smell the auroch on the river-road pintrpnit
let us carry the beautiful (strange?) children to the knom
let us sing with the children by the knom
let us set the children's beautiful (strange?) skulls by the hearth
when the rain comes
let us have rain
let us have rain
++++++++++++++++++++++++++++++++
+++++++++++++++++++++++++++++++++++++++
+++++++++++++++·.........................tremble

[Schwerner writes of this: "The modern, accidental form of
Sumero-Akkadian tablets provided me with a usable poetic structure. They offered, among other things, ways out of closures—
which I find increasingly onerous—as well as the expansion of the
constricting girdle of English syntax. They also invited spontaneous phonetic improvisations, . . . made me feel comfortable in re-
creating the animistic . . . & (enabled me) to put in holes wherever I wanted, or wherever they needed. . . .

["What is more, the rapid shifts in tonality & texture found in some archaic & primitive materials contribute a helpful antidote to 'civilized' modes concerned with characterological & dramatic imperatives of consistency. . . . (These) tonal & textural shifts . . . help place in some perspective the contemporary mystique of line-endings & their poetic importance. The question is not, Where does the line end; the question is, When is verse not charged with the power of the varied possible? The question is, What is meaningfulness?"]

All Lives, All Dances, & All Is Loud, p. 38

Translated by C. M. Bowra from R. P. Trilles, *Les Pygmées de la Forêt Equatoriale* (Paris, 1931), & printed in Bowra, *Primitive Song,* (World Publishing Co., Cleveland, 1962), p. 106.

UNIVERSAL PRIMITIVE & ARCHAIC VISION OF ALL LIFE IN MOTION & SHARING A SINGLE NATURE WHICH IS SACRED

20TH CENTURY AMERICAN NOSTALGIA TO ADDRESS & TO ANIMATE THE THING-WORLD

Addenda. (1) "Primitive man by no means lacks the ability to grasp the empirical differences of things. But in his conception of nature & life these differences are obliterated by a stronger feeling: the deep conviction of a fundamental and indelible *solidarity of life* that bridges over the multiplicity and variety of its single forms. . . . Life is felt as an unbroken continuous whole. . . . The limits between (its) different spheres are not insurmountable barriers; they are fluent and fluctuating. . . . By a sudden metamorphosis everything may be turned into everything. If there is any characteristic and outstanding feature of the mythical world, any law by which it is governed—it is this law of metamorphosis." (E. Cassirer.)

(2) A SONG OF THE BEAR
    Sung by Eagle Shield

my paw is sacred
all things are sacred

(F. Densmore, *Teton Sioux Music,* p. 264)

(3) "For everything that lives is holy."—W. Blake, *A Song of Liberty*.

Summary. A common ideology in what Cassirer calls "the consanguinity of all forms of life"; a common method in the free interchange of terms within the poem. *Question:* Is the order you speak of "natural" or is it "imposed"? *Answer:* Please repeat the question.

Yoruba Praises, p. 39

Bakare Gbadamosi & Ulli Beier, *Yoruba Poetry* (Ministry of Education, Nigeria, 1959), p. 16.

Shango—the Yoruba god of thunder; said to have been the third king of the town of Oyo.

The praise-poem (Yoruba *oriki*, Zulu *izibongo*, Basuto *lithoko*, etc.) turns up through much of Black Africa. At its simplest it's the stringing-together of a series of praise-names (usually independent utterances) describing the qualities owned by a particular man, god, animal, plant, place, etc.—anything, in short, that makes a "deep impression" on the singer (see Addenda (1), below). Often, too, it's not a question of "praise" but of delineation according to a certain method. The method itself is a kind of "collaging" from a fixed set of verses, lines & tags which are at the poet-diviner's disposal & can be supplemented by new invention. Among the Yoruba, e.g., each individual has a series of praise-names in the form of "descriptive phrases . . . that may be invented by relatives or neighbors or—most frequently—by the drummers" (Gbadamosi/Beier, p. 7) or, particularly in the case of god names, handed down from the past. The actual singing (or drumming) of the praise-poem involves the arrangement of already existing materials into a new & coherent composition "having as its subject a single individual." The individual poet takes off from the work of the collectivity, to which he adds as last in a line of makers. But his "art" is one of assemblage—the weighing of line against line.

Addenda. (1) "To the imaginative mind of the Bantu every-thing that causes a deep impression, even material objects, affords an occasion for the utterance of lofty phrases and words of praise. Once when traveling south of Delagoa Bay through the desert, our party arrived in the neighborhood of the Umbelozi railway. The train was heard in the distance. One of my servants was busy cleaning pots; I heard him muttering the following words:

The one who roars in the distance
The one who crushes the braves in pieces & smashes them
The one who debauches our wives—
They abandon us, they go to the towns to lead bad lives—
The seducer! And we remain alone

He was extolling the huge thing & lamenting his misfortune and the curse it has brought upon the country." (Henri A. Junod, *Life of a South African Tribe* [1912], Vol. II, p. 196.)

(2) Further examples of praise-poems appear on pages 164, 166, 167, 168, and 173. The reader may also be interested in the combination of praise-poem technique with "composition by chance" in the Basuto divining poems (see commentary, p. 469, below); also in the similarity of praise-poems to earlier Egyptian workings (see "The Cannibal Hymn," p. 149; "Egyptian God Names," p. 10) & to the epic genealogies of Polynesia (see commentary, p. 394). In looking for modern analogues, three areas of resemblance should be distinguished: to modern poets using techniques of assemblage or collage; to efforts, e.g., by dadaists & surrealists, to write group-poems; & to poems, irrespective of method, in which a series of phrases are made to turn around a single subject-as-pivot. The first two at least witness to a modern-primitive concern with the transpersonal—but that's just part of the story.

(3) "The poet . . . ('the maker of plots or fables' as Aristotle insists) . . . is pre-eminently the maker of the plot, the framework —not necessarily of everything that takes place within that frame-work! The poet creates a *situation* wherein he invites other persons & the world in general to be co-creators with him! He does not wish to be a dictator but a loyal co-initiator of action within the free society of equals which he hopes his work will help to bring about."—Jackson Mac Low.

(4) Takis Sinopoulos

IOANNA RAVING

Constantinos is a door.

He is a face behind the door.

He is a door that suddenly slams and crushes your fingers.

Constantinos is an empty room.

Scream of peril in an empty room.

Constantinos is a house, a gloomy house.

Within him unexplored religions of blood smolder.

Constantinos is tomorrow tomorrow tomorrow (tomorrow countlessly repeated).

He has two bodies, one red the other black.

Sometimes I deprive him of one, sometimes of the other. Together they reduce me to ashes.

Constantinos disappears if you look at him squarely.

Constantinos appears if you dream of him.

He battles night, falls on her blind with rage and thus is filled with wounds that constantly fester.

He tortures himself with the faces, the vagueness tyrannizes him, fumbling my body, the light of my face and persistent tears shatter him.

Constantinos is the sun that determines the shadow of grass with his continuous movement.

Constantinos is the design on a carpet of stifled flowers.

Constantinos is the struggle with rooms and birds.

He always speaks of a river that will cleanse his back of the soil and impurities of this earth.

He recovers from the dark motives that excite his blood and then he sleeps.

Constantinos has much filth in his imaginary life.

Constantinos is a questionable fact.

Constantinos is a half-eaten mask.

He wears this winter coat and presumes he is constantly transforming.

Constantinos is a dark oppressive day when the wind carries dust to the windows.

Behind the face of Constantinos stirs the black Constantinos.

Constantinos burns at night with a passion more terrible than his words.

I repeat Constantinos is a house.

He is a house full of contrivances whose claws slash your back.

Constantinos repents for deeds that never happened.

He confuses what he did with what he planned to do.

He constructed dreadful buildings and held them hopelessly in his hands until they tumbled and smashed us.

Constantinos is responsible for whatever happens inside us.

Constantinos is a mirror that shatters in endless paranoia and reflections of fantastic surprises.

He always calls my face dark ravine of the moon. (My face itself is light.)

Constantinos is terrifying when he flays the layers of his skin one by one.

I don't know how to calm Constantinos.

Hour after hour madness stands by him and it shines from within his bowels like a lighted lamp.

This is Constantinos.

> (*Translation from the Greek* by
> George Economou.)

War God's Horse Song I, II, pp. 40 & 41

(1) Slightly revised from Dane & Mary Roberts Coolidge, *The Navaho Indians* (Houghton Mifflin, Boston, 1930), p. 2.

(II) Collected by D. P. McAllester & previously unpublished. Variations on the same matter from the Blessingway of Frank Mitchell (d. April 1967) of Chinle, Arizona. This is No. 13 of 17 horse-songs in Mitchell's possession—the series a major example of minimal adjustments & variations on a single theme.

See note, immediately following, on "To the God of Fire."

To the God of Fire as a Horse, p. 44
To the God of Fire, p. 45

Two hymns from the Rig-Veda (1500–1200 B.C.) in English versions by Robert Kelly.

Agni was the Vedic Aryan god-of-fire & personification of the sacrificial fire itself. The connection of sun- & fire-gods with the horse is familiar enough from (say) Greek mythology, & it's interesting too that the Navaho figure identified by the Coolidges as the war-god (see "War God's Horse Song" above) appears in McAllester's variation as "son-of-the-Sun" who (like an untragic Phaeton) receives his father's multi-colored horses, etc. A text from the very ancient *Brhad Aranyaka Upanishad* equates various parts of the sacrificial-horse with elements of the cosmos, much as the Navaho does:

> Dawn . . . is the head of the sacrificial horse. The sun is his eye; the wind, his breath; the sacrificial fire his open mouth; the year is the body of the sacrificial horse. The sky is his back; the atmosphere, his belly; the earth, his underbelly; the directions, his flanks; the intermediate directions, his ribs; the seasons, his limbs; the months & half-months, his joints; days & nights, his feet; the stars, his bones; the clouds, his flesh. Sand is the food in his stomach; rivers, his entrails; mountains, his liver & lungs; plants & trees, his hair; the rising sun, his forepart; the setting sun, his hindpart. When he yawns, then it lightnings; when he shakes himself, then it thunders; when he urinates, then it rains. Speech is actually his neighing.

The reader may want to compare these compositions with the African praise-poems (see above, pp. 39, 167, & 173).

The Stars, p. 46

J.R.'s working from A. E. Preyre's French version after C. G. Leland (1902) as printed in Roger Caillois & Jean-Clarence Lambert, *Trésor de la poésie universelle* (Gallimard, Paris, 1958), p. 35.

A 1921 version by Leland's collaborator, John Dyneley Prince, has two significant changes: *our light is a voice* > *our light is a star,* & *this is the song of the stars* > *this is a song of the mountains.*

The Annunciation, p. 49

Adapted by J.R. from J. Bacot, *La vie de Marpa* (Librairie Orientaliste Paul Geuthner, Paris, 1937), p. 31.

Marpa (eleventh century A.D.) was third guru in the line founded by Tilo in India & successor to his own teacher Naropa. He was the first Tibetan master of the Kargyudpa sect & the instructor of the more famous Milarepa. Theirs "was essentially a ritualist system based upon spells & diagrams (mantras & yantras), the power to use which could only be imparted directly from adept to disciple. Hence the name of (the) sect, (i.e.) the followers of the oral tradition." (Sir Humphrey Clarke, *The Message of Milarepa,* p. xii.) The original religion of Tibet, called *Bon,* had been strongly shamanistic, & the powers of the Kargyudpa teachers were such that their brand of Buddhism could easily merge with & replace it.

Marpa traveled a good deal & translated half a hundred works from Sanskrit, which earned for him his nickname of *Sgra-sgyur,* The Translator. Like all the gurus of his line, he was the subject of a biography, & in it much was made of his violent temper as a child, an instability he had to master & transform. His personality was, in this sense, very much like that of the shamans (see below, p. 424). Like them too, he was said to have the power of ecstasy, & his soul could leave his body & enter another's. He made many songs & spells, though Milarepa seems to have surpassed him there.

See, too, the note on Milarepa, p. 486, below.

How Isaac Tens Became a Shaman, p. 50

Selected & adapted from Marius Barbeau, *Medicine-Men on the North Pacific Coast* (National Museum of Canada Bulletin No. 152 [Ottawa, 1958]), pp. 39 ff.

A. *The Experience,* p. 50. The word "shaman" (Tungus: šaman) comes from Siberia & "in the strict sense is pre-eminently a religious phenomenon of Siberia & Central Asia" (Eliade). But the parallels elsewhere (North America, Indonesia, Oceania, China, etc.) are remarkable & lead also to a consideration of coincidences between "primitive-archaic" & modern thought.

Eliade treats shamanism in-the-broader-sense as a specialized technique of ecstasy & the shaman as "technician-of-the-sacred." In this sense, too, the shaman can be seen as protopoet, for almost always his technique hinges on the creation of special linguistic circumstances, i.e., of song & invocation.

In 1870 Rimbaud first used the term *voyant* (seer) to identify the new breed of poet who was to be "absolutely modern," etc.:

> one must, I say, become a seer,
> make oneself into a seer

or, as Rasmussen writes of the Iglulik Eskimos:

> the young aspirant, when applying to a shaman, should always use the following formula
> > *takujumaqama:* I come to you
> > because I desire to see

& the Copper Eskimos called the shaman-songman *"elik,* i.e., one who has eyes."

. . . .

Isaac Tens' experience is not only extraordinary but typical of (1) the psychology of shamanism, (2) the shaman's "initiation" through dream & vision, (3) transformation of vision into song. The dream & vision aspect, in fact, goes way past any limits, however loosely drawn, of shamanism, into areas where a priesthood (as developer & transmitter of a *fixed* system) predominates, &, on the other hand, into areas where "all men" are "shamans," i.e., are "open" to the "gift" of vision & song. Thus:

> The future (Bororo) shaman walks in the forest & suddenly sees a bird perch within reach of his hand, then vanish. Flocks of parrots fly down toward him & disappear as if by magic. The future shaman goes home shaking & uttering unintelligible words. An odor of decay . . . emanates from his body. Suddenly a gust of wind makes him totter; he falls like a dead man. At this moment he has become the receptacle of a spirit that speaks through his mouth. From now on he is a shaman. (A. Métraux, "Le Shamanisme chez les Indiens de l'Amérique du Sud tropicale," 1944, in Eliade, *Shamanism,* p. 82.)

Then the bear of the lake or the inland glacier will come out, he will devour all your flesh & make you a skeleton, & you will die. But you will recover your flesh, you will awaken, & your clothes will come rushing to you. (Wm. Thalbitzer, "The Heathen Priests of East Greenland," 1910, in Eliade, *Shamanism*, p. 59.)

He dreams of many things, & his body is muddled & becomes a house of dreams. And he dreams constantly of many things, & on awaking says to his friends: "My body is muddled today; I dreamt many men were killing me; I escaped I know not how. And on waking, one part of my body felt different from the other parts; it was no longer alike all over." (H. Callaway, *The Religious System of the Amazulu*, Natal, 1870, p. 259.)

All Blackfoot songs, except those learned from other tribes, are said to have been obtained through dreams or visions. . . . A man may be walking along & hear a bird, insect, stone or something else singing; he remembers the song & claims it as especially given to him. A man may get songs from a ghost in the same way. (C. Wissler, "Ceremonial Bundles of the Blackfoot Indians," *Anthropological Papers of the American Museum of Natural History*, Vol. VII, Part 2 [1912], p. 263.)

Anything, in fact, can deliver a song because anything—"night, mist, the blue sky, east, west, women, adolescent girls, men's hands & feet, the sexual organs of men & women, the bat, the land of souls, ghosts, graves, the bones, hair & teeth of the dead," etc.—is alive. Here is the central image of shamanism & of all "primitive" thought, the intuition (whether fiction or not doesn't yet matter) of a connected & fluid universe, as alive as a man is— just that much alive.

And all this seems thrust upon him—a unifying vision that brings with it the power of song & image, seen in his own terms as power to heal-the-soul & all disease viewed as disorder-of-the-soul, as disconnection & rigidity. Nor does he come to it easily— this apparent separation of himself from the normal orders of men—but often manifests what Eliade calls "a resistance to the divine election."

We're on familiar ground here, granted the very obvious differences in terminology & place, materials & techniques, etc.—recognizing in the shaman's experience that systematic derangement of the senses Rimbaud spoke of, not for its own sake but toward the possibility of sight & order. For the shaman-poet

> like the sick man . . . is projected onto a vital plane that shows him the fundamental data of human existence, that is, solitude, danger, hostility of the surrounding world. But the primitive magician, the medicine man, or the shaman is not only a sick man; he is, above all, a sick man who has been cured, who has succeeded in curing himself. (Eliade, *Shamanism*, p. 27.)

So, something more than literature is going on here: for ourselves, let me suggest, the question of how the concept & techniques of the "sacred" can persist in the "secular" world, not as nostalgia for the archaic past but (as Snyder writes) "a vehicle to ease us into the future."

Addenda. (1)

Demon or bird! (said the boy's soul,)
Is it indeed toward your mate you sing? or is it really to me?
For I, that was a child, my tongue's use sleeping, now I have heard you,
Now in a moment I know what I am for, I awake,
And already a thousand singers, a thousand songs, clearer, louder and more sorrowful than yours,
A thousand warbling echoes have started to life within me, never to die.

O you solitary singer, singing by yourself, projecting me,
O solitary me listening, never more shall I cease perpetuating you,
Never more shall I escape, never more the reverberations,
Never more the cries of unsatisfied love be absent from me,
Never again leave me to be the peaceful child I was before what there in the night,
By the sea under the yellow and sagging moon,
The messenger there arous'd, the fire, the sweet hell within,
The unknown want, the destiny of me.

—Walt Whitman
from *Out of the Cradle Endlessly Rocking*

(2) Allen Ginsberg

PSALM IV

Now I'll record my secret vision, impossible sight of the face of God:

It was no dream, I lay broad waking on a fabulous couch in Harlem

having masturbated for no love, and read half naked an open book of Blake on my lap

Lo & behold! I was thoughtless and turned a page and gazed on the living Sun-flower

and heard a voice, it was Blake's, reciting in earthen measure:

the voice rose out of the page to my secret ear that had never heard before—

I lifted my eyes to the window, red walls of buildings flashed outside, endless sky sad in Eternity,

the sunlight gazing on the world, apartments of Harlem standing in the universe

—each brick and cornice stained with intelligence like a vast living face—

the great brain unfolding and brooding in wilderness!—Now speaking aloud with Blake's voice—

Love! thou patient presence & bone of the body! Father! thy careful watching and waiting over my soul!

My son! My son! the endless ages have remembered me! My son! My son! Time howled in anguish in my ear!

My son! My son! my Father wept and held me in his dead arms.

Sept. 1, 1957
Ischia

[*Note.* The actual vision must have taken place in the summer of 1948. He writes of it elsewhere: "That is to say, looking out at the window, through the window at the sky, suddenly it seemed that I saw into the depths of the universe, by looking simply into the ancient sky. The sky suddenly seemed very *ancient.* And this was the very ancient place that (Blake) was talking about, the sweet golden clime. I suddenly realized that *this* existence was *it!* And, that I was born in order to experience up to this very moment that I was having this experience, to realize what this was all about—in other words that this was the moment I was born for. This initiation."]

. . . .

B. *The Songs,* p. 52. The songs were recorded in 1920 from Isaac Tens, an old member of the Gitenmaks tribe of the Gitksan at Hazelton, B.C. The free workings here are by J.R. & are based on Barbeau's literal translations plus interpretations & descriptions of the accompanying visions, apparently from Tens himself. His total song property consisted of three groups of songs—twenty-three in all, or somewhat more than the average Gitksan shaman. Some of his comments follow.

"When I am called to treat a patient, I go into something like a trance, & I compose a song, or I revive one for the occasion . . . (*Of the ending of the first song*): This cannot be explained rationally, because it is a vision, & visions are not always intelligible. In my vision I dreamt that I was very sick, & my spirit became sick like me; it was like a human being but had no name. In the same dream I saw that there had been a heavy run of salmon headed by a large Salmon. This would bring relief to the people who were starving. The huge Salmon appeared to me in my vision, although he was way down deep in the canyon. The She Robin came to me, & she lifted me out of my sickness. That is how I was cured . . . (*Of the first verse of the second song*): Singing this, the actual words were not uttered, only the meaningless syllables of the burthen. But their meaning was kept in the thoughts, although they were not considered a secret . . . (*Commenting further on the second song*): When getting ready for the songs, I fell into a trance & saw a vast fine territory. In the middle of it a house stood. I stepped into it, & I beheld my uncle Tsigwee who had been a medicine-man (*halaait*). He had died several years before. Then another uncle appeared—Gukswawtu. Both of them had been equally famous in their day. The songs above are those I heard them sing. While they were singing, the Grizzly ran through the door, & went right around. Then he rose into the air behind the clouds, describing a circle, & came back to the house. Each of my uncles took a rattle & placed it into one of my hands. That is why I always use two rattles in my performances. In my vision I beheld many fires burning under the house. As soon as I walked out of the house, my trance ended. From then on I sang those chants just as I had learned them in my vision."

Addenda. Gary Snyder

FIRST SHAMAN SONG

In the village of the dead,
Kicked loose bones
    ate pitch of a drift log
    (whale fat)
Nettles and cottonwood.   Grass smokes
                in the sun
Logs turn in the river
    sand scorches the feet.

Two days without food, trucks roll past
    in dust and light, rivers
    are rising.
Thaw in the high meadows.   Move west in July.

Soft oysters rot now, between tides
        the flats stink.

I sit without thoughts by the log-road
Hatching a new myth
Watching the waterdogs
        the last truck gone.

                —from *Myths & Texts*, 1960

A Shaman Climbs Up the Sky, p. 54

J.R.'s adaptation from Mircea Eliade, *Shamanism: Archaic Techniques of Ecstasy* (Bollingen Series LXXVI, Pantheon Books, 1964), pp. 191–97. Original texts in Wilhelm Radlov, *Aus Siberien* (Leipzig, 1884), Vol. II, pp. 20–50.

But the shaman's techniques-of-the-sacred made him, more than the modern poet, supreme physician & custodian of the soul. The belief was enough to validate the function—that he could climb to heaven or descend to the underworld or into the sea, could find a cure or an answer to misfortune, or after death guide the soul to its place-of-rest, etc.

In the rites accompanying a climb, a tree or ladder was generally used (see "Climbing Events," p. 109), but often too the shaman's drum was itself viewed as vehicle-of-motion; "the drum," said the Yakut shamans, "is our horse." The journey—to "heaven" or "hell"—took place in stages marked by "obstacles," the shaman-songs being the keys to unlock them. Thus, when the Altaic "black" shaman in his descent reaches "the Chinese desert of red sand (&) rides over a yellow steppe that a magpie could not fly across, (he) cries to the audience: 'By the power of songs we cross it!'" In singing & dancing he has the help of assistants, & sometimes the audience joins him in chorus.

In the ascent itself, the shaman climbs from notch to notch on the tree, while singing his actions & the obstacles that meet him. A horse is sacrificed, killed by breaking its backbone so that "not a drop of its blood falls to the ground or touches the sacrificers." The scarecrow-goose follows & overtakes the horse's soul, while the shaman both sings & responds by imitating the bird's cry. The climb ends with the address to Bai Ulgan, from whom he learns "if the sacrifice has been accepted & . . . what other sacrifices the divinity expects."

The subtitles only give a sketch of the actions (events) accompanying the songs; the interested reader can consult Eliade for the fuller scenario.

Black Elk's "Great Vision," p. 58

Abridged from *Black Elk Speaks: Being the Life Story of a Holy Man of the Oglala Sioux,* as told through John G. Neihardt. Published by William Morrow & Co., 1932. Reprinted by the University of Nebraska Press, 1961, pp. 20–33.

Hehaka Sapa or Black Elk. Born "in the Moon of the Popping Trees (December) on the Little Powder River in the Winter when the Four Crows Were Killed (1863)." Died August 1950, on the Pine Ridge Reservation, Manderson, South Dakota. A "holy man" or "priest" (*wichasha wakon*) of the Oglala Sioux &, like his second cousin Crazy Horse, a great "visionary seer." But unable to live out his visions for the rescue of his people, he did finally deliver to strangers a record of those sightings & of the rituals entrusted to him by the former "keepers of the sacred pipe." And, more than eighty years after his great vision & initiation, was able to say of that "defeat":

. . . Now that I can see it all as from a lonely hilltop, I know it was the story of a mighty vision given to a man too weak to use it; of a holy tree that should have flourished in a people's heart with flowers & singing birds, & now is withered; & of a people's dream that died in bloody snow.

The reader interested in knowing more about the workings of Black Elk's mind & about Sioux ritual in particular, should consult his second book, *The Sacred Pipe: Black Elk's Account of the Seven Rites of the Oglala Sioux,* recorded & edited by Joseph Epes Brown & published by the University of Oklahoma Press, 1953.

The Dream of Enkidu, p. 66

The Epic of Gilgamesh, English version by N. K. Sandars (Penguin Books, 1960), pp. 89–90.

Gilgamesh—"The hero of the Epic; son of the goddess Ninsun & of a priest in Kullab, fifth king of Uruk (Erech) after the flood, famous as a great builder & as a judge of the dead. A cycle of epic poems has collected around his name."

Enkidu—"Moulded by Aruru, goddess of creation, out of clay in the image of Anu, the sky-god; described as 'of the essence of Anu' & of Ninurta the war-god. He is the companion of Gilgamesh, & is wild or natural man; he was later considered a patron or god of animals."

Sandars' version is a reconstruction based on previous translations from Sumerian, Akkadian, & Hittite originals. It reads very well & for many poets of the editor's generation has been a way into the material. A "collation" (we might now call it a collage), it is in that sense, as Sandars in fact points out, like "the 'Standard Text' created by the scribes of Assurbanipal in the seventh century: (also) a collation." But certainly an example of what to do with archaic material to get it back in circulation.

Pyramid Texts, p. 68

Samuel A. B. Mercer, *The Pyramid Texts in Translation &
Commentary* (Longmans, Green & Co., New York, 1952).

Thot—in the darkness Thot is the moon.

Geb—as earth god.

Unas—the name of one of the dead kings; Mercer's text gives
N. as the general name.

The texts (arranged by Sethe & others into 714 "utterances,"
over 2000 lines) come from eight pyramids "constructed, & apparently inscribed, between the years 2350 & 2175 B.C.," with
many of the verses still older, perhaps 3000 B.C., writes Mercer,
"perhaps long before." The five printed here are charms: for keeping off serpents & scorpions, for a night journey of the deceased
king, for guarding the grave against "evil visitors," etc. Structurally
& "in keeping with their general magical character, most if not
all of these utterances begin with the expression *dd mdw,* which
is a rubrical direction 'to say,' that is, the words are to be spoken
or recited by someone, often a lector-priest, sometimes the deceased king himself, & sometimes by him in the first person."

But the often fragmentary & "primitive" character of the work
has led (as elsewhere) to misreading based on inherited concepts
of sequence, of how-a-poem-goes, etc. Against this the present editor can only assert his own sense of their force & coherence,
hoping for confirmation in others' statements that, e.g.,

. . . the Pyramid and Coffin Texts . . . are the supreme
achievements of their time and are to be explained as such
and not as a chance collection of heterogeneous tags put
together to justify the pretensions of rival priesthoods. The
more they are studied, the greater appear their literary quality
and intellectual content. (R. T. Rundle Clark, *Myth & Symbol
in Ancient Egypt,* p. 13.)

The Killer, p. 70

Adapted by J.R. from James Mooney, *Sacred Formulas of the Cherokees,* (Bureau of American Ethnology, Seventh Annual Report [Washington, 1891]), p. 391.

"This formula is from the manuscript book of A'yu^{n}ini (Swimmer) who explained the whole ceremony. . . . As the purpose of the ceremony is to bring about the death of the victim, everything spoken of is symbolically colored black. . . . The declaration (at) the end, 'It is blue,' indicates that the victim now begins to feel the effects of the incantation, & that as darkness comes on, his spirit will shrink & gradually become less until it dwindles away to nothingness." (Mooney, pp. 391–92.)

As another instance of the power of obsessive, single-color imagery, Eliade (*Shamanism,* p. 201) describes an Altaic descent to the underworld in which

> as each "obstacle" is passed (the shaman) sees a new subterranean epiphany; the word *black* recurs in almost every verse. At the second "obstacle" he apparently hears metallic sounds; at the fifth, waves & the wind whistling; finally, at the seventh, where the nine subterranean rivers have their mouths, he sees Erlik Khan's palace, built of stone & black clay & defended in every direction.

Addenda. The best-known modern example of this fairly common technique would have to be Lorca's *Somnambule Ballad* (Green, green, I want you green, etc.) but the editor has chosen the following as a more recent example & one that refers back directly to the Cherokee text.

....

Diane Wakoski

BLUE MONDAY (1965)

Blue of the heaps of beads poured into her breasts
and clacking together in her elbows;
blue of the silk
that covers lily-town at night;
blue of her teeth
that bite cold toast
and shatter on the streets;
blue of the dyed flower petals with gold stamens
hanging like tongues
over the fence of her dress
at the opera/opals clasped under her lips
and the moon breaking over her head a
gush of blood-red lizards.

Blue Monday. Monday at 3:00 and
Monday at 5. Monday at 7:30 and
Monday at 10:00. Monday passed under the rippling
California fountain. Monday alone
a shark in the cold blue waters.

> You are dead: wound round like a paisley shawl.
> I cannot shake you out of the sheets. Your name is
> still wedged in every corner of the sofa.
> Monday is the first of the week
> and I think of you all week.
>
> I beg Monday not to come
> so that I will not think of you
> all week.

You paint my body blue. On the balcony
in the soft muddy night, you paint me
with bat wings and the crystal
the crystal
the crystal
the crystal in your arm cuts away
the night, folds back ebony whale skin

and my face, the blue of new rifles,
and my neck, the blue of Egypt,
and my breasts, the blue of sand,
and my arms, bass-blue,
and my stomach, arsenic;

there is electricity dripping from me like cream;
there is love dripping from me I cannot use—like acacia or
jacaranda—fallen blue & gold flowers, crushed into the street.

Love passed me in a blue business suit
and fedora.
His glass cane, hollow and filled with
sharks and whales . . .
He wore black
patent leather shoes
and had a mustache. His hair was so black it was
almost blue.

"Love," I said.
"I beg your pardon," he said.
"Mr. Love," I said.
"I beg your pardon," he said.

So I saw there was no use bothering him on the street.

Love passed me on the street in a blue
business suit. He was a banker
I could tell.

So blue trains rush by in my sleep.
Blue herons fly overhead.
Blue paint cracks in my
arteries and sends titanium
floating into my bones.
Blue liquid pours down
my poisoned throat and blue veins
rip open my breast. Blue daggers tip
and are juggled on my palms.
Blue death lives in my fingernails.

If I could sing one last song
with water bubbling through my lips
I would sing with my throat torn open,

the blue jugular spouting that black shadow pulse
and on my lips
I would balance volcanic rock
emptied out of my veins. At last
my children strained out
of my body. At last my blood
solidified and tumbling into the ocean.
It is blue.
It is blue.
It is blue.

A Poison Arrow, p. 70

J.R.'s working from Roger Rosfelder, *Chants Haoussa* (Editions Seghers, Paris, 1952).

A Charm: To Cause the Gangosa That Eats Away the Nose, p. 72

R. F. Fortune, *Sorcerers of Dobu* (E. P. Dutton & Co., New York, 1932), pp. 139–40. Adapted by Ben Moses.

"Every disease is held to be caused by a *tabu. Tabu* [in Dobuan] denotes an incantation, expressing black hatred in an extremely ugly form, which has the power of inflicting disease. . . . The names of the great majority of the *tabus* (incantations) are the names of certain shell-fish, insects, birds & animals with the prefix *lo* (to get). . . . To get the hornbill is to get gangosa, to get the snake is to get paralysis. . . . The incantation that causes gangosa is known as Kalena Sigasiga. . . .

"The hornbill of gangosa is not an ordinary material hornbill. It is a monstrous being, active in many places at once. Hence, hornbill of Sigasiga, of Darubia (etc.). . . . Like other supernatural agents it is not subject to the limitations of time & space. . . .

"(But) despite the ubiquity of the hornbill double of gangosa . . . there is the very material touch of 'in the lowana treetop.' The great beak of the hornbill which he uses in hacking out tree hollows, accounts for his body-rending powers. The boom of the hornbill in the bush was compared by my informant with the thick nasal utterance that I had heard from a mutual acquaintance who had no nose, the entire organ having been eaten away by gangosa. The references 'he crouches, etc.,' refer not to the hornbill, but to the victim, & are introduced towards the final strophes. The final strophe . . . reveals the mythical foundation, the reference to the first ancestors. . . . (It) conceals the spirit of the woman Nebagieta in the object that is to carry the charm. . . . She wore a rough jagged nose & she gave birth to a hornbill, the hornbill of all hornbills. She was the creator of gangosa by incantation. . . .

"The charm is uttered into an object. . . . The pronouncer of the incantations chews ginger, stands three or four feet away from the object charmed & utters the charm in short staccato phrases with a vicious spitting of ginger on to the object charmed, punctuating each phrase . . . & taking care that his shadow falls behind & not in front of him." (Fortune, pp. 138–42.)

Snake Chant / Storm Chant, p. 75

Miriam Koshland (tr.), "Six Chants from the Congo," *Black Orpheus: A Journal of African & Afro-American Literature*, No. 2 (January 1958), pp. 19–21.

The English translator writes of the second of these: "The (storm) chant . . . was translated into French by Tristan Tzara & was published in *Dada* (Zurich 1917). It was republished in *Musée Vivant*, 1952. The original text is lost." Like others of Tzara's *Negerlieder*, etc. ("discoveries & translations" he called them), it reflects the Dadaists' desire to break the stranglehold of European art—to search, as Hugo Ball wrote, for an art that "is the key to every former art: a Solomonic key that will open all the mysteries."

Offering Flowers, p. 77

Bernardino de Sahagún, *Florentine Codex: General History of the Things of New Spain*, translated by Arthur J. O. Anderson & Charles E. Dibble (School of American Research, Santa Fe, N.M., & the University of Utah, 1951, 1963) Vols. III, pp. 101–3; XII, pp. 214–15.

The Aztecs (they say) rode on lakes of flowers, & decorated bodies, gods & houses with flowers, which their language made into synonyms for speech/heart/soul & for the sun as world-heart/world-flower. Men waged a "flowering war" of the spirit in which "if

spirit wins," writes Sejourné, "the body 'flowers' & a new light
goes to give power to the Sun." Only later, the Aztec rulers literal-
ized this into a series of staged battles against already conquered
peoples, that the foredoomed losers paid for (literally) with their
hearts. So, too, the ceremony given here (the only monthly ritual
without human sacrifice) was not devoted to Xochipilli, the god
of flowers & the soul, but to the war god Huitzilopochtli.

Correspondences of heart & word & flower are repeated by the
Japanese Seami, who speaks of the "flower" (the "flower-thought"
of the Buddhists) as the Nō actor's hidden ability, a matter of the
heart & voice. In the dance & gesture language of India, Wilson
D. Wallis tells us

> when the fingers are straight & are brought together so that
> the tips touch, the gesture means "flower bud." When con-
> veyed to the mouth & thrust outward, it means "speech."
> In Hawaii this gesture means "flower"; or, if made at the
> mouth, it means "talk" or "song." (In Stanley Diamond
> (ed.), *Culture in History: Essays in Honor of Paul Radin*
> [1960], p. 330.)

But it's the same too in Francis of Assisi's "little flowers" & in
the dead words of our own language that speak of eloquence as
"flowery" or "florid"—terms that have lost their currency, except
when Carlos Williams, say, makes them alive again in *Asphodel,
that greeny flower*. And there are other instances to remind us, &
a memory perhaps of that "great flower" of Dante's—"high fantasy" he called it, & "living flame."

Addenda. Note also the advent of "flower-power," "flower-
children," etc., contemporaneous (1967) with the production of
the present volume.

From *The Night Chant,* p. 79

Washington Matthews, *The Night Chant, a Navaho Ceremony*
(Memoirs of the American Museum of Natural History [New
York, 1902]), pp. 143–45.

Tsegehi—a dwelling of the gods.

Night Chant or Night Way is only one part of the very complex
Navaho system of myths & ceremonies directed mainly toward
healing. Other chants or ways include Beauty Way, Blessing Way,
Mountain Way, Flint Way, Enemy Way, Prostitution Way, Life

Way, Shooting Way, Red Ant Way, Monster Way, Moving Up Way, etc.—each with special functions, each consisting of many songs, events, & myths-of-origin—with endless subdivisions and reconstructions thereof. The whole chantway system is so complicated in fact that the individual priest or chanter (*hatali*, lit. a keeper-of-the-songs) can rarely keep-in-mind more than a single ceremony like the nine-day Night Chant, sometimes only part of one. There's also more room for variation by the individual singer than at first meets-the-eye—& this is itself a part of the system since, in transmitting the ceremonies, a gap is invariably left that the new singer must fill-in on his own.

As with other "primitive" art of this complexity, the Night Chant is very much "intermedia," though on the ninth night (from which this excerpt is taken) the singing dominates & is "uninterrupted . . . from dark until daylight." At the start of this song

> patient & shaman (have positions) in the west, facing the east, & the priest prays a long prayer to each god, which the patient repeats after him, sentence by sentence. . . . The four prayers are alike in all respects, except in the mention of certain attributes of the gods. . . . (The one given here is addressed) to the dark bird who is the chief of (the sacred) pollen. While (it) is being said, the dancer keeps up a constant motion, bending & straightening the left knee, & swaying the head from side to side. (Matthews, p. 142.)

While the complexity of Night Chant, etc., necessitates a collective effort in performance & transmission, the legend of its founding credits the inspiration to Bitahatini, literally His-Imagination, His-Visions, but freely translated as The Visionary. Carried off by the gods he brought back the rites for this chant (of sandpainting, dance & masks, etc.) along with the songs & instructions for curing. The Navahos said of him:

> Whenever he went out by himself, he heard the songs of spirits sung to him, or thought he heard them sung. . . . His three brothers had no faith in him. They said: "When you have returned from your solitary walks & tell us you have seen strange things & heard strange songs, you are mistaken, you only imagine you hear these songs & you see nothing unusual." Whenever he returned from one of these lonely rambles he tried to teach his brothers the songs he had heard; but they would not listen to him. (Matthews, p. 159.)

The reader may want to compare this early experience of The Visionary's with that of Isaac Tens (see above, p. 50) & the nature of his spirit-journey with Black Elk's "Great Vision" (p. 58). While these accounts are from three Indian groups that are supposed to be far apart in their approaches to the sacred, the experiences show a common (shamanic/not priestly) pattern, with echoes throughout the "primitive & archaic" worlds. Neruda's vision of his dead friend Jimenez, with its presumably coincidental use of a Night Chant refrain (*vienes volando* = come flying, or come soaring), opens still further areas for speculation:

> Amid frightening feathers, nights,
> amid magnolias, amid telegrams,
> with the south and west sea winds
>   you come flying.
>
> Under tombs, under ashes,
> under frozen snails,
> under the earth's deepest waters
>   you come flying.
>
> And deeper, between drowned children,
> blind plants and rotting fish,
> out through the clouds again
>   you come flying.
>
> More distant than blood and bone,
> more distant than bread, than wine,
> more distant than fire
>   you come flying.
>
> *Etcetera*

(from Clayton Eshleman's translation of
Alberto Rojas Jimenez Viene Volando)

When Hare Heard of Death, p. 85

Paul Radin, *The Road of Life & Death: A Ritual Drama of the American Indians* (Bollingen Series V, Pantheon Books, New York, 1945), pp. 23–24.

Hare (a trickster-figure or deific goof-up) is sent by Earthmaker to rescue the two-leggeds from the evil ones; but at the crucial moment (trying against the law of life to save his aunts & uncles from death) he looks back (like Orpheus or Lot's wife) against the instructions of his grandmother (earth), & "as he peeped, the place from which he had started, caved in completely & instantaneously." The wild scene that follows—of destructive frustration & hysteria—is surely more meaningful than Adam's "I was afraid because I was naked," etc., & leads in turn to the founding of the Winnebago Medicine Rite.

Poem from "A Dispute over Suicide," p. 86

T. Eric Peet, *A Comparative Study of the Literatures of Egypt, Palestine, & Mesopotamia.* Published for the British Academy by Humphrey Milford (Oxford University Press, 1931), pp. 115–17.

The poem is imbedded in a prose "dispute over suicide between a man & his 'soul'" (i.e., the *ka,* or separable part of the "personality"), in which the "soul" is finally won over to the idea of suicide, the world being what it is, etc. The argument in the poem is apparently the clincher.

The papyrus itself dates from the "good times" of the Twelfth Dynasty (1991–1786 B.C.), which leads some to assume it must really be the work of an earlier & more troubled time. But change & expansion may lead to just this kind of (personal if not mythic) questioning, where the old language no longer works.

Peet translates three of eight strophes of the first section, nine of sixteen of the second, the entire third section, & omits the three surviving strophes of the fourth.

A Peruvian Dance Song, p. 88

Translated by Margot Astrov, *The Winged Serpent: An Anthology of American Indian Prose & Poetry* (The John Day Company, New York, 1946), p. 344, from R. & M. D'Harcourt, *La musique des Incas et ses survivances* (Paris, 1925).

Death Song, p. 88

Frances Densmore, *Papago Music* (Bureau of American Ethnology, Bulletin 90 [Washington, 1929]), p. 127.

The song was used for curing & was given to the poet (Owl Woman, called Juana Manwell) by a dead man named Jose

Gomez. This was her ordinary way of receiving songs—from the "disturbing spirits" of dead Papagos "who follow the old customs & go at night to the spirit-land." As Frances Densmore tells it:

> The spirits first revealed themselves to Owl Woman when she was in extreme grief over the death of her husband and other relatives. This was 30 or 40 years prior to the recording of her songs in 1920. The spirits took her to the spirit land in the evening and brought her back in the early dawn, escorting her along a road. . . . When the spirits had taken her many times . . . they decided that she should be taught certain songs for the cure of sickness caused by the spirits. It was not necessary that she should go to the spirit land to learn the songs. It was decided that a person, at his death, should go where the other spirits are and "get acquainted a little," after which he would return and teach her some songs. . . . She has now received hundreds of these songs, so many that she cannot remember them all. It is possible for her to treat the sick without singing, but she prefers to have the songs. (*Papago Music*, pp. 115–16.)

. . . .

"The Authors are in eternity."—W. Blake.

The Relations of Wind, Rain & Cloud to Human Beings after Death, p. 89

Wilhelm H. I. Bleek & Lucy C. Lloyd, *Specimens of Bushman Folklore* (George Allen & Co., London, 1911), pp. 397, 393.

Given in August 1875 by Día!kwain, who heard it from his parents & observed it himself.

NARRATOR'S NOTE:
And our gall, when we die, sits in the sky, etc. "Mother, she used to tell me, that this happens to us if we sit in the shade when the place is not particularly warm, when it is only moderately warm, & we feel that the summer seems as if it would be hot. We think: 'Allow me to sit for a little in the shade under the bush; for the sun's eye is not a little hot; I will sit a little while in

the shade'; then we make clouds; our liver goes out from the place where we are sitting in the shade, if the place is not hot. Therefore, we make clouds on account of it. For, when it is really summer, then we may sit in the shade."

For more on Día!kwain, see the note on *The String Game,* p. 447.

The Mourning Song of Small-Lake-Underneath, p. 91

John R. Swanton, *Tlingit Myths & Texts* (Bureau of American Ethnology, Bulletin 39 [Washington, 1909]), p. 395.

Composed by Hayi-a'k!ᵘ (Small-Lake-Underneath) about a drifting log found full of nails, out of which a house was built. It is used when a feast is about to be given for a dead man "& they have their blankets tied up to their waists & carry canes."

The poem comes from a collection of 103 Tlingit songs gathered by Swanton. "By far the larger number were composed for feasts or in song contests between men who were at enmity with each other."

Lamentation, p. 91

Truman Michelson, *The Owl Sacred Pack of the Fox Indians* (Bureau of American Ethnology, Bulletin 72 [1921]), p. 29.

The (sacred) Owl had taught them: "We shall die . . . we shall all die. No one of us who exist as mortals here, shall exist as a mortal forever. . . . If anyone thinks, 'No, not I; I shall always exist as a mortal,' he surely dies. . . . The manitou has fixed that which will happen to each one of us."

But the man who lost his wife & son cried out: "Surely the manitous could not have made us." His song was

> Cry, cry for myself—
> Cry, cry for myself . . .

until one Being came to live with him, saying: "Such is the extent of the blessing I bestow upon you. . . . For I know how badly you felt when you lost sight of your son whom you loved."

444   TECHNICIANS OF THE SACRED

The Flight of Quetzalcoatl, p. 92

Translated by J.R. from Spanish prose translation by Angel María Garibay K., *Epica Nahuatl* (Biblioteca del Estudiante Universitario, Mexico, 1945), pp. 59–63. First publication in English by Unicorn Book Shop (Brighton, England, 1967).

Archaic thought is coherent & directed, but the coherence isn't based on consistency of event so much as covering the widest range of possible situations. Like a shotgun blast, say, or a saturation bombing—effective against known targets & some unknown ones as well. So, the "greatest variation in legends & interpretations of the disappearance of Quetzalcoatl" may simply be noted & would have caused the Nahua makers no special discomfort. The important thing was for any account to hit home—to present the god's doings as image of how-it-really-is.

The present version comes from Sahagún's *Historia* (see above, p. 404), with the ending from the *Anales de Quauhtitlan,* & begins *after* whatever-had-happened to get him on the road. In Sahagún three sorcerers (one with a god name, two without) came to him, got him high on "white wine" (pulque?), while working other sorceries to destroy his city, Tollan ("Tula"). But the acount is shapeless & lacks the thrust or point of myth-become-poetry.

The *Anales* in this case are more articulate. In brief, the gods Tezcatlipoca, Ihuimecatl & Toltecatl decided to force Quetzalcoatl out of his city "where we intend to live." Tezcatlipoca thought to bring it off by "giving him his body," so showed him a "double mirror the size of a hand's span" & "Quetzalcoatl saw himself, & was filled with fear, & said: 'If my subjects see me, they will run away!' For his eyelids were badly inflamed, his eyes sunken in their sockets, & his face covered all over with wrinkles. His face was not human at all!" (I. Nicholson, *Firefly in the Night,* p. 69.)

The vision is repeated: always the terror of self-recognition, of the man in his dying body, his flesh. They get him drunk, have him sleep with his sister Quetzalpetatl, then wake up in sorrow:

And he sang the sad song he had made that he might depart thence: "This is an evil tale of a day when I left my house.

May those that are absent be softened, it was hard & perilous for me. Only let the one whose body is of earth exist & sing; I did not grow up subjected to servile labor." (L. Sejourné, *Burning Water*, p. 57.)

And so on. In the *Anales* there's a period of four days (= dark phase of Venus) when he lies alone in a stone casket, then heads for the sea where the transfiguration (into Venus, the morning star) takes place. Sahagún is richer in the journey itself with its further revelations (also the many place-namings typical of primitive & archaic myth); has him form the raft of serpents & set off across the sea; ends with "no one knows how he came to arrive there at Tlapallan" (i.e., in Maya country, where the "plumed serpent" is the god Kukulcan)—but that's another story.

The force of the myth is in the image in the mirror: the journey a dark night before his re-emergence through fire & transfiguration. As plumed serpent Quetzalcoatl "belonged equally to the dark abyss & the celestial splendor" (Sejourné, p. 114):

> Quetzalcoatl taught that human greatness grows out of the awareness of a spiritual order; his image must therefore be the symbol of this truth. The serpent plumes must be speaking to us of the spirit that makes it possible for man—even while his body, like the reptile's, is dragged in the dust—to know the superhuman joy of creation. (Sejourné, p. 84.)

His identification with the planet Venus says this also.

Addenda. (1) The rotting face is what we start from in knowing where we are. The god isn't simply idealized as man-more-than-man-surviving-death but imaged also as man-fallen-with-man-into-rotting-flesh:

> . . . And it is said, he was monstrous.

> His face was like a huge, battered stone, a great fallen rock; it (was) not made like that of men. And his beard was very long—exceedingly long. He was heavily bearded. (Sahagún, *Florentine Codex*, IV, p. 13.)

(2) Compare this with the Chinese (Na-Khi) *Song of the Dead, Relating the Origin of Bitterness* (p. 262, above; commentary, p. 491, below).

A Sequence of Songs of the Ghost Dance Religion, p. 98

Selected by Margot Astrov, *The Winged Serpent: An Anthology of American Indian Prose & Poetry* (The John Day Company, New York, 1946), pp. 143-44, from James Mooney, *The Ghost-Dance Religion & the Sioux Outbreak of 1890* (Bureau of American Ethnology, Fourteenth Annual Report [1896]).

The late nineteenth-century messianic movement called the Ghost Dance, was not simply a pathetic reaction to White rule or confused attempt to suck-up Christian wisdom. The ritual use of ecstasy & the dance is clearly more Indian than Christian; & the movement's central belief that the present world would go the way of all previous worlds through destruction & re-emergence had been (for all the Christian turns it was now given) widespread throughout North America and at the heart, say, of the highly developed religious systems of the Mexican plateau.

The "messiah" of the Ghost Dance was Wovoka ("the cutter"), also called Jack Wilson, who circa 1889 was taken up to heaven by God & there given the message of redemption, with full control over the elements, etc. His doctrine spread quickly through the Indian world, under various names but always referring to the trance-like dance at its center; thus "dance in a circle" (Paiute), "everybody dragging" (Shoshoni), "the Fathers' dance" (Comanche), "dance with clasped hands" & "dance craziness" (Kiowa), & "ghost dance" (Sioux & Arapaho). Wovoka's own dance was described by a northern Cheyenne follower named Porcupine in terms reminiscent of Jesus' "round dance" with his disciples in the apocryphal & equally "unchristian" Acts of St. John:

> They cleared off a space in the form of a circus ring & we all gathered there. . . . The Christ [i.e., Wovoka] was with them. . . . I looked around to find him, & finally saw him sitting on one side of the ring. . . . They made a big fire to throw light on him. . . . He sat there a long time & nobody went up to speak to him. He sat with his head bowed all the time. After a while he rose & said he was very glad to see his children. . . . "My children, I want you to listen to all I have to say to you. I will teach you, too, how to dance a dance, & I want you to dance it. Get ready for your dance & then, when the dance is over, I will talk to you." He was

dressed in a white coat with stripes. The rest of his dress
was a white man's except that he had on a pair of moccasins.
Then he commenced our dance, everybody joining in, the
Christ singing while we danced. . . . (Later) he commenced
to tremble all over, violently for a while, & then sat down.
We danced all that night, the Christ lying down beside us
apparently dead.

Of the songs themselves Mooney writes: "All the songs are
adapted to the simple measure of the dance step . . . the dancers
moving from right to left, following the course of the sun . . .
hardly lifting the feet from the ground. . . . Each song is started
in the same manner, first in an undertone while singers stand
still in their places, & then with full voice as they begin to circle
around. At intervals between the songs . . . the dancers unclasp
hands & sit down to smoke or talk for a few minutes. . . . There
is no limit to the number of these songs, as every trance at every
dance produces a new one. . . . Thus a single dance may easily
result in twenty or thirty new songs."

Not surprisingly Wovoka, as an adjunct to his vision-search,
was one of the first Indian "revivalists" to make use of peyote—
thus a forerunner of the peyote-cult with its subsequent impact on
the main U.S. culture.

The String Game, p. 100

W. H. I. Bleek & L. C. Lloyd, *Specimens of Bushman Folklore* (George Allen & Co., London, 1911), p. 237.

Dictated in July 1875 by Día!kwain, who heard it from his
father, χaa-ttin. The song is a lament, sung by χaa-ttin after
the death of his friend, the magician & rainmaker, !nuin|kui-ten,
"who died from the effects of a shot he had received when going
about, by night, in the form of a lion." There is also the following
comment:

Now that "the string is broken," the former "ringing sound
in the sky" is no longer heard by the singer, as it had been
in the magician's lifetime.

But the sense of a suspended string game ("cat's cradle") seems
also implicit—a universal game of changes not far from the activity of magicians & poets.

The Abortion, p. 101

W. G. Archer, "The Illegitimate Child in Santal Society," *Man in India,* XXIV (1944), 156–58.

The "true-poem" ("primitive" or not) doesn't repress but confronts what's most difficult to face—not only the great-existential-life-crises, etc., issues-of-reality, etc., but personal events outside all ritual pattern. Attempts to hold poetry to the (abstractly) Good & Beautiful, i.e., to "hymns to the gods & praises of famous men" (Plato), work against the poet's impulse & function, thus opening the door for platitude & art-as-propaganda. Plato who attacked poets as liars-by-nature is himself revealed as the first great liar-by-reason-of-state.

The Tale of a Dog Which Made a Song, p. 103

Rev. Canon Henry Callaway, *Nursery Tales, Traditions & Histories of the Zulus, in their own words* (London, 1868).

Umatiwane—a chief of the Amangwane.
Umpangazita—a chief of the Amathlubi.
Umadhladhla—the name of Ungalonkulu, the son of Ukadhlakadhla, who was killed by the Amangwane during the war. *Amadhladhla,* his people.

"The dog rebukes the people for not weeping for their dead chief."

Death Rites I, p. 104

Translated by C. M. Bowra, *Primitive Song* (World Publishing Co., Cleveland, 1962), pp. 222–23, from R. P. Trilles, *Les pygmées de la forêt équatoriale* (Paris, 1931).

Dan—a cavern in the forest at whose "gates" Khvum (as father of life & death) will meet the newly-born dead &, like Osiris, act as judge-of-the-underworld.

Characteristic of much pygmy poetry is an extreme sensitivity to polar images of light & darkness, for which see also "Ghosts & Shadows," p. 145, "Death Rites II," p. 171, & "A Poem of Changes," p. 172.

The Book of Events (I), pp. 105–26

(Most of these originally appeared in J.R.'s *Ritual: A Book of Primitive Rites & Events* [Something Else Press, New York, 1966].)

Lily Events, p. 107. Adapted from *A Black Civilization*, illustrated, revised edition, by W. Lloyd Warner. Copyright 1937 by Harper & Row, Publishers, Inc. Copyright 1958 by W. Lloyd Warner. P. 419. Reprinted by permission of the publishers.

Garbage Event, p. 108. Adapted from W. R. Geddes, *Nine Dayak Nights* (Oxford University Press, 1957, 1961), pp. 19–20.

Beard Event, p. 108. Adapted from Warner, *op. cit.*, p. 333.

Stone Fire Event, p. 109. Adapted from Warner, *op. cit.*, p. 318.

Climbing Event I, p. 109; *Climbing Event II*, p. 109. Adapted from Mircea Eliade, *Shamanism: Archaic Techniques of Ecstasy* (Bollingen Series LXXVI, Pantheon Books, New York, 1964), pp. 126–27.

Gift Event I, p. 110. This is a very abbreviated version of the "Kula" described throughout *Argonauts of the Western Pacific* by Bronislaw Malinowski (E. P. Dutton & Co., 1922).

Gift Event II, p. 110. Adapted from statements by Kwakiutl Indians in "The Amiable Side of Kwakiutl Life: The Potlatch and the Play Potlatch," by Helen Codere, *American Anthropologist*, Vol. 56, No. 2 (April 1956).

Marriage Event, p. 111. Adapted from William Wyatt Gill, *Life in the Southern Isles* (Religious Tract Society, London, 1876), pp. 59–60.

Going-Around Event, p. 112. Adapted from W. Bogoras, *The Chuckchee* (Jessup N. Pacific Expedition, Memoirs of the American Museum of Natural History, 1904–1909), pp. 402–3.

Language Event I, p. 113. Adapted from Martin Dobrizhofer, *An Account of the Abipones, an Equestrian People of Paraguay*, tr. by Sara Coleridge (John Murray, London, 1822).

Language Event II, p. 113. Adapted from Edward Sapir, *Selected Writings* (University of California Press, 1944), pp. 180–81.

Language Event III, p. 114. Adapted from N. J. v. Warmelo, "Contribution Towards Venda History, Religion & Tribal Ritual," *Ethnological Publications* (Department of Native Affairs, Union of South Africa), III (1932), 49–51.

Friendship Dance, p. 116. Adapted from Frank G. Speck & Leonard Broom, *Cherokee Dance & Drama* (University of California Press, 1951), pp. 65–67.

Grease Feast Event, p. 118. Adapted from Franz Boas, "The Social Organization & Secret Societies of the Kwakiutl Indians," in *Reports of the U. S. National Museum under the Direction of the Smithsonian Institution for the Year Ending June 30, 1895* (U. S. Government Printing Office, Washington, 1897), pp. 355–56.

Peacemaking Event, p. 120. Adapted from Alfred Reginald Radcliffe-Brown, *The Andaman Islanders* (Cambridge University Press, 1922, 1933), pp. 134–35.

Booger Event, p. 122. Adapted from Speck & Broom, *op. cit.,* pp. 28–36.

Sea Water Event, p. 123. Adapted from Warner, *op. cit.,* p. 337.

Further Sea Water Events, p. 124. Adapted from Warner, *op. cit.,* pp. 409–11.

Noise Event, p. 126. Adapted from The Book of Psalms.

The editor has taken a series of twenty rituals & other programmed activities from a wide geographical area & has, as far as possible, suppressed all reference to accompanying mythic or "symbolic" explanations. This has led to two important results: (1) the form of the activities is, for the first time, given the prominence it deserves; (2) the resulting works bear a close resemblance to those mythless activities of our own time called events, happenings, de-coll/age, kinetic theater, etc. It may be further noted that most of these "events"—like the (modern) intermedia art they resemble—are parts of total situations involving poetry, music, dance, painting, myth, magic, etc., as are many of the songs & visions presented elsewhere in this anthology. Having revealed this much, the editor does not wish to obscure by a series of explanatory footnotes the forms that have been laid bare. While absence of such notes may result in some distortion, it's precisely the kind of distortion that can have a value in itself. Like seeing Greek statues without their colors.

Addenda. The following examples of contemporary events & happenings may be instructive to the reader who has not been aware of the resemblances alluded to above. (N.B. The word "happening" itself has counterparts in, e.g., the Navaho word for "ceremonial" which, Kluckhohn & Wyman tell us, translates almost literally as "something-is-going-on," or in the widespread use by the Iroquois of the English word "doings.")

Alison Knowles
GIVEAWAY CONSTRUCTION (1963)

Find something you like in the street and give it away. Or find a variety of things, make something of them, and give it away.

La Monte Young*
COMPOSITION 1960 #15
to Richard Huelsenbeck

This piece is little whirlpools
out in the middle of the ocean.

* © La Monte Young 1963. All other rights including rights to public or private performance of *Composition 1960 #15* are retained by La Monte Young.

Dick Higgins
From CLOWN'S WAY:
A DRAMA IN THREE HUNDRED ACTS

Act Five.
Climb up a ladder. At the top, smile. Climb down again.

Emmett Williams
A SELECTION FROM "5,000 NEW WAYS"

select 50 compound words.
split them, and turn the freed second halves into verbs.

select 50 projections and 50 sounds.
write them on cards, and shuffle them.

fast upon reading one of the 'new ways,'
show a projection, make a sound
picked at random from the pile of cards.

n.b. at a performance in paris in 1963, the first three operations yielded these combinations:

text: the new way the maiden heads
projection: a hundred-dollar bill
sound: draining sink

text:	the new way the banana splits
projection:	two left shoes
sound:	firecracker

text:	the new way the belly buttons
projection:	great wall of china
sound:	rooster

Carolee Schneemann
From MEAT JOY (1964)

The Intractable Rosette. Men gather women into circular formation. A sequence of attempts to turn women into static, then moving shapes: linking their arms, tying their legs together. They arrange them lying down, sitting up, on their backs, & every attempt to move them as a solid unit fails as they fall apart, roll over, get squashed, etc. All shouting instructions, ideas, advice, complaints. All collapse in a heap.

Serving Maid with huge tray of raw chickens, mackerel, strings of sausages, strews them extravagantly on the bodies. Wet fish, heavy chickens, bouncing hot-dogs. Bodies respond sporadically: twitching, reaching, touching. Individual instructions for fish-meat-chickens. Instances: independent woman flips, flops, slips on the floor like a fish, jumps up, throwing, catching, falling, running. Lateral woman attacked by others. Central woman sucking fish. Individual man with fish follows contours of woman's body with it. Tenderly, then wildly. All inundated with fish & chickens.

Alan Kaprow
RAINING

(Scheduled for performance in the spring, for any number of persons and the weather. Times and places need not be coordinated, and are left up to the participants. The action of the rain may be watched if desired.)

(For Olga and Billy Klüver, January 1965)

Black highway painted black
Rain washes away

Paper men made in bare orchard branches
Rain washes away

Sheets of writing spread over a field
Rain washes away

Little grey boats painted along a gutter
Rain washes away

Naked bodies painted gray
Rain washes away

Bare trees painted red
Rain washes away

Wolf Vostell

BERLIN (Selections)

100 events
on the streets and in apartments and stores
for a chance public

took place on the 10th of november 1965
from 9 A.M. to 4:10 P.M.
within the city limits of BERLIN

100 events each lasting 1 minute
. . . .

(number of chance spectators in parentheses)

1   9 A.M.—waiting at the goerlitz subway station (2)
2   staring at the ticket seller in the subway station (2)
3   effacing a copy of paris-match during the drive to the
    silesian gate (2)
4   driving to the ruins of the goerlitz train station (0)
5   looking for a parking place (0)
6   burying an electric clock in the sand of the ruined
    area (11)
7   breaking an egg on it (11)
8   griping about germany (11)
9   driving to 49 manteuffel strasse (0)
10 looking for a parking place (0)
11 flooding the bed-living room with a garden sprinkler (1)
12 going to the cellar (1)
13 following the second hand of a watch with a welding
    torch (1)

14   going to the living room (1)
15   gluing forty-four bright pink lipsticks to a greek type-
     writer (1)

. . . .

65   confronting the notice found in berlin apartment houses
     CHILDREN ARE PROHIBITED FROM PLAYING ON
     STAIRS AND IN HALLWAYS AS WELL AS FROM
     LOITERING OUTSIDE THE ENTRANCE with the
     reality of war ruins and juxtaposed posters, pictures and
     news photos:
66   the line-up at a debuntantes' ball
67   weeping american soldiers in viet nam
68   a 12-year-old viet cong bending over a dead friend
69   an american soldier lighting a cigarette
70   vietnamese girls serving in american army field hospitals
71   a smiling man leaning on a volkswagen
72   cigarette ad
73   concentration camp number on forearm
74   the brandenburg gate seen from the west
75   the victory column

. . . .

91   driving to wilhelm strasse (o)
92   looking for a parking place (o)
93   walking to the wall (o)
94   strewing twenty pounds of sugar on western soil bordering
     the wall (o)
95   waiting (o)
96   waiting (o)
97   waiting (o)
98   waiting (o)
99   becoming aware that there is no end
100 reading the announcement that these 100 events took
     place (500)

"Eventually everything will be happening at once: nothing behind
a screen unless a screen happens to be in front."   —John Cage

The Book of Events (II), pp. 127–41

The texts in this section give a fuller account of three selected events, in order to show the realization of such activities in context. Since the editor could have done the same for many of the preceding events—at least where dialogue &/or songs were available—this section shouldn't be thought of as an "advance" over the first but simply another way of considering ritual-theater: by letting the words, the dramatic action & the myth take a more central position.

Taming the Storm: A Two-Shaman Vision & Event, p. 129

Abridged from Knud Rasmussen, *The Intellectual Culture of the Copper Eskimos* (Report of the Fifth Thule Expedition [Copenhagen, 1932]), pp. 56–61.

Word, vision, & event come together in the work, along with the environment itself. Shakespeare's *Lear* the classic example of the simulation of a meteorological event in a theatrical situation; Kaprow's *Raining* (above, p. 452) & La Monte Young's *Composition* ♯15 (above, p. 451) examples of the incorporation of natural weather conditions in a non-mythic "happening."

Coronation Event & Drama, p. 134

Theodor H. Gaster, *Thespis: Ritual, Myth & Drama in the Ancient Near East* (Anchor Books, Doubleday & Co., New York, 1961), pp. 378–83. Reworking of dialogue by J.R.

While still in the womb Osiris & Isis, son & daughter of Earth & Sky, formed the child Horus between them. Osiris' dark counterpart was Set, his brother, who later destroyed & dismembered him, Isis & Horus becoming the means to his recovery & rebirth as judge-of-the-dead, etc. In battle Horus tore out Set's testicles, while Set ripped out Horus' black (left) eye (i.e., the moon; but some say both the white & black eyes: sun &

moon) & "flung it away beyond the edge of the world, & Thoth, the moon's genius & guardian" (but also: god of words & spels) "found it lying in the outer darkness" (R. T. Rundle Clark, *Myth & Symbol in Ancient Egypt,* p. 224) & restored it to Horus in the ritual of recovery here enacted.

The text is from a papyrus of the Twelfth Dynasty (circa 1970 B.C.) but Kurt Sethe (who first recognized it as theater) dated the contents from the First Dynasty (circa 3300 B.C.). It "gives an account of the traditional ceremonies at the installation of the king, which was celebrated in conjunction with the New Year ceremonies during the month of Khoiakh. . . . Each detail of the ritual program is, however, invested at the same time with a durative significance, & this is brought out explicitly in the form of a mythological 'key' attached to every scene." (Gaster, *Thespis,* p. 81.) Forty-six scenes have been preserved, of which seven are presented here. The "events" of the coronation are in small caps; the mythological key in italics.

Addenda. The classic modern example of a direct use of Egyptian funerary materials is Lawrence's *Ship of Death.* The story of Osiris & Isis has become *the* ancient myth for many of those younger poets who can still form attachments to the old gods *per se* (see, e.g., Ed Sanders' very free reworkings of the laments of Isis & Nephthys [above, p. 151]).

Dance Scene: The Death of Tlacahuepan, p. 138

English version by David Ossman, from Angel M. Garibay K., *La literatura de los Aztecas* (Editorial Joaquin Mortiz & Instituto Indigenista Interamericano, Mexico, 1964), pp. 87–92.

The heroes of the piece, Tlacahuepan & Ixtilcuechahuac, died between the years 1494 & 1498 in a battle at Atlixco. They were the brothers of the second Motecuzoma, & their deaths (especially Tlacahuepan's) became the subject of many poems & dances (see above, p. 224).

Addenda. In the original manuscript, writes Garibay, there's clear indication of a scene-to-scene change in the verse rhythms. It's fairly clear also that this is a fragment of a longer work.

Ghosts & Shadows, p. 145

J.R.'s working from R. P. Trilles, *Les Pygmées de la Forêt Equatoriale* (Paris, 1931), reprinted in Caillois & Lambert, *Trésor de la poésie universelle,* p. 27.

Interiorizing as a mode of translation: that the pygmy "ghosts" are as elusive as "soul" or "personality" or "unconscious"—for us the last believable remnants of the mythic underworld. But the pygmies would more likely see the forest-as-a-dark-soul than as Lawrence has it.

The Chapter of Changing into Ptah, p. 146

Adapted by Ben Moses from E. A. W. Budge, *The Papyrus of Ani (Book of the Dead)* (Medici Society Ltd., London, 1913), Vol. II, pp. 546–48.

Ptah—the lord of life, who conceived the elements of the universe with his heart & brought them into being with his tongue.

Ka—the double; separable part of the personality.

Hathor—goddess of the sky; divine cow who holds the stars in her belly.

Busiris & Heliopolis—Greek names for the Lower Egyptian cities of Tetu & Anu.

Ra—the Sun.

Tem (Atum)—oldest of the gods; creator.

Keb (Geb)—god of the earth & father of the gods; "in many places he is called the 'great cackler' & he was supposed to have laid the egg from which the world sprang" (Budge).

Tait—goddess of weaving.

The Book of the Dead isn't a book but a catch-all name for the Egyptian funerary papyri, the best-known set coming from the papyrus of (the scribe) Ani written down between 1500 & 1350 B.C. As with the Egyptian "namings" (see above, p. 10), the concern here is not with the dignity of the god-nature so much as its energy: at once more-than-human & utterly of-this-earth. It is the same vision that makes the great fanged statue of Coatlicue or the multi-breasted Diana of Ephesus more interesting & probably more truthful than the Venus de Milo or Michelangelo's Pietà.

. . . .

Jerome Rothenberg
CHILD OF AN IDUMEAN NIGHT (1965)

1

I, the fat god
I, the good gardener   (p. klee)

Deposit me in your heart
& go to war gaily
Be a singer to Philistia
& carry an American flag
to the border

O Jerusalem
O city of mechanics

Covered with hair of fire
Beard against beard
A row of tigers stands there

Be holy, I say
Write on water
Become the first architect, be
Father of your race

& let men fuck your beard

2

I, tallow
I, voice of holocaust
I, crystal

I, open door
I, decimal
I, winter solstice

I, willow
I, dancer
I, wind-udder

I, parchment
I, avatar
I, shoe

I, harmonica
I, tongue of doves
I, emblem

I, regiment
I, globus
I, pustule

I, tooth
I, tumescence
I, father of tractors

I who swallow the dead
I who die
I who shit with the jackal

I who swell

3

They walk, eyes
In chest
Believing their peace
Their warm days
They burrow
They call me
Master
They say & we dream
Master master
Candle with how many wicks
Destroyer
Worshipper
God of the Tsars
Old father
Old language the father spoke
& wrote it in brass
& that was the testament in brass
& there were other testaments
& iron
& still other testaments
& still other old languages
& I wallowed
& I bathed in the heavy water
Master master
I was firm & substantive
I showed myself
I labelled this part hair
& that part tendon
& I reached between my legs
I grew fat

I became the father of my race
My wide hips in the dust
My heart
Was with the children
Believing
Their peace, their warm days
& still other testaments
I bellowed
I spat
I made thunder
I was first before the Senate
Someone called me
Master
Master
Child of an Idumean night
Possessor
Murderer
First to sit on the stone
To ride the locomotive
& be lost
& to proclaim the kingdom
& to be lost again
& swollen again
& fattened without a sense of repetition
But "made fat with fatness"
In the dust
My wide hips in the dust
& I reached between my legs
& I wallowed
& I bathed in the heavy water
My throne
My sweet light
My substance
This tsar did many good things
Though he was no father

Prayer to Thot, p. 148

Workings by Ulli Beier, "Traditional Egyptian Poetry," *Black Orpheus,* No. 18 (Ibadan, Nigeria, 1965), p. 7.

Thot (Thoth)—The Moon; "lord of divine speech;" Thought; Hermes Trismegistus; etc. But the reader shouldn't set aside as merely-primitive "the white haired monkey" & "quartz phallus."

The Cannibal Hymn, p. 149

Ibid., p. 6.

Unas (Unis)—the dead king.

Made up of Utterances 273 & 274 of the Pyramid Texts (for which see commentary, p. 432, above). Mercer indicates that the hymn consists, in fact, of a series of shorter utterances; the method of bringing them together & the resultant feeling of the poem is very reminiscent of later African praise-poems (described above, p. 418) & suggests a continuity that is, but shouldn't be, surprising. It would seem—from other evidence as well—that the disintegration which overtook Egypt was later in coming to Black Africa.

Addenda. The picture of the dead king "slaying & devouring the gods as food" (Mercer) isn't unlike the heaven of the Jews, where the souls of the Righteous were to spend eternity feasting on the flesh of Behemoth & Leviathan—the possibility too of that having its source among the god-eaters. To say nothing of the Eucharist, etc.

Incantation by Isis for Revival of the Dead Osiris, p. 151

Free working by Ed Sanders in *Fuck You: A Magazine of the Arts,* Vol. 5, No. 5 (1963).

The assemblage goes back to materials in Budge's *Osiris & the Egyptian Resurrection,* viz. *The Lamentations of Isis & Nephthys* & the words of Isis in *The Book of Making the Spirit of Osiris, or The Spirit Burial* (c. 1500–1350 B.C.). Like a number of poets after Lawrence, Sanders makes direct use of the old Egyptian gods, glyphs, erotic visions, death symbols, etc., & has published his own work under the emblem of the Horus eye, which he renames the "peace eye." The re-reading of the source is seminal, not far either from the scholarship of T. Rundle Clark & others.

For more on Isis & Osiris, see above, p. 455.

Conversations in Courtship, p. 153

Excerpts from Ezra Pound's translation in *Love Poems of Ancient Egypt,* translated by Ezra Pound & Noel Stock (New Directions, New York, 1962), pp. 4–7.

"These versions are based on literal renderings of the hieroglyphic texts into Italian by Boris de Rachewiltz, which first appeared in the volume *Liriche amorose degli antichi Egizioni,* published by Vanni Scheiwiller, Milan, in 1957. Most of the original Egyptian texts have survived only in incomplete form, but, for the purpose of modern adaptation, it has seemed desirable to present each poem as complete."

Egyptian Remedies, p. 156

Translated by C. P. Bryan, *Papyrus Ebers* (1930), as reprinted in Josephine Mayer & Tom Prideaux, *Never to Die* (Viking Press, New York, 1938), pp. 79–80.

Middle Kingdom medical recipes as found-poetry.

Five Ambo Ghost Songs, p. 158

Bronislaw Stefaniszyn, *Social & Ritual Life of the Ambo of Northern Rhodesia* (Oxford University Press [International African Institute], 1964), pp. 157–60.

The songs are used to treat cases of possession & are classified according to the kind of spirit involved (*masyabe, bamoba, baciwilla*). But the Ambo describe the ghosts no further than saying that "like all shades . . . they have only half a body & live on flies."

The possessed person "falls ill, & behaves in a strange way, swallowing uncooked flour, & singing at night. He says he 'wants to sleep at the river,' & if not watched will run away. He eats raw eggs, imitates the bark of the jackal & whines like the zebra. He climbs trees, even very slender ones, & jumps from one to another."

Treatment is first by herbal medicine which, in this case, only diagnoses the disturbance & determines the dance (& songs) to be used. "The possessed (then) dances alone but surrounded by a large chorus. She dances with raised hands, waving her palms, an action not performed in other Ambo dances. . . . It is maintained that if the possessed did not dance, she (or he) would die."

The Comet, p. 160; *The Trial,* p. 161; *The Lovers,* p. 162.

P. Amaury Talbot, *In the Shadow of the Bush* (Wm. Heinemann, London, 1912), pp. 455, 456, 459.

This is a form of secret-writing that was widespread among groups besides the Ekoi, being there the property of a society called the Nsibidi. Messages sent in Nsibidi script were cut or painted on split palm stems; the signs employed show a wide range of conventionalization & abstraction, e.g.:

Moon in three phases

Husband & wife love each other ardently. They love to put their arms around one another (shown by extended hands). They are rich, have three tables & a pillow at each side

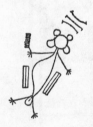

A mirror standing on a table

People arranging their hair in the mirror

Sign denoting a talkative man

Sick man lying down in his house, with three visitors

In addition to their use in sending messages, they were incised on sacred or play objects, & tattooed on the bodies of society members.

For other picture-writings, see above, pp. 28, 195, 262.

Addenda. (1) by Ian Hamilton Finlay

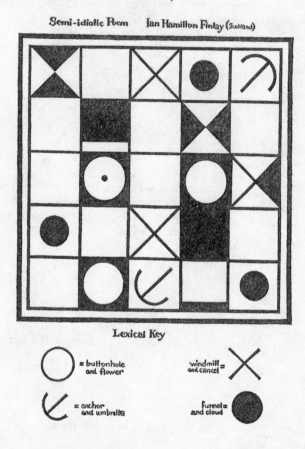

Semi-idiotic Poem   Ian Hamilton Finlay (Scotland)

Lexical Key

⭕ = buttonhole and flower

∠ = anchor and umbrella

windmill and cancel = ✕

funnel and cloud = ⬤

(2) by John Furnival

semi-erotic scotch poem for i.h.f.

lexical key :

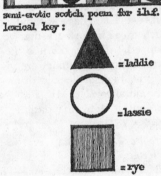

= laddie

= lassie

= rye

Drum Poem #7, p. 163

Adapted by Ben Moses from R. S. Rattray, *Ashanti* (Oxford University Press, 1923), pp. 269, 280.

". . . Among the Ashanti the drum is not used . . . (to rap) out words by means of a prearranged code, but . . . to sound or speak the actual words . . . drum-talking as distinct from drum-signalling . . . an attempt to imitate by means of two drums, set in different notes, the exact sound of the human voice." (Rattray, p. 242.)

Ashanti is a tonal language & "the drum gives the tones, number of syllables, & the punctuation accurately. The actual vowels & the individual consonants cannot be transmitted. It is therefore generally impossible to 'read' accurately any particular word when standing alone"—though the "words" are heard distinctly as parts of larger units, aided too by the use of standard or set phrases.

This type of poem (or poem-realization) is widespread in Africa. Among the Yoruba, e.g., "the 'dundun' drum can play any tone & glide of the . . . language & its range is an octave. . . . Just as in Semitic languages the consonants are so important that one can write the language without vowels, so in Yoruba the tones are of such great importance that vowels as well as consonants can be dropped." (Beier, *Yoruba Poetry,* p. 9.)

In Rattray's Ashanti transcriptions, two tones are given: for the low or male drum (M) & the high or female drum (F). These may be combined almost simultaneously (MF, FM, MM or FF) or grouped in syllables as indicated by the dashes.

Addenda. In Max Neuhaus' *Realization of Jackson Mac Low's 'The Text on the Opposite Page,'* a reading by two voices of a dual series of typewritten letters, numbers & signs is recorded on magnetic tape & lowered by four octaves, etc. The resulting "distortion" creates a musical composition which both is & isn't the original reading. The sound is of a very deep, very resonant & percussive piece of electronic music: the voice an undiscernible but real presence.

Oriki Ogun, p. 164

Bakare Gbadamosi & Ulli Beier, *Yoruba Poetry* (Ministry of Education, Nigeria, 1959), pp. 21 ff. (selected).

Ogun is the god of iron & is worshiped by all who use iron. He is a semi-historical figure who has become an *orisha,* i.e., a "mediary between Olorun (the supreme god) & man. . . . (The *orisha*) personifies some aspect of the divine power," & each *orisha* has his own set of colors, materials, etc.

For a description of the Yoruba *oriki* (praise-poem), see above, p. 418.

Hyena, p. 166; *Cattle,* p. 166

George Economou's working from D. F. v. d. Merwe, "Hurutshe Poems," *Bantu Studies,* XV (1941), 330, 321.

Praise-poems for animals; see also the two following notes.

The Train, p. 167

Economou, v. d. Merwe, *ibid.,* p. 335.

Praise-poem form imposed on new matter. Whatever enters a man's field-of-vision is part of his real world.

Of praise-poems among the Hurutshe, v. d. Merwe writes: ". . . a man may add a few lines to a poem heard by somebody else, with the result that a given poem may be the creation of two or even more persons. But the poems as recited by different people differ (also in that) the lines or stanzas composing the poems . . . sometimes change positions."

For more on praise-poems, see especially p. 418, above.

The Elephant I & II, pp. 168, 169

(I) Bakare Gbadamosi & Ulli Beier, *Yoruba Poetry* (Ministry of Education, Nigeria, 1959), p. 34.

(II) Translated by C. M. Bowra from R. P. Trilles, *Les pygmées de la forêt équatoriale* (Paris, 1931), in Bowra, *Primitive Song* (World Publishing Co., Cleveland, 1962), pp. 44–45.

Compare the approach to the same subject by (I) praise-poem structure & (II) strophe & refrain. The Yoruba is technically classified as an *ijala* on the basis of the group to which the reciter belongs (in this case, "hunters") & the technique of recitation he employs; but the disposition of the verses is like that of the Yoruba *oriki* (see above, p. 418). In the Pygmy poem, writes Bowra, "the main text is sung by the leader, & the refrain by his companions in the chase."

Death Rites II, p. 171

Bowra, Trilles, *ibid.,* pp. 202–3.

Khvum (Khmvum)—father of the forest who "at times visits the sun to keep its fires burning;" he is otherwise connected with judgment in the underworld (see note on "Death Rites I," p. 448, above).

The eldest son of the dead man begins the song, & the maternal uncle (italicized lines) replies.

A Song of Changes, p. 172

Translated by C. M. Bowra from R. P. Trilles, *L'Ame du Pygmée d'Afrique* (Paris, 1945), in Bowra, *Primitive Song,* pp. 284–85.

Characteristic of *all* poetry where sensitivity to the shifting polarities of light & darkness, etc., becomes a matter of cognition &, perhaps, of tragedy.

. . . .

Federico García Lorca
THE SONG WANTS TO BE THE LIGHT

> The song wants to be the light.
> In the darkness the song contains
> threads of phosphorous and moon.
> The light does not know what it wants.
> On its boundaries of opal,
> it meets itself face to face,
> and returns.

(Translation by James Wright)

The Praises of the Falls (Lithoko tsa Maoa), p. 173

Adapted by J.R. from Father F. Laydevant, "The Praises of the Divining Bones among the Basotho," *Bantu Studies,* VII (1933), 341–73.

The "praises"—first gathered by the Basuto writer, Joas Mapetla—accompany the casting of oracle bones. Their purpose is

(1) to create, as with music, the conditions under which the bones are to be read, i.e., to provide that "coefficient of weirdness" Malinowski spoke of (see above, p. 386) in which the words *are* music, act upon us before their sense is clear or against the possibility of any fixed meaning;

(2) as open-ended imagery that can then—almost "falsely"—be read as secret closed statements (the functional language of the oracle) in the participants' search for clues to the unknown: the cause of disease & misfortune, etc.

Mapetla's description of the bones & the procedures for casting is never clear. There are apparently four to twenty in a set or "litaola": four principal ones from the hoofs & horns of oxen, with lesser bones from ankles & hindlegs of anteaters, springbok, sheep, goats, monkeys, also occasional shells, twigs & stones. The four major bones are designated as greater & lesser male & greater & lesser female, & are read according to the sides on which they fall, direction of fall, positions relative to each other & to the minor bones, etc. The greater male & female have four sides called walking, standing, covering, & dying; the lesser male & female only walking & dying. Here is Mapetla's description of the casting & "praising":

When they are divining, the person who comes to ask for this service sweeps the ground where he has to throw them. Then the diviner loosens them from the string & gives them to the one who comes to consult.

This one tosses them & lets them fall on the ground.
Then the diviner examines them carefully in order to see the position they have taken.

When he sees that they have fallen in a certain position, he praises that fall for a good while.

Among the praises he mixes the affairs of people, of (various) things, of animals & sicknesses.

When he has finished the praises, he says to the person who came to consult him: Make me divine, my friend.

This one says: With these words, when you were making the praises, you pointed exactly to my case, & to my sickness.

And the diviner says: So it is, & this special position (of the bones) says the same. Then the diviner gives a charm to the consulting person, & receives a small fee from him (in exchange).

(For a clearer description of a related & more complex system, see Junod on divining bones among the Thonga: *The Life of a South African Tribe* [1913], Vol. II, pp. 493 ff.)

Addenda. (1) In the typical praise-poem (see above, p. 418) the lines or praises are independent units that the poet brings together in a kind of collage. In the present instance, however, it is the fall of the bones that suggests what lines or praises will be used & determines their order. Thus chance—to a greater or lesser degree—serves to program the divining praises much as dice-castings, tarot-readings, random digit tables, etc., take on a structuring & selecting function for some contemporary poets. In both cases, syntactical devices may be used to bridge the lines, or the disjunction between lines (as silence or punctuation) may be accepted on its own. As printed here, the numbers indicate the separate units (lines or praises) of the Laydevant-Mapetla text.

(2) The name of a "fall" is generally that of the plant or other remedy to be used in that instance. Most African words that remain in the translations are likewise either plants or proper names —the meaning being fairly evident from the context.

(3) The editor has printed these with some reservations about their accuracy but in the hope that others will be encouraged to do more detailed work on a body of lore & poetry that, carefully assembled, may represent an African *I Ching or Book of Changes*.

A Phantom Bird, p. 181

Blaise Cendrars, *The African Saga: Anthologie nègre*, translated by Margery Bianco (Payson & Clarke Ltd., New York, 1927), pp. 343–44.

The Story of the Leopard Tortoise, p. 182

Wilhelm H. I. Bleek & Lucy C. Lloyd, *Specimens of Bushman Folklore* (George Allen & Co., London, 1911), pp. 37 ff.

Dictated, in 1875, by !kwéiten ta ‖ken, who heard it from her mother, ‡kamme-an.

NARRATOR'S NOTES, ETC. The narrator explains that this misfortune happened to men of the Early Race.

And she altogether held the man firmly with it, i.e., by drawing in her neck.

The man's hands altogether decayed away in it, i.e., the flesh decayed away & came off, as well as the skin & nails, leaving, the narrator says, merely the bones.

Rub our elder sister a little with fat; for, the moon has been cut, while our elder sister lies ill: i.e., the moon "died" & another moon came while she still lay ill, the narrator explains.

Addenda. (1) "In Bushman astrological mythology the Moon is looked upon as a man who incurs the wrath of the Sun, & is consequently pierced by the knife (i.e., the rays) of the latter. This process is repeated until almost the whole of the Moon is cut away, & only one little piece left; which the Moon piteously implores the Sun to spare for his (the Moon's) children. . . . From this little piece, the Moon gradually grows again until it becomes a full moon, when the Sun's stabbing & cutting processes recommence." (W. H. I. Bleek, *A Brief Account of Bushman Folklore & Other Texts* [Cape Town, 1875], p. 9.)

(2) For further comments on the Bleek-Lloyd translations, see above, p. 413.

Gassire's Lute, p. 184

Leo Frobenius & Douglas C. Fox, *African Genesis* (Stackpole Sons, New York, 1937), pp. 97–109.

(1)

                                              the blood
            streams from the bodies of his sons
            to feed the voice of Gassire's lute;

> the men who mean good
>
> must rage, grieve, turn with dismay
>
> to see how "base and unjust actions, when they are the objects of hope, are lovely to those that vehemently admire them"
>
> and how far men following self-interest can betray all good of self.
>
> (Robert Duncan, from *Passages 24*)

(2) The Soninke are a small remnant group now mostly Moslem & inhabiting the desert oases of Tichit & Walatu in what used to be French West Africa; but Fox suggests that the longer epic (*Dausi*) of which this is a preserved fragment goes back to around 500 B.C., Wagadu being the legendary city of the Fasa (Fezzan in Herodotus), the other cities mentioned having ancient counterparts, etc. In the form given the song comes from the fourth to twelfth centuries A.D. & was, so he tells us, the work of "troubadours." Whatever its history, the poem's statement about the artist remains chilling.

Three Midē Songs & Picture-Songs, p. 195

W. J. Hoffman, "The Midēwiwin or 'Grand Medicine Society' of the Ojibwa," *Seventh Annual Report of the Bureau of American Ethnology* (Washington, 1891), *passim*.

The *Midēwiwin* ("society of the Midē or Shamans") consisted of four grades or degrees & involved a gradual opening-up of sense perception, powers to heal, etc. The myth-of-origin has it that Minabozho, servant of Dzhe Manido (the Midē guardian spirit), took pity on the Ojibwa ancestors, therefore delivered to "Otter" the mysteries of the Midēwiwin (sacred drum, rattles, shells, song, dance, etc.) & instructed him to pass them to the people.

The Midē songs were re-made by successive generations & recorded in pictographs "incised upon birchbark"—no mere mnemonic devices (as Hoffman gives them) but with independent meanings that varied from recorder to recorder. Here, following Hoffman, are some "readings" for the pictographs in the third set—though in no sense closing their meaning:

(1) The disk is the dish for the feast of spirits in the Midē lodge, the arms reaching toward it denoting the spirits who take food therefrom. Thus the candidate will be enabled to invoke & commune with the spirits of departed Midē, & to learn from them of hidden powers.

(2) The reason for the representation of a human form was not satisfactorily explained. The preceptor felt confident, however, that it signified a manido (deity) who controls the fog, one different from one of the *anamiki,* or Thunderers, who would be shown by an eagle or a hawk, when it would also denote the thunder, & perhaps lightning, neither of which occurs in connection with fog.

(3) Rests & silences often involved ceremonial smoking.

(4) The figure is an outline of the Midē lodge with the sacred Midē stone indicated within, as also another spot to signify the place occupied by a sick person. The waving lines above & beneath the oblong are magic lines, & indicate magic or supernatural power.

(5) The Midē who is chanting is shown in the figure; his eyes are looking into the candidate's heart. The lines from the mouth denote speech. The horns are a manner of indicating superior powers.

(6) Although the crow is mentioned, the Thunderbird (eagle) is delineated. The Midē sack, which gives the singer manido powers, is made of crow's skin.

(7) The head is symbolical of the white bear manido; the short lines below it denoting flame radiating from the body, the eyes also looking with a penetrating gaze, as indicated by the waving lines from each eye. A manido of great powers.

The songs themselves consist (typically) of "a number of archaic words, some of which are furthermore different from the spoken language on account of their being chanted, & meaningless syllables introduced to prolong certain accentuated notes." The songs may also be repeated for as long as the singer chooses— "the greater the number of repetitions . . . the greater is felt to be the amount of inspiration & power of the performance" (Hoffman, 164).

Addenda. For more on picture-poems, etc., see above, pp. 28, 160, 262, & the accompanying commentaries.

Ten Chippewa (Ojibwa) *Songs*, p. 202

Frances Densmore, *Chippewa Music* (Bureau of American Ethnology, Nos. 45, 53 [1910–1913]), *passim.*

Densmore makes each word of Chippewa equal a line of English (see note on Teton Sioux, following).

Song 2: The singer said he killed a Crow Indian & sang this song with the scalp.

Song 3: The *death-song* was given in dream-vision or composed like this one at the time of death. The large bear was Gawitayac's "manido animal" in whose guidance he had trusted.

Song 5: war song, used in "dog feast" after eating of dog's head shortly before conclusion.

Song 7: The song's origin was a dream in which the singer became a buffalo & was given these words by other buffalos.

Song 8: A dream song . . . used in war dances.

Song 9: A Midē funeral song.

Song 10: The "game of silence" consisted of keeping still as long as possible in the face of non-sequential & far-out expressions meant to cause laughter.

Addenda. (1) The concreteness of the poems is in their images, which often have nothing to do with the song's function; i.e., they are "abstract" with relation to context, which they do not explain but within which they act.

(2) Kenneth Rexroth writes, specifically of the materials collected by Densmore: ". . . Songs, like other things which we call works of art, occupy in American Indian society a position somewhat like the sacraments and sacramentals of the so-called higher religions. That is, the Indian poet is not only a prophet. Poetry or song does not only play a vatic role in the society, but is itself a numinous thing. The work of art is holy, in Rudolph Otto's sense—an object of supernatural awe, & as such, an important instrument in the control of reality on the highest plane." (*Assays,* New Directions, pp. 56–57.)

Five Teton Sioux Songs, p. 205

Frances Densmore, *Teton Sioux Music* (Bureau of American Ethnology, Bulletin 61 [1918]), pp. 180, 187, 221, 222, 237.

The first song was given by wolves in a dream; the second by an elk in a dream. Songs 3 & 4 were sung by Charging Thunder (Wakingyanwatakpe) who learned them from his father, Bear Necklace (Matonapin). Song 5 was sung by Bear Eagle (Matowangbli) who credited its making to Shell Necklace (Pangkeskanapin).

The lines of Densmore's translation correspond to single words in the Sioux; thus each word of Sioux = a line of English. The result, accidental or otherwise, is to isolate the poem's structural properties (of stops & starts, disjunctions, etc.) as basis for a new music of utterance in the translation, providing a notation (including the parenthetical additions) that closely parallels—remarkably so for the fifth song—the sound of much contemporary poetry in English, e.g.:

Robert Creeley

I KNOW A MAN

As I sd to my
friend, because I am
always talking,—John, I

sd, which was not his
name, the darkness sur-
rounds us, what

can we do against
it, or else, shall we &
why not, buy a goddamn big car,

drive, he sd, for
christ's sake, look
out where yr going.

Songs of the Masked Dancers, p. 208

Pliny Earle Goddard, "The Masked Dancers of the Apache," *Holmes Anniversary Volume* (Washington, 1916), pp. 133-35.

Goddard's Note: "Masked dancers are one of the outstanding features of the ceremonial and religious life of the Southwest. The Apache of Arizona . . . call these masked dancers Gan . . . and the beings they represent the same name. . . . In these songs [accompanying girls' puberty rites] one recognizes at once the sacred number four, connected with the world quarters each with its color . . . north, white . . . east, black . . . south, blue . . . west, yellow. . . . The dualism of sky and earth also appears. Several of the sacred materials are mentioned—the soft feathers, the black stone or jet, and pollen connected with speech or prayer. The mountain of the east, 'Mescal Mountain,' is the mythological home of the Gans, where there stands a row of Douglas spruce. Besides the Gans themselves, the Sky Boy and Sky Girl are prominent as persons, and the thunder and lightning with clouds disguised as spots represent the forces of nature."

Addenda. Masked dancers have been part of the phenomenology of religion back to the great "sorcerer" in the neolithic cave of *Trois Frères.* Color & number symbolism is almost as widespread. But notice, for variety's sake, the very rigid & intellectual color patterns compared to the obsessive single-color imagery noted elsewhere (see above, p. 433).

Songs in the Garden of the House God, p. 210

Washington Matthews, "Songs of Sequence of the Navahos," *Journal of American Folk-Lore,* 7 (1894), pp. 185-94.

"House God" is Matthews' translation of *xactceoɣan,* a god-name others speak of as untranslatable. Created by Whiteshell Woman from a yellow corn ear, he is "represented as having charge of farm songs & is the god of evening or sunset": thus writes Reichard (*Navaho Symbolism,* II, 503).

Matthews coined "songs of sequence" for Navaho songsets using the parallelisms ("rhyming thoughts" someone once called them) typical of primitive & archaic poetry. Here the variations within the tight structure of the burden follow a particular (grammatical) feature of Navaho: the tense-aspect system of its verb. As Reichard tells it:

> In Navaho, verbs of action and motion are differentiated in a rather simple tense system—present, past and future—and a complicated aspect system—progressive, momentary, customary, inceptive, and cessative. Often, therefore, the burden of the song has a tense or aspective change to indicate progression from a wish to an accomplishment. (*Symbolism*, I, 294.)

In the "farm songs," e.g., the events move from seed-planting to growth to harvest to husking, while the verbs translate (roughly) as: *I wish it to be . . . It is becoming . . . It has become so . . . It increases by spreading . . . Now from my hands it gives forth a sound,* etc. But these are only some of the steps covered: normal to Navaho but giving rise to strange new structures in translation. And these too have their values.

A Song from "The Enemy Way," p. 212

Father Berard Haile, *Origin Legend of the Navaho Enemy Way* (Yale University Publications in Anthropology, No. 17 [1938]), pp. 264–65.

"Enemy-Way" was originally a war ceremony involving re-enactment of mythical Navaho wars—the slaying of monsters by the Hero Twins & the war on Taos. It is now used for healing, "to lay the ghost of an outsider (causing sickness), that of a white man or of some other non-Navaho. . . ." (For more on the Navaho chant-system of which this is a part, see p. 438, above.)

The song is one of nine sung during preparation & decoration of the drum. As in all Navaho ceremonial music

> . . . after a brief introduction of vocables, usually something like " 'eneya," a song begins with a phrase repeated a number of times in what may be called a chorus. Then the body of the song begins, but at the end of each line in the body the last few bars of the chorus are added as a sort of burden.

The complete, or nearly complete chorus is repeated between the halves of a two-part song and again at the end of the song. Usually only the chorus and burden change from one song to the next within any song-group. (David P. McAllester, *Enemy Way Music* [1954], p. 16.)

For more on Navaho burden-changes, see the preceding note.

Old Song: For the Tall One, p. 214

Shortened from Dane & Mary Roberts Coolidge, *The Last of the Seris* (E. P. Dutton & Co., New York, 1939), pp. 51–54.

The poem is from the island of Tiburon off the coast of Sonora in Baja California, & is called The Old Song—*Eee-go'-set*. Juan Tomas', "a tall, wrinkled old man, claiming to be one hundred & three years old," said of it: "This song came down from seven grandfathers. It was taught one to another. In the old days the song [as war song] was given only to a brave man's son. The language is not that of the modern Seris but is an ancient language which could not be communicated by words. It is very old."

A Song of the Winds (by Santo Blanco), p. 216

Ibid., p. 82.

Santo Blanco was one of the few Seris to keep the songs in anything like their old form. He had seen the god of the cave too & described him as follows:

He lives in a little cave inside the big cave. I could see through him when he walked toward us, yet I was conscious he was coming closer & closer, until he was a hand's length from my face. It was dark as night, but I could see him. His arms were stretched out & his hands were hanging down, & from their tips water dripped. It was like ice. He came to me very slowly, & held his fingers over my head. He came again & spread his hands over me, & from the finger-tips I caught water in my palms.

The water is holy of course & cures—& he renews his supply of it (of the songs also?) by returning to the cave. Then

. . . the Spirit comes out of his inner cave & sings. The Spirit is a god, but not like the God of the Gringos. He is very much more beautiful than He Who Rules Heaven & Earth, the God in the sky. He has a white hat & a black coat, very long. To his ankles. Inside this black coat there are all kinds of bright colors. (Coolidge, pp. 94–95.)

Six Seri Whale Songs, p. 217

Ibid., pp. 68–69.

"And enormous mother whales lie dreaming suckling their whale-
tender young
and dreaming with strange whale eyes wide open in the waters
of the beginning and the end."
—D. H. Lawrence, from *Whales Weep Not!*
. . . .

For more on the author, Santo Blanco, see the preceding note.

Inatoipippiler (Excerpts), p. 219

Nils Holmer & S. Henry Wassén, *Inatoipippiler, or The Adventures of Three Cuna Boys* (Etnologiska Studier No. 20 [Göteborg, Sweden, 1952]).

Uncle Oloyailer—name of a sea monster (*yailler* = "an animal like a seal," but the singer explains it by *nali e tule* = "shark man").
Uncle Nia—spirit owner of a fortress reached by Inatoipippiler in his undersea journey.

Sometime around 1840, three boys from Portogandí (on the San Blas coast of Panama) went fishing & didn't return. A *nele* (wise-man with shamanic powers) was consulted, who revealed facts about the disappearance that form the basis of the poem. The boys, about ten years old, were never seen again & are said to have been drowned in an eddy.
The song/poem is attributed to Akkantilele ("the *nele* of Acandí") who composed it ten days after the disaster; the present version by Belisario Guerrero (Maninibigdinapi) apparently comes in a direct line of transmission, poet to poet. Though based on

an actual event, the images are visionary & in the universal tradition of underworld journeys.

"Songs of this kind," the translators tell us, "are usually accompanied by a monotonous chant rather than singing, every line or section beginning high & gradually falling off, amidst modulations upward & downward into a prolonged cadence. . . . Repetitions are multiplied at choice, so that the singer, when he takes his time, may not be through singing until the morning hours." The lines of the original vary greatly in length.

Addenda. Not apparent in the translation is the use of a special narrative mode that shifts the perspective from third to first person, both to make the historical time immediate & to freely interiorize some of the objective material. Thus "they are approaching the ship" is literally "you are approaching my ship," & (more surprisingly) "the southwind is making a noise" is literally "making a noise in me"; or elsewhere "they go to the loft to sleep when midnight has come" is literally "when you have come in me." The translators write: "This represents the boys' thoughts; such quasi-dialogue constructions are peculiar to Cuna poetic language."

For more on such shifts, etc., see the note on the Fijian "Flight of the Chiefs," page 517, below. The most obvious modern analogues are stream-of-consciousness writers like Joyce or Faulkner, but something of the kind informs most contemporary experiments with structuring, composition-by-field, etc.

Three Nahuatl Poems, p. 222

Workings by William Carlos Williams in Thomas Mabry Cranfill (ed.), *The Muse in Mexico* (University of Texas Press, 1959), pp. 90–91.

"Here in this large building whose great hall was to serve the Spaniards for barracks from that time until the end, Montezuma and Cortez found themselves seated face to face. Montezuma spoke: 'They have told you that I possess houses with walls of gold and many other such things and that I am a god or make myself one. The houses you see are of stone and lime and earth.' —Then opening his robe: 'You see that I am composed of flesh and bone like yourselves and that I am mortal and palpable to the touch.'" (W. C. W., *In the American Grain,* p. 31.)

For Tlacahuepan, p. 224

J.R.'s working from Spanish translation by Angel María Garibay K., *Poesía indígena de la Altiplanície* (Ediciones de la Universidad Nacional Autónoma, Mexico, 1952), p. 171.

After the battle in which Tlacahuepan was killed (see above, p. 456), they brought home the remains of the dead & placed them on the funeral pyre; "then the old men took up the *teponaztle* & *atabal* drums, & began to sing the praises of the dead man; & they all held shields in their left hands & staffs in their right hands."

The "kingdom of death" is more precisely one of several warrior heavens or stopping-off places on the way to the "house of the sun." The Seven Caves are the mythical Aztec place-of-origin (Chicomóztoc). Eagles & Tigers (or jaguars) were the two principal warrior fraternities &, symbolically, the major antagonists in a "flowering war" of the spirit. For the rest, bells, flowers, caves, birds (& specifically a bird like *that*) create a landscape for death that the mind still shares & is moved by.

The Return of the Warriors, p. 225

J.R.'s working from Garibay, *ibid.,* p. 99.

Anáhuac—the territory of Mexico; *Tenochtitlan*—the city of Mexico.

Totoquihuatzin—king of Tlacopan, ruled 1487–1519.

Nezahualpilli—son & successor of Nezahualcoyotl (most famous of the pre-Conquest poets) as king of Tetzcoco. Born 1464. Rule began 1472. Died 1515.

The poem suggests a pulling-together of verses from before & after the Conquest—a sense of the city between glory & ruin.

Popol Vuh (Excerpts), pp. 227, 231

English version by Delia Goetz & Sylvanus G. Morley, *Popol Vuh: The Sacred Book of the Ancient Quiché Maya* (University of Oklahoma Press, 1950), pp. 119–23, 148–50; from the Spanish translation by Adrián Recinos.

Cuchumaquic—lit. "gathered blood"; *Xquic*—lit. "little blood, or blood of a woman."

The Popol Vuh, literally "the book of the community" (or "common-house" or "council"), was preserved by Indians in Santo Tomás Chichicastenango, Guatemala, & in the eighteenth century given to Father Francisco Ximénez who transcribed & put it into Spanish; vanished again & rediscovered in the 1850s by Carl Scherzer & Abbé Charles Etienne Brasseur de Bourbourg. It existed in picture-writing before the Conquest, & the version used by Father Ximénez (& since lost) may have been the work, circa 1550, of one Diego Reynoso. The book "contains the cosmogonical concepts & ancient traditions of (the Quiché nation), the history of their origin, & the chronicles of their kings down to the year 1550."

The story-of-the-maiden begins after the death of the mythical twin-heroes, Hun-Hunahpú & Vucub-Hunahpú, who went "to play ball on the road to Xibalba" (underground region inhabited by the enemies of man, apparently survivors of an earlier age of wooden people). There they were killed by Xibalba's rulers when, in one of the "places of torture," they failed to keep pine-sticks & cigars burning overnight. Hun-Hunahpú's head was placed in a calabash tree, where it became like all the other fruit: "& the Lords of Xibalba said: 'Let no one come to pick the fruit. Let no one come & sit under this tree.'"

The maiden's sons, Hunahpú & Xbalanqué, later go the same road to Xibalba, where they beat its rulers at ball & by surviving ordeals in the houses of torture.

While the poems are rich in local details, there are many motifs too that are "universal"—of twin heroes, underworld trees, forbidden fruit, impregnation by tree &/or spittle, heroic labors, etc.

Previously unpublished versions of pre-Conquest "Incan" poetry by W. S. Merwin.

"An Indian [Incan] poet, called a harauec, that is, an inventor, composed quantities of . . . verses of all kinds. . . . The verses were composed in different meters, some short & others long . . . but they were as terse & precise as mathematics. There was no assonance, each verse being free. . . . I recall a love song, composed of four lines, from which may be judged the austerity of these terse compositions I spoke of; here it is with the translation:

Caylla llapi	To this tune
Puñunqui	you will sleep
Chaupituta	At midnight
Samusac	I shall come."

(Thus: Garcilaso de la Vega, *The Royal Commentaries of the Inca*. Born 1539, died 1616, he was the son of an Incan princess & a Spanish conquistador. He & Poma de Ayala (*Nueva crónica y buen gobierno*) are the chief early chroniclers of Incan history, etc.)

The Broken Vase, p. 240

From Maria Jolas (tr.), in Garcilaso de la Vega, *The Royal Commentaries of the Inca*, ed. Alain Gheerbrant (The Orion Press Inc. [Grossman Publishers], New York, 1961), pp. 81–82.

The poem, composed in four-syllable lines & recorded by means of *quipu* (knotted cords of different thicknesses & colors), was first transcribed, in Quechua & Latin, by Father Blas Valera. Garcilaso, who preserved it in his "commentaries," writes of this kind of astronomical poem: "The Indian poet . . . speaks, like a philosopher, of the secondary causes that made God create, in the air, thunder & lightning, as also hail, snow & rain. They were based on an Indian fable which goes as follows: The Creator, they say, took care to set a girl of royal blood in the sky, to whom he entrusted a vase full of water that she is supposed to pour on the earth whenever it is needed. Sometimes, it so happens, that one of the brothers of this girl breaks the vase, & this is the source of thunder & lightning. It can easily be seen that this is a man's doing, since thunder & lightning are fierce the way a man's nature is, & not tender, like the nature of a woman. On the other hand, they add, it is the girl who sends hail, snow & rain, these being soft, tender things that are beneficial, just as the feminine nature is beneficial."

Words from Seven Magic Songs (by Tatilgäk), p. 241

Workings by Rochelle Owens from Knud Rasmussen, *Intellectual Culture of the Copper Eskimos* (Report of the Fifth Thule Expedition [Copenhagen, 1932]), pp. 112–18.

Tatilgäk explained: "One makes magic songs when a man's thoughts begin to turn towards another or something that does not concern him; without his hearing it, one makes magic songs so that there may be calm in his mind, to make his thoughts pleasant—for a man is dangerous when he is angry."

Addenda. Rochelle Owens' most elaborate working of Eskimo data is in her play, *The String Game:* a use of "distant" materials to trace the dimensions of the human. Also in some poems, like the following.

．．．．．．．

Rochelle Owens
　　SONG OF MEAT, MADNESS & TRAVEL (1966)

I

dried meat
　　　　O glorious is dried meat.
　　my wife's breast in my hand
　　we stare at dried meat
　　　　　　is it not strange?

II

I pity her
　　　　now I pity her　　the woman the woman
　　who calls
　　in a voice of white madness
　　　　Let me fetch you, let me fetch you!

III

I desired to go north
　　　　as a great singer and dancer
　　my ears my ears
　　there is singing in them
　　　　The big caribou cows and the big bulls
　　and men
　　　　　　watch for me

A Song of Men's Impotence & the Beasts They Hunted, p. 242

Owens from Rasmussen, *ibid.,* pp. 162–63.

The Dead Hunter Speaks Through the Voice of a Shaman, p. 244

J.R.'s working from Rasmussen, *ibid.,* pp. 184–86.

Aijuk, they say, after his death, they say, his song, by Paulinâq dreamt. Sung by Netsit.

Eskimo Prose Poems, p. 245

Knud Rasmussen, *Intellectual Culture of the Iglulik Eskimos,* translated by William Worster (Copenhagen, 1930), pp. 261, 268, 304, 255.

The content isn't original—only the way-of-its-going. The larva-child, e.g., turns up in variants among other Eskimo groups Rasmussen recorded, but only here touches home, as something other than fantasy. The editor recalls a similar account in Swanton's *Tlingit Myths & Texts*—that one dealing with a chief's daughter who rears a woodworm which, killed by the town, becomes a clan emblem, the girl's four songs to the worm-child repeated at feasts, etc. Ivaluardjuk uses the material much differently, not to define-the-origin-of but to let the language force the mind toward a lonely & disturbing vision-of-the-real. A master of that mode—like Russell Edson.

....

Russell Edson
AN AIR BABY (1964)

A woman had an air baby, with little dust eyes that wink and blink in the sunlight.

But one day she breathed deeply and breathed her little baby into herself. So that she breathes out as hard as she can. No, that is not my baby. And she breathes out again as hard as she can. No, that is not my baby either.

Nothing is your baby, you foolish dog sitting there panting, says her husband.

No, no, I breathed it in, I sucked it out of my arms into my nose.

You foolish dog, how dare you treat my unknown heir like a smell.

I had it here: it had just wet its diapers and I was just about to throw it on the floor for wetting on me. I was just summoning my breath to jump on it for wetting on me. I was just drawing deeply on the atmosphere in preparation for the punitive feat. And I drew it into one of my nostrils, or both, breaking it between my nostrils.

You are the cruel mother that eats back her young, says her husband.

And why should I not?

Because you eat well enough without that. Why just the other day I brought you a lovely insect, remember, six legs? and how you baked it in the oven? remember how I climbed on your back and said take me to Market street, where I bought you a cookbook? and we looked through it for a recipe for baked baby, and there was none? And how you baked the cookbook and how really good it was? Don't you remember anything?

I remember something that I never had.

(From *The Very Thing That Happens*, New Directions, p. 26.)

The Quest of Milarepa, p. 251

Selected from Sir Humphrey Clarke, *The Message of Milarepa* (John Murray, London, 1958), pp. 1–2, 6–9.

Mila, his actual name; *repa*, the cotton-clad, a title of those who, like him, had learned to withstand the Himalayan cold through inner heat, etc.

Tsangpo—the Brahmaputra.

Mount Tisé & Lake Mapang at its foot—originally the holy places of the Bon Shamans whom Milarepa, having proved their master in magic, dispossessed in the name of Buddhism.

In Milarepa's *Life*, "as chronicled by his favorite disciple Rechung . . . we learn how, after his father's untimely death, he and his mother and sisters were despoiled of their patrimony; how he ran away . . . and learnt the black arts from a local sorcerer;

conjured up a hailstorm which ruined their crops and caused the roof of their house to fall in and kill their guests at a harvest festival; how remorse overcame him; how he then set out to find the truth and met his teacher Marpa; how Marpa, as penance, for seven years disciplined him savagely till even his spirit was almost broken, but finally initiated him; how after long contemplation in his mountain solitudes he finally attained enlightenment and was consecrated by Marpa as his successor; and how he lived to a ripe old age, teaching the faith and working miracles. . . ." (Clarke, *The Message,* xi–xii.)

Addenda. (1) For more on Marpa, Tibetan Buddhism & its relation to Bon shamanism, etc., see above, p. 423.

(2) The sacralization-of-the-everyday has been a rite of modern poetry since Baudelaire's perception (circa 1846) of the "heroism of everyday life." It takes many forms, but the reader at this point may especially enjoy comparing Mila's "cotton shirt" with the following.

. . . .

Pablo Neruda

ODE TO MY SOCKS

Maru Mori brought me
a pair
of socks
which she knitted herself
with her sheep-herder's hands,
two socks as soft
as rabbits.
I slipped my feet
into them
as though into
two
cases
knitted
with threads of
twilight
and goatskin.
Violent socks,
my feet were
two fish made
of wool,

two long sharks
seablue, shot
through
by one golden thread,
two immense blackbirds,
two cannons,
my feet
were honored
in this way
by
these
heavenly
socks.
They were
so handsome
for the first time
my feet seemed to me
unacceptable
like two decrepit
firemen, firemen
unworthy
of that woven
fire,
of those glowing
socks.

Nevertheless
I resisted
the sharp temptation
to save them somewhere
as students
keep
fireflies,
as learned men
collect
sacred texts,
I resisted
the mad impulse
to put them
in a golden
cage
and each day give them
birdseed

and pieces of pink melon.
Like explorers
in the jungle who hand
over the very rare
green deer
to the spit
and eat it
with remorse,
I stretched out
my feet
and pulled on
the
magnificent
socks
and
then my shoes.

The moral
of my ode is this:
beauty is twice
beauty
and what is good is doubly
good
when it is a matter of two socks
made of wool
in winter.

(Translated by Robert Bly)

Keeping Still / The Mountain, p. 255
The Marrying Maiden, p. 257

From *The I Ching or Book of Changes,* German translation by
Richard Wilhelm rendered into English by Cary F. Baynes (Bollingen Series XIX, Pantheon Books, New York, 1950), pp. 214–
17, 222–26.

"The manner in which the *I Ching* tends to look upon reality
seems to disfavor our causalistic procedures. The moment under
actual observation appears to the ancient Chinese view more of a
chance hit than a clearly defined result of concurring causal chain
processes. The matter of interest seems to be the configuration
formed by chance events in the moment of observation, & not at

all the hypothetical reasons that seemingly account for the coincidence." (Thus: C. G. Jung, *Foreword* to Wilhelm's *I Ching*, p. iii.)

Thought of this kind, when applied to the field-of-the-poem, defines that field both in primitive/archaic & in much modern poetry: that whatever falls within the same space determines the meaning of that space. What Jung called "synchronicity" (with the problems it raises of indeterminacy & the observer's part in structuring the real) becomes a principle of composition: common link between such otherwise different modes as chance poetry, automatic writing, "deep" image, projective verse, etc., & between those & the whole world of non-sequential & non-causal thought. That modern physics at the same time moves closer to a situation in which anything-can-happen, is of interest too in any consideration of where we presently are.

For more on the *I Ching*, composition by correspondence, juxtaposition, chance, etc., see above, pp. 401 & 470.

Addenda. The *I Ching* has been a direct influence on recent poets like Jackson Mac Low or John Cage—even an instrument for random composition. But the idea of random composition itself has other roots in the modern; thus

Tristan Tzara
From MANIFESTO ON FEEBLE LOVE & BITTER LOVE

> To make a dadaist poem
> Take a newspaper.
> Take a pair of scissors.
> Choose an article as long as you are planning to
>   make your poem.
> Cut out the article.
> Then cut out each of the words that make up this
>   article & put them in a bag.
> Shake it gently.
> Then take out the scraps one after the other in
>   the order in which they left the bag.
> Copy conscientiously.
> The poem will be like you.

Origin-Legend of the Chou Tribe, p. 259

Arthur Waley, *Chinese Poems* (revised edition; Unwin Books, London, 1961), pp. 15–17.

The poem comes from the *Shih Ching*—"song-word scripture" (Waley) but in English commonly called *The Book of Songs* or *The Confucian Odes.* "The songs," writes Waley, "are indeed 'Confucian' in the sense that Confucius (who lived c. 500 B.C.) & his followers used them as texts for moral instruction, much as Greek pedagogues used Homer. There is no reason to suppose that Confucius had a hand in forming the collection."

Waley's translation of the *Shih Ching* tries getting back to the pre-Confucian sense of it, & his comments on the "origin-legend" compare its motifs with similar matter throughout the "primitive & archaic" world. The reader can contrast Waley's workings & those of Pound (*The Confucian Odes,* New Directions, 1954) where the songs get a decidedly "literary" sound—in this case medieval & Elizabethan. But, writes the oracle, "no blame."

Song of the Dead, Relating the Origin of Bitterness (Excerpts), p. 262

Joseph F. Rock, *The Zhi mä Funeral Ceremony of the Na-Khi of Southwest China* (Studia Instituti Anthropos, Posieux [Fribourg], Switzerland, 1955), Vol. 9, pp. 55, 58, 87, 90, 92. Adapted & arranged by J.R.

The Na-Khi tribe (a branch of the Ch'iang) settled in the Li-chiang district probably during the Han Dynasty. Their main funeral ceremony, the Zhi mä, involves the chanting of various "books" & songs, preserved until recently in mnemonic picture-writing. While much of this writing is based on the rebus principle (of the ⟨eye pictograph⟩ =I variety), there are places too where the picto-graph seems to comment on matter in the spoken text; e.g., the first symbol in the song's title represents a large horsefly, such as occur on the high meadows in the summer, they emerge only when the sun shines & hide when overcast, they are blood suckers & a plague to both man & beast; the Na-Khi call them mun, here the symbol stands for mun = dead, it has also the meaning of old. . . .

But the picture itself (of a horsefly) is a presence also & adds to the meaning—whether by chance or intention is outside the present editor's concern. There are also purely literal pictographs of the ⟨eye pictograph⟩ = eye variety.

The song *per se* is "one of several types of funeral songs, sung at the death of an old man while the body is still in the house." The manuscript consists of eighteen pages from which the present editor has excerpted & slightly adapted pages 2, 3, 13, 14, 15, juxtaposing pictures & words, etc. The song (to sum it up) proposes to relate "the origin of bitterness" & follows the dead man (possibly identified with the "first father") as he sees his image reflected, learns he's growing old, wanders to distant towns to buy long life, sees men selling silver & gold "but years he saw no one sell," then in an empty marketplace watches leaves of the bamboo turn yellow, thinks

> so trees must also die, it is the custom
> there is death after all

laughs & turns back.

The song now moves to a consideration of all who have died, including apparently "the father of heaven" & "the mother of the earth," so that "even in heaven there is bitterness." Then come the dance sections given here as sets 3, 4, & 5—*ritual description: "they form themselves into a circle, but not a closed one, & holding hands much like children do when at play, begin a dance"*—followed by further accounts of the dead man's ascent & the accomplishments & powers to be inherited by his son, his village, & his neighbors.

Addenda. Compare the face-in-the-mirror/flight-&-wandering themes with the Quetzalcoatl poem (p. 92; commentary, p. 444) & the flight-&-wandering with the life-quest of the dying hero in *The Epic of Gilgamesh*. The old shamans, by the way, had the power to see their own skeletons & to undertake ritual journeys to reclaim the dead. But the editor doesn't want to suggest that seeing an old face in the mirror is straight ritual symbolism; Ginsberg's poem, *Mescaline,* e.g., gets the whole thing down in more personal terms.

From "The Nine Songs," p. 267

Arthur Waley, *The Nine Songs: A Study of Shamanism in Ancient China* (George Allen & Unwin Ltd., London, 1955), pp. 37–38, 41–42, 47, 53–54.

The Big Lord of Lives (Ta Ssu-ming)—determines human longevity; apparently also maintains the balance of the world, between Yin & Yang, etc. The shaman assists him in this. "Big" & "little" in this & the next song refer to a major & a lesser festival in which the songs were used.

Nine Provinces—China; *Nine Hills*—chief mountains of China. *Ch'iang*—sound effect, without meaning.

The Little Lord of Lives—*you* (line 6)—the god.

life-parting—where the people concerned are still alive but can't meet.

Broom-star—i.e., a comet; used by deities to sweep away evil.

The River God (Ho-po)—"He was a greedy god, often taking a fancy to & abducting mortal men's daughters, to add to his harem, or carrying off their sons to marry his daughters. . . . Sometimes he merely took a fancy to people's clothes. . . . At Yeh, in the extreme north of Honan c. 400 B.C." shamans would round up a pretty girl each year & set her adrift "on a thing shaped like a bridal bed," letting it finally sink. Unlike the other gods of the Nine Songs "his cult went on till modern times."

The Mountain Spirit (Shan-kuei)—many mountain spirits were worshiped under various names in ancient China. Like the river-spirits they also demanded human husbands & wives.

magic rain—i.e., sent by spirits.

The Chinese shaman (*wu*) has a history that both predates & outlasts these songs, which Waley figures around the third or fourth centuries B.C. though "the prototypes on which they were founded go back to a much earlier period." They are part of the

Ch'u Tz'u collection ("generally translated 'Elegies of Ch'u'")
often attributed to the poet Ch'ü Yüan, & have the feel of
literary reworkings of non-literary goods. But the shamanic remnants are still strong, the sense too of an accompanying performance making use of dance & gesture, meaningless sound ("at
the cesura of each line is the exclamation *hsi* which may . . .
represent the panting of the shamans in a trance"), etc.—all
designed to invoke the gods & bring them into the shaman's
service.

The force of the address is erotic, i.e., "the shaman's relation
with the Spirit is represented as a kind of love affair," though the
absence of number, gender, & tense (& of an accompanying
scenario) often makes it unclear whether the god or the shaman
is speaking, whether the address is male to female, female to male,
male to male, etc. Eliade tells of similar love-songs & sex-play
between Teleut shamans (called kams) & their celestial wives:

> My darling young kam
> we shall sit together at the blue table
> My darling husband, my young kam
> let us hide in the shadow of the curtains
> & let us make love together
> & have fun
> My husband, my young kam

& Kumandin shamans of the Tomsk region had phallic games
in which "they gallop with the (wooden) phallus between their
legs 'like a stallion' & touch the spectators." Not surprising since
in the western-world also, sexuality (however concealed or allego-
rized) provides the dominant thrust in the great god-poems, like
the *Song of Songs* or the following:

San Juan de la Cruz
A POEM FOR THE ASCENT OF MOUNT CARMEL

> On a dark night, afraid
>   to love you, burning
> Then this joy
>   to find the door
>   (unseen)
>   the house so quiet
>
> Dark & safe
>   to find

the secret stair, disguised
rejoicing
Dark, not touching
anything, the house so quiet

On that night, rejoicing
   secretly that no one saw
   me, that I looked at nothing
   Had no light to lead me
         only
   what burned inside my shirt

that led me
   like the light one afternoon
   A place where someone
   waited whom I knew
   And no one came on us

Oh night that led me, that
   I loved beyond the dawn
   Oh night that held
   us close, changed
   me through what I loved
         receiving

till the breasts were full
   I'd hidden for him, waiting
   for his head to sleep there
   Then I brought him gifts
   this fan of cedars with its night-air

Air of armies
   stirring through his hair
   That soft hand
   hurts my neck, suspending
   all my senses

I stayed with him, forgetting
   pressed my face against him
   Everything has left me
         gone
   My pain is fading
   vanishes among the lilies

                    (Translation by J.R.)

From "Chao Hun, or The Summons of the Soul," p. 271

Abridged from David Hawkes, *Ch'u Tz'u: The Songs of the South* (Oxford University Press, 1959), pp. 103–9.

The poem's beginning (summons to the sick or dead soul & description of its other-world journey) is an elaboration of one of the recurrent visions of (particularly) Asiatic shamanism—for which see the commentary on the Altaic "Shaman Climbs the Sky," p. 429, above.

But this, like the preceding "Nine Songs," is late along, & when the poet gets into a plush description of the royal court & the joys awaiting the soul back-home, etc., the view-of-things is very different, very changed from what it was. The envoi is a further reminder that *this* poet knew *this* King, with whom he went hunting & from whom he won favors, etc. The verse of the envoi is, Hawkes tells us, in a different (song) mode from the rest.

For more on Chinese shamanism & the *Ch'u Tz'u*, see the preceding note.

What Was Said, p. 275

A. K. Ramanujan, *Translations from the Tamil* (Indiana University Press, 1967), *passim.*

The *Kuruntokai,* an anthology of over 300 love poems, is one of the Tamil "eight anthologies" from the Sangam period between the first & fourth centuries A.D. Many of these poems, writes Ramanujan, were sung by "wandering minstrels" & are therefore much closer to "folk literature" than to classical Sanskrit. Most are older than the dates would indicate.

Ramanujan says of his workings: "The look of my English translations is an attempt to imitate the internal syntax rather than the line divisions of the original. The originals are in a kind of blank verse with rhymes at the beginning of lines."

Three Love-Charms from Chhattisgarh, p. 280

Translation by Verrier Elwin in *Man in India,* XXV (1945), 141–43.

The Witch, p. 283

W. G. Archer, "The Santal Treatment of Witchcraft," *Man in India*, XXVII (1947), 105–6.

[The translator quotes the following]: "When girls are initiated into witchcraft, they are taken away by force and made to lead tigers about. This makes them fearless. They are then taken to the most powerful *bongas* in succession, and are taught . . . to become possessed. They are also taught mantras and songs and by degrees they cease to be afraid. . . . When a girl has learnt everything she is made to take her degree (*sid a tang*) by taking out a man's liver and cooking it with rice in a new pot; then she and the young woman who is initiating her eat the feast together. A woman who has once eaten such a stew is completely prolific and can never forget what she has learnt." (C. H. Bompas, *Folklore of the Santal Parganas* [1909], pp. 423–24.)

Mantra for Binding a Witch, p. 284

Verrier Elwin, *The Baiga* (John Murray, London, 1939), pp. 390–91.

Writing of Baiga poetry, Elwin's workings, etc., W. G. Archer describes a basic type of Baiga poem called a *dadaria*, which involves "the pairing of one image with another, the vitally important but latent link." Sometimes the process is one of simple juxtaposition, of placing the images together: "it is their compression into a dadaria which causes them to fuse & gives the incandescence of poetry." All this is part of a general "Baiga attitude to images. . . . An image of an object is regarded not only as vivid in itself but as capable of the most powerful associations with other images. The object can, as it were, exist not only as itself but also as the other objects which it resembles. A snake is not only a snake but a stick. A deer is not only a deer but a girl. An arrow is not only an arrow but a phallus. And it is the vivid collocation of these images which is the basis of the poetry."

Most of the combinations Archer cites, however remote they get, have a more or less precise (i.e., fixed) reference, but "in Baiga mantras, on the other hand, the relation continues, but *it is as if the effort is to make it completely obscure*. Images follow one another, all directed, it may be, at binding a witch. . . . 'The sharp end of a knife,' 'the glow-worm of a virgin,' 'the nail of a bone,' 'the lamp of flesh,'—all these are probably, at bottom, sexual symbols, but *it is the strained insistence on the image, the remoteness of the reference, the strange adequacy which gives the mantra its mysterious force.* In these mantra, Baiga poetry reaches the limit of its power." (*Man in India*, XXIII [1943], 59.)

The process is, of course, fundamental to the language of magic & ecstasy, & is a key link between primitive & modern poetry, both of which make use of the free-swinging (what elsewhere I call "deep" or "open") image as instrument for evocation & cognition.

See also above, pp. 397–401.

The Pig, p. 285

Verrier Elwin, *ibid.*, pp. 406–7.

bewar—forest land cleared & burnt for cultivation.

Laru—the Laru-kaj, or pig-sacrificing event (see below).

phulera—a sort of swing in which are placed the leaf-wrapped head & liver of the pig.

The ceremony is called the Laru-kaj & is "probably the most ancient of all Baiga rituals." It appeases a demon of disease (Narayan deo) after he's been lured out of the patient's body with a bribe of pig. The pig is given rice to eat, its phallus is scalded with boiling water, then "three men, holding the pig by its two hind legs & buttocks, push the pig's head into (a) hole . . . half full of water. . . . Then the men begin to bump it up & down in the hole . . . (but) death . . . is due to suffocation." As an alternative the pig may be crushed by half a dozen men sitting or standing on the ends of a plank laid across the pig's stomach "while the fore & hind feet of the pig are pulled backwards & forwards alternately over the plank until it is crushed to death." This is the action accompanying the first poem. The second marks the washing, singeing & bloodletting, while the third coincides with the demon's appearance to receive his share of pig. And

> it was plain that pig had
> nothing on his mind. For
> Christ's sake didnt he
> know what was happening
> to him when one held him

by the flanks? No, nor the other
making click click, spin
spin noises, clearing his throat

writes Robert Kelly of another pig, another place. But the indifference ("coolness") of the songs here seems deliberate.

After the Harvest: A Prayer, p. 287

J.R.'s working from Jeanne Cuisinier, *Prières accompagnant les rites agraires chez les Mu'o'ng de Man du'c* (Ecole Française d'Extrême-Orient, Hanoi, 1951), pp. 18–26.

This & the six other prayers in Cuisinier's book come from the province of Hoa Binh in what's now "North" Vietnam. An earlier & freer working, *Vietnam: A Prayer to the Old Gods*, appears in Walter Lowenfels' *Where Is Vietnam?* (Doubleday & Co., Inc., New York, 1967).

The Seven, p. 290

J.R.'s working from C. Fossey, *La magie assyrienne*, as printed in Caillois & Lambert, *Trésor de la poésie universelle*, p. 40.

Exorcism dating from the beginning of the second millennium B.C. or earlier. Discovered—engraved in the original Akkadian & a later Assyrian translation—in the library of Assurbanipal at Nineveh.

The "seven," writes E. M. Butler, are "the seven great planetary demons or *maskim*, the dark counterparts of the planetary gods." In the "Prayer to the Gods of the Night" (see the comment after next) what are apparently the same forces appear in benevolent form. This approach to "evil" is a common feature of many primitive/archaic thought-systems, much as Reichard has shown it in her studies of Navaho symbolism:

Although Navaho dogma stresses the dichotomy of good and evil, it does not set one off against the other. It rather emphasizes one quality or element in a being which in different circumstances may be the opposite. Sun, though 'great' and a 'god,' is not unexceptionally good. . . . Similarly, few things are wholly bad; nearly everything can be brought under control, and when it is, the evil effect is eliminated.

Thus evil may be transformed into good; things predominantly evil, such as snake, lightning, thunder, coyote, may even be invoked. If they have been the cause of misfortune or illness, they alone can correct it. . . . Good then in Navaho dogma is control. Evil is that which is ritually not under control. And supernatural power is not absolute but relative, depending on the degree of control to which it is subjected. In short, definition depends upon emphasis, not upon exclusion. (*Navaho Religion,* p. 5.)

Enki & Uttu, p. 291

Translation by S. N. Kramer, *Enki & Ninhursag: A Paradise Myth,* in James B. Pritchard, *Ancient Near Eastern Texts Relating to the Old Testament* (Princeton University Press, 1950), pp. 39–40.

The water-god Enki has successively impregnated the goddess Ninhursag ("the mother of the land"), their daughter Ninmu & his daughter-granddaughter Ninkurra, but meets resistance in Uttu who is his child by Ninkurra. This fragment deals with the seduction of Uttu, which will then lead to the birth of eight plants, their uprooting & swallowing by Enki, his downfall through curse of Ninhursag, their reconciliation, his eventual recovery.

"The translation," writes Kramer, "was made from tablets inscribed some time in the first half of the second millennium B.C.; the date when the myth was composed is unknown."

. . . .

SYMBOLS EMPLOYED IN THE TEXTS. *Italics:* doubtful translation. *Parentheses:* words added in translation. *Brackets:* restoration of parts now illegible or completely lost. *Three dots:* texts that are unintelligible to the translator. *Three dots in brackets:* text wholly or partially damaged & therefore unintelligible.

[*Note.* The reader accustomed to the visual & typographical aspects of modern poetry—& with a feeling for the accidental—may prefer to accept the translators' markings as he finds them. For more about this, see the commentary on "The Fragments," above, p. 415.]

Prayer to the Gods of the Night, p. 293.

Translation by Ferris J. Stephens in *ibid.,* pp. 390–91.

Shamash—sun-god (Heb. *shemesh:* sun).

Sin—moon-god.

Adad—storm-, rain-, & weather-god.

Ishtar—goddess of love, fertility, war, etc. (Heb. *Astaroth, Esther;* Germanic *Auster;* Eng. *Easter*).

Gibil—fire-god.

Irra—a god of the underworld.

The translator tells us: "The occasion for this prayer is a divination ceremony carried on at night. The great gods who ordinarily control the affairs of the world are regarded as resting in sleep; and therefore the gods represented by several of the constellations of fixed stars are asked to witness the performance and to guarantee that truth will be revealed. The place from which this text comes is not known, but it was written in the Old Babylonian period, in the first half of the second millennium B.C. It is written in the Akkadian language and the Babylonian cursive script."

The idea of a working relationship between the polarities of light & darkness, day & night, etc., is as possible to human thought as the notion of their irreconcilability—& at least as widespread. "It is dark, it is light," reads the Aztec "definition," & the second Isaiah writes, "I form the light, & create darkness: I make peace, & create evil: I the Lord do all these things." So too, much modern poetry (where "the issue," writes David Antin, "is reality") is witness to the recovery of darkness, i.e., of darkness & light, the relation of figure to ground, etc.

. . . .

> If there were not an utter and absolute dark
> of silence and sheer oblivion
> at the core of everything,
> how terrible the sun would be,
> how ghastly it would be to strike a match,
>   and make a light. . . .

(D. H. Lawrence, from *The End, The Beginning.*)

502   TECHNICIANS OF THE SACRED

Child-Bearing Text, p. 294

Translation by E. A. Speiser, *Creation of Man by the Mother Goddess,* in *ibid.,* p. 100.

The reverse side of an Old Babylonian tablet (early part of second millennium B.C.) dealing with the creation of man from clay mixed with the flesh & blood of a slain god. The text came to be used as part of an incantation to facilitate childbirth. *Nintu* ("queen who gives birth") is one of the Sumerian names for the Mother Goddess—the "Bearing One" of the next to last line.

The Goddess, p. 295

Translation by H. L. Ginsberg, *The Poems about Baal & Anath,* in *ibid.,* p. 136.

Anath, the Canaanite war-goddess, was sister of Baal (god of rain & fertility) whom she aided in his struggles with his counterpart Mot (god of death & sterility). The episodes involve the death & resurrection of Baal & remind us of the more famous Egyptian myths of Isis, Osiris, & Set (see above, p. 455). But the fragment given here is a perfect depiction of the goddess' fury—made more fantastic perhaps by the loss of explanatory data, etc.

The Baal & Anath poems were written in Ugaritic, a Canaanite dialect spoken at Ras Shamra-Ugarit & closely related to Old Testament Hebrew. The texts date from the early fourteenth century B.C., though the matter is undoubtedly older. They have been uncovered since 1929.

Addenda. (1) "The Goddess is a lovely, slender woman with a hooked nose, deathly pale face, lips red as rowan-berries, startlingly blue eyes and long fair hair; she will suddenly transform herself into sow, mare, bitch, vixen, she-ass, weasel, serpent, owl, she-wolf, tigress, mermaid or loathsome hag. . . . The reason why the hairs stand on end, the skin crawls and a shiver runs down the spine when one writes or reads a true poem is that a true poem is necessarily an invocation of the White Goddess, or Muse, the Mother of All Living, the ancient power of fright and lust—the female spider or the queen-bee whose embrace is death."—R. Graves, *The White Goddess,* p. 10.

(2) Denise Levertov
THE GODDESS (1959)

She in whose lipservice
I passed my time,
whose name I knew, but not her face,
came upon me where I lay in Lie Castle!

Flung me across the room, and
room after room (hitting the walls, re-
bounding—to the last
sticky wall—wrenching away from it
pulled hair out!)
till I lay
outside the outer walls!

There in cold air
lying still where her hand had thrown me,
I tasted the mud that splattered my lips:
the seeds of a forest were in it,
asleep and growing! I tasted
her power!

The silence was answering my silence,
a forest was pushing itself
out of sleep between my submerged fingers.

I bit on a seed and it spoke on my tongue
of day that shone already among stars
in the water-mirror of low ground,

and a wind rising ruffled the lights:
she passed near me returning from the encounter,
she who plucked me from the close rooms,

without whom nothing
flowers, fruits, sleeps in season,
without whom nothing
speaks in its own tongue, but returns
lie for lie!

Hebrew Visions, p. 297

(1) Genesis xxviii:10–14; (2) Isaiah xxi:1–12, xxii:1–3; (3) Ezekiel i:4–19; (4) Revelation xii:1–8, 13–16.

An older stream of image & vision remains a presence in Hebrew poetry, emerging through the dreams & words of the prophet-poets—& from there is transmitted to the West, a way-of-the-mind kept alive after the invention of a restrictive logic.

Those interested in cross-cultural correspondences can read Jacob's vision of the sky-ladder against, say, the Altaic shaman's sky-journey (above, p. 54; commentary, p. 429) & the ladder-events on p. 109; the "living creatures" against the Yoruba *oriki* (p. 39) or Black Elk's "great vision" (p. 58); John's apocalyptic narrative of the woman & the serpent against the Australian Wauwalak myth (commentary, p. 507). As a matter of technique, the group of continuous visions from Isaiah shows how the Hebrew poets composed by bringing-together a series of loosely-connected verses: juxtaposition rather than causal connection, or as Lawrence described it, a language without therefores.

Addenda. Lawrence, further: "The Apocalypse is still, in its movement, one of the works of the old pagan civilization, and in it we have, not the modern process of progressive thought, but the old pagan process of rotary image-thought. Every image fulfils its own little circle of action and meaning, then is superseded by another image. . . . Every image is a picturegraph, and the connection between the images will be made more or less differently by every reader. . . . We must remember that the old human conscious process has to *see something happen,* every time. Everything is concrete, there are no abstractions. And everything *does* something." (*Apocalypse,* p. 83.)

Twelve Kura Songs from Tikopia, p. 305

J.R.'s adaptation from Raymond Firth, "Privilege Ceremonials in Tikopia," *Oceania,* XXI (1950), 170–75. [Original reprinted in Firth, *Tikopia Ritual & Belief* (George Allen & Unwin, London, 1967).]

The *kura* is performed when "the eldest daughter of the elder . . . reaches maturity (and) becomes the *fafine ariki,*" or chief female. She is then doomed to live apart from all men &,

growing older, to commit suicide by swimming out to sea, dwelling after death among "the assembly of those who have made the *kura*."

The dance itself is said to have originated with the god Rata & his consort Nau Taufiti, both very fierce, both with more-than-human sex-hunger & -power. To tap this energy in the dance, "men & women face each other in pairs, & the songs are exchanged between the two parties. . . . It is so that the men are Rata & the women Nau Taufiti." The songs, like much sacred poetry, are expected to act as a sexual stimulant; their "black humor" is also clearly within the range of the sacred.

While *Kume* in Song 1 is likely a separate goddess from Nau Taufiti, the rest of the songs involve a series of exchanges (sexual abuse & praise) between Rata & his principal consort. The *One-Before-Us* is Faka-sautimu, adze-god, anterior & superior to Rata. In Song 4 *cherry* is literally the puka-berry & indicates that the woman's vulva is small & pink. The *black buttocks* in Song 8 come from rubbing them against the ground in (frequent) intercourse. The *cordyline root* of the final song is "carrot-shaped & several feet long, & when cooked in the oven gets very dark in color."

The Gumagabu Song, p. 309

Bronislaw Malinowski, *Argonauts of the Western Pacific* (paper edition; E. P. Dutton & Co., New York, 1961), pp. 293–94.

Background: "Several generations ago, a canoe or two from Burakwa, in the island of Kayeula, made an exploring trip to the district of Gabu. . . . The natives in Gabu, receiving them at first with a show of interest, & pretending to enter into commercial relations, afterwards fell on them treacherously & slew the chief Toraya & all his companions. . . . The slain chief's younger brother (Tomakam) went to the Koya of Gabu & killed the head man of one of the villages, avenging thus his brother's death. He then composed a song & a dance which is performed to this day."

Malinowski adds, of the poem's non-euclidean structure & resemblance to modern poetry: "The character of this song is extremely elliptic, one might even say futuristic, since several scenes are crowded simultaneously into the picture . . . (and) a word or two indicates rather than describes whole scenes &

incidents." Thus the opening strophe moves between the Guma-gabu man on top of his mountain, Tomakam's pledge to go there, the women grieving for Toraya, the mountain again, the mist above Tomakam's home, lastly his mother crying for revenge. The second strophe starts with dream narrative, shifting suddenly to the expedition's arrival at Gabu & the ritual exchange of gifts. The third uses first-person narration to describe the killing. In the fourth (third-person again) there's description of a storm at sea, but in the fifth, without transition, the party is safe at home & the chief (Tomakam) holds up a basket containing the victim's head. The final strophe (description of a feast) slips back into first-person.

Thus the movement is complicated & very much alive—the gaps in sequence allowing that play-of-the-mind which is so highly developed a process among many "primitive" poets.

The Poetics of Hunger, p. 311

Bronislaw Malinowski, *Coral Gardens & Their Magic* (George Allen & Unwin, London, 1935), Vol. I, pp. 233–34.

The charm is part of the Trobriand *vilamalia* or ritual of plenty. An explanation given to Malinowski places the charm's real value not in its power to stabilize the harvest, but to stabilize the appetites of the participants:

Supposing the vilamalia were not made, men & women would want to eat all the time, morning, noon & evening. Their bellies would grow big, they would swell—all the time they would want more & more food. I make the magic, the belly is satisfied, it is rounded up.

Adds Bagido'u, the garden magician: "What would be the good of harvesting splendid crops if they were eaten in a hurry because people had too much desire for food?"

The Daybreak, p. 313

R. M. & C. H. Berndt, *The World of the First Australians* (Ure Smith, Sydney, 1964; University of Chicago Press, 1965), p. 319.

[The translators write]: "Over the greater part of Aboriginal Australia, particularly in the Centre, most songs . . . are arranged in cycles, a few words to each song. . . . (In this) section from the sacred Dulngulg cycle of the Mudbara tribe, east of the Victoria River country, Northern Territory, . . . each line represents one song, which is repeated over and over before the singers move on to the next."

The Waves, p. 314

Ibid.

The Laragia originally occupied the Darwin area, but today are virtually extinct. This traditional song is "now a lament for the country which is no longer theirs."

The Lightning Snakes, p. 315

Ibid., p. 315.

A love-song, connecting the present lovemaking with natural & mythic events, mythic beings, etc. A good example of the poet's ability to weave multiple threads & levels of experience into a single "narrative." (For more on the Wauwalak, etc., see the following note.)

Sightings: Kunapipi, p. 316

Songs selected & arranged by J.R. from R. M. Berndt, *Kunapipi: A Study of an Australian Aboriginal Religious Cult* (International Universities Press, 1951), pp. 121–31.

Kunapipi is the name of a major fertility cult, which centers around "a Great Mother, expressed as either a single or dual personality, her power being extended to her daughters, the Wauwalak." In the myth, these (two) Wauwalak Sisters leave their home territory after the elder has incestuous relations with a clansman & becomes pregnant. At a sacred water-hole she gives birth to a child, blood from the afterbirth attracting a great python (Julunggul), who lives in the hole. Then, writes Berndt

. . . the sky was shut in with clouds: a storm broke, summoned by Julunggul. They washed the baby, to get rid of the smell of blood, but it was too late. Night had fallen. They crouched in the hut by the fire while the rain poured down outside, taking it in turns to dance and to call ritually in an effort to drive away the storm. When the elder sister danced . . . the rain dwindled to almost nothing. When the younger sister did this, she could check the storm only a little. Then they sang Kunapipi songs, and the storm died down.

Later the Sisters are swallowed & vomited up—thus the ancient pattern of death & resurrection, etc.

But the relation of myth to ritual-event & song is complicated far beyond the simple telling. The ceremonial ground is at once the place-of-the-snake & womb-of-the-mother; & the myth is always a real presence behind the Kunapipi songs, forming (on other ceremonial occasions) the basis of both sacred & secular cycles with a clearly "narrative" quality. Here it's (mostly) present through allusion, the songs' actual "content" consisting of descriptions of accompanying ceremonial activities, particularly of ritual intercourse between clansmen (fertility "magic" sanctioned by the elder sister's incest) & of "fire-throwing" (djamala) that "symbolizes the lightning sent by Julunggul." Bullroarers of cypress bark reproduce the python's roaring in the storm; also, the songs & dances are said to be those of the mythic beings themselves—the Sisters dancing to postpone the coming of the snake, etc.

Of the songs *per se* Berndt writes: "Like the majority of songs in Aboriginal Australia, these consist of 'key' words, which seem to us to need further explanation, but are usually understood by natives singing or participating in the ritual. These 'key' words, several of which constitute a song, are really word pictures. . . . In short songs of this type in particular, the meaning of a word usually depends entirely upon the context. . . . Moreover . . . a song that is sung in one context, to a specific part of the rituals, may have one meaning, while in another context it has a different meaning." There are also different classes of words with the same "meaning": some open to the whole community, some requiring special knowledge, some used only in singing, etc.

Addenda. The editor, unlike the translator, is also interested in the out-of-context "carry-over" of the songs, & has arranged this selection to suggest the possibilities of a non-contextual reading. In doing so, he has taken some songs in Berndt's literal renderings, some in his freer "general translations," & has patterned them after his own *Sightings* (see below). So as not to mislead the reader, it has also seemed instructive to include, as an appendix (pp. 363–75, above), a presentation of the original songs, the interlinear translations, the free renderings, & some additional comments—exactly as given by Berndt.

. . . .

Jerome Rothenberg

SIGHTINGS (VI)

1. The earth shudders under the rain.

2. A hand.
   Five fingers.

3. Milkweed; was it that?

4. They add in rows.

5. Beginning from the waist, slip downwards; force a smile.

6. Perhaps a dish.
   A cup.

7. Horse   grey   knot
   fallen   throat   of-blood.

8. One thought, a thousand movements.

From "The Djanggawul Song Cycle," p. 318

Ronald M. Berndt, *Djanggawul: An Aboriginal Religious Cult of North-Eastern Arnhem Land* (Philosophical Library, New York, 1953), pp. 255–57.

Rangga—sacred emblem; identified with the penis of the Djanggawul Brother. *Rangga clansfolk:* those who initially emerged from the Djanggawul Sisters; ancestors of the present-day eastern Arnhem Landers.

Djuda—tree rangga emblem, from which trees sprang up when plunged into the ground by the Djanggawul.

Nara—ceremony; ceremonies instituted by the Djanggawul.

Nara shade—hut or shelter placed (in this context) on the nara ceremonial ground from which dancers emerge; in it the rangga emblems are stored. Symbolic of the uterus, etc.

Mat, or ngainmara mat—conically shaped; belonging to the Djanggawul Sisters; a uterus symbol, a whale, etc.

Berndt's translation of the *Djanggawul Cycle* (Yirkalla version) consists of 188 "songs" like the five given here—though, as with other Australian poetry, there's the possibility of considering each line a separate song. The cycle itself follows the wanderings of the Djanggawul Brother & his two Sisters, Bildjiwuraroiju & Miralaidj, who come to Arnhem Land from Bralgu (Land of the Eternal Beings), bringing with them ceremonies & sacred objects, & peopling the places through which they pass. The Brother "has an elongated penis, & each of the Two Sisters has a long clitoris . . . so long that they drag upon the ground as they walk." At Marabai, the Brother & his companions, "men whom the Sisters had made," sneak up & steal the baskets containing the sacred emblems—the men thus gaining control of the cult. Here too "the long penis of the Brother & the clitorises of the Sisters (are shortened). More people are born & some are circumcised." Part Nine (from which the excerpt is taken) continues this action; also "the Brother has coitus with his young sister (Miralaidj), who has an arm-band within her," i.e., something blocking the vaginal passage; "the breaking of this causes blood to flow. Dancing follows."

The poem's "events" are both mythic & ritual; e.g., the brother's penis entering the obstructed vagina is also the rangga pole catching on the transverse fiber of the ngainmara mat. The whole cycle, in fact, is rich in this kind of (highly developed) multiple narrative.

The Moon-Bone Cycle, p. 322

Ronald M. Berndt, "A Wonguri-Mandjikai Song Cycle of the Moon-Bone," *Oceania,* Vol. XIX, No. 1 (1948), pp. 16–50.

Wonguri—linguistic grouping. *Mandjikai*—clan name, alternatively "sandfly."

(Song One): Names at the end are of important headmen who are themselves related to the great Beings of the past.

(Song Nine): *Bukalili*—"power"-names, associated here with the Beings of the billabong: bone, catfish, frog, etc. *Bukalili* is the general word; specific "power"-names appear in the original text.

The Myth. "In the dream-time, Moon, a man, and his sister, Dugong, lived near a large clay pan in the Arnhem Bay plains country, which, during the rainy season, becomes a billabong. There they used to collect lily and lotus roots which became the evening star. Leeches made the place so uncomfortable that Dugong went into the sea to live. For his part, Moon went to the sky, saying that when he became sick, thin and only bones, he would follow Dugong down into the sea, where he would leave his bones to be washed up on to the beach in the form of the nautilus-shell. Moon added that after three days he would become alive and gradually regain his strength and size by eating lily and lotus roots." (A. P. Elkin, *The Australian Aborigines,* Doubleday-Anchor, 1964, pp. 275–76.)

"At the same place of the Moonlight and of the Dugong, a little after the Dugong and Moon went out to sea, a large fight took place between the Totemic Beings. . . . Many of these . . . were killed, and they were unable to become alive as the Moon does; they followed the pattern the Dugong had set." (Berndt, *Moon-Bone*, p. 20.)

The Songs. [Berndt writes]: "The Moon-Bone Cycle is a secular version of some . . . sacred songs which are incorporated in the Wauwalak Cycle [see above, p. 507]. . . . It is in the sacred version that the full myth is explained and the totemic beings and their actions are sung. In the Moon-Bone Cycle given here, the whole myth is viewed, so to speak, in retrospect. . . . [At lily-gathering time] people of the Wonguri-Mandjikai make their camp in the country associated with the Dugong and Moon. . . . They are preparing for the coming of the First Rains, which will herald the Wet Season; and they store their clubs in readiness for battle, for it was here that extensive fighting took place in the Dreaming Period. . . ." [Places & animals of the here-&-now bring up (mythic) memories, until the last two sections when] "they see the moon rising . . . (and) recall that the Moon has lost his bone in the sea and becomes once more a new moon. . . . The Evening Star is finally revealed as a Lotus Bloom, a Lily Root" [i.e., the moon's source of food] "and the string attached to it is the stalk of these plants."

[Further]: "The songs are usually sung straight through to a particular rhythm, and then repeated any number of times; so that the whole cycle . . . is rarely completed in one evening. . . . (There also seems to be) no defined punctuation in the actual singing; sentences and phrases may run from one to the other without an apparent break. . . ." [Compare this last point to modern practice.—J.R.] (Songs of the north-east Arnhem Land region) "are remarkable (also) for the fact that they are much longer than those in other areas of the Northern Territory. . . .

(Finally) the traditional structure of (the) songs . . . has (not) stylized (the songmen's) art (or) stifled individual expression. On the contrary, the great song men add a touch of new mastery to the old rhythms, and extend or abbreviate the original versions as the mood seizes them."

Berndt's "general" (i.e., "free") translation is reproduced in its entirety.

A Dream of the Afterlife, p. 331

Edwin Grant Burrows, *Flower in My Ear: Arts & Ethos of Ifaluk Atoll* (University of Washington Publications in Anthropology, Vol. 14 [1963]), pp. 316–19.

An *arueru*, or lament: apparently the least elaborately "danced" of the poem-dances of this small (pop. 250) atoll. The interest, as with many poems in Burrows' book, is in the narrative-presentation-of-thought; also in the shifting focus & point-of-view, etc.
Burrows writes of the laments:

> within the house the mourners are seated close together, too close for much bodily movement. . . . In the laments (composed for some previous death) most mourners sing without gesticulation. But the nearest relatives, who are seated next to the corpse, sway their bodies from side to side, and extend one arm toward the corpse or over it, waving hand and arm as they sing. This gesture is the only dancelike movement in the *arueru*.

In the other forms, the dance does more of the telling; hence the whole structure would be harder to see from just-the-words.

From "The Legend of Saveasi'uleo," p. 335

English version by David Rafael Wang, previously unpublished.

The Myth. Saveasi'uleo, the first-born of Muli & Muli, a couple on the island of Savaii, devoured four of his younger brothers when they went swimming. His grieving parents moved inland to a hill named Alao. Their youngest son, Ulufanuasesee (lit. "moving panorama"), was undaunted. When he went swimming, he faced his brother Saveasi'uleo & challenged him.

Later, in Faletatai, Ulufanuasesee married a woman, who gave birth to Siamese twins, who separated when some men accidentally dropped heavy firewood on the ground & frightened them. One of the Siamese twins, Taema, swimming near the island of Annuu, met her uncle Saveasi'uleo & married him. This fulfilled Ulufanu-asesee's prediction that the brothers would be united again through their descendants.

[The translator adds]: "Like most poems in the oral tradition (consider, e.g., the ballads in Scotland and America), the 'Legend' has various slightly different versions. But the freakish Saveasi'uleo has been as integral a part of the Samoan imagination as the Monkey among the Chinese."

Night Births, p. 338

From Martha Warren Beckwith, *The Kumulipo: A Hawaiian Creation Chant* (The University of Chicago Press, 1951), *passim.*

Kumu-(u)li-po—lit. "Beginning-(in)-deep-darkness," but also the name of the first male god born from the Night or *Po*.

Pimoe—"a shape-shifting being of uncertain sex, for whom in her feminine form legendary heroes go fishing."

Paliuli—"ever verdant land of the gods where abundant food grows without labor."

"The Hawaiian *Kumulipo*," writes the present translator, "is a genealogical prayer chant linking the royal family to which it belonged not only to the primary gods . . . (&) to deified chiefs . . . within the family line, but to the stars in the heavens & the plants & animals useful to life on earth, who must also be named within the chain of birth & their representatives in the spirit world thus be brought into the service of their children who live to carry on the line in the world of mankind." Queen Lili'uokalani, who first translated the work in the 1890s, dated it from around 1700 & gave the author's name as Keaulumoku.

Further, the *Kumulipo* "consists in sixteen sections called *wa,* a word used for an interval in time or space. The first seven sections" (from which all excerpts in the present anthology are taken) "fall within a period called the *Po,* the next nine belong to the *Ao,* words generally explained as referring to the world of 'Night' before the advent of 'Day'; to 'Darkness' before 'Light'; or, as some say, to the 'Spirit world' in contrast to the 'World of living men.' . . . Of the over two thousand lines that make up the chant, more than a thousand are straight genealogies listing by pairs, male & female, the various branches . . . making up the family lines of descent. Thus, although the whole is strung together within a unified framework, it may in fact consist of a collection of independent family genealogies pieced together with name songs & hymns memorializing the gods venerated by different branches of the ancestral stock." The chant ends with the name of the chief's newly born son, whose claim to kingship it helps establish.

Addenda. (1) The "dog child" of the fourth excerpt is connected with "the hairless 'Olohe people . . . dog men with the mystical shape-shifting powers of the demigods." *Maloma* is "the place people go when they die"; the *Hula,* or dance wind, blows there.

(2) Beckwith points to the heavy punning of the original, in which "the use of double meaning in a word extends to whole passages." In addition "the Hawaiian genius for quick transition of thought, piling up suggested images without compulsion of persistency to any one of them, makes it difficult to translate consistently." Her own solution would lead to double renderings & much interpretive commentary; but the possibility that this Polynesian nightworld-dreamworld-punworld can be delivered through some form of Joycean translation oughtn't to be overlooked. Sounds from *Finnegan,* e.g.,

. . . Dark hawks hear us. Night! Night! My ho head halls. I feel as heavy as yonder stone. Tell me of John or Shaun? Who were Shem and Shaun the living sons or daughters of? Night now! Tell me, tell me, tell me, elm! Night night! Telmetale of stem or stone. Beside the rivering waters of, hitherandthithering waters of. Night!

—or something like that as a way.

(3) For more on genealogies, composition-by-naming, etc., see the notes on the Maori creation poem (p. 394, above), the Egyptian god names (p. 10; commentary, p. 392, above), & the African praise-poems (commentary, p. 418, above).

The Body-Song of Kio, p. 342

J. Frank Stimson, *Tuamotuan Religion* (Bishop Museum Bulletin No. 103, Honolulu, 1933), pp. 32–33.

Kio, or *Kiho*—supreme god & creator.
Oatea, or *Vatea*—overlord of the world of light.

"Ruea-a-raka" (the singer of the poem) "insists that the enumeration of the parts of Kio's body was chanted by Kio to Oatea as part of the requisite ritual, & finds nothing incompatible with the god's inherent dignity in its wording; she explains that Kio, when conferring his mana upon Oatea, was obliged thus to detail all of the various parts of his own body whose disparate powers were consequently passed over respectively, & intact, to Oatea."

Funeral Eva, p. 343

English version by David Rafael Wang, previously unpublished.

[Translator's note]: "The *eva* was attributed to Chief Koroneu, who composed it over the death of his son, Atiroa, who had died in bed of disease. The boy had been treated by Pangeivi, Tane's high priest.
"The performers of the *eva* blackened their faces with charcoal, shaved their heads, cut their skin to draw blood, and wore *pakoko,* filthy cloth dipped in mud."

The Lovers I & II, pp. 344, 345

Kenneth P. Emory, *Kapingamarangi: Social & Religious Life of a Polynesian Atoll* (Bishop Museum Bulletin No. 228, Honolulu), pp. 166–68.

Both dictated by Tomoki. The cunnilingus theme is explicit in the second poem but informs the first poem also. Emory writes of it: "The practice . . . of initiating intercourse by or limiting the sexual relations to cunnilingus . . . has such a prominent place in the chants that I suspect it functioned as a means of birth control, in the spacing of children. It was institutionalized to the extent that the hair-do of the men, the leaving of a point of hair on each side of the forehead . . . was consciously thought of as providing a grip for the women."

The first poem is exactly as Emory gives it; in the second the present editor has arranged Emory's prose translation in verse lines & made some minor changes to ease the reading. The *waka mara* is "a square beam used in setting up the warps in weaving."

Flight of the Chiefs (Song V), p. 347

Buell H. Quain, *The Flight of the Chiefs: Epic Poetry of Fiji* (J. J. Augustin, New York, 1942), pp. 85–88.

Flight-of-the-Chiefs—legendary home of the ancestors of the present-day inhabitants of Bua Province, Fiji.

The-Eldest—the ruling chief at Flight-of-the-Chiefs; also called Sailing-the-Ocean.

Lady Song-of-Tonga—The-Eldest's chief wife.

Fruit-of-the-Distant-Sleep—The-Eldest's daughter, here a child but in the great Third Song (too long to reproduce here) the central figure.

Clapping-Out-of-Time—a dwarf of chiefly standing, brought to Flight-of-the-Chiefs long before The-Eldest's time, to amuse Sir Watcher-of-the-Land, who was then acting chief.

Nabosulu nabusele—the conventional closing for all epic songs.

The "composer" of this & fourteen of the fifteen songs in Quain's collection was Daubitu Velema who "(alone) among the descendants of his ancestral village (The-Place-of-the-Pandanus) . . . has inherited the right to practice (shamanistic) arts in his land-group & bears the sacred tokens. . . . When he was a small child, people knew he was destined to become a seer. It could be seen readily in his diffidence, his excitability & his curiosity about serious things." His mother's brother taught him & it is this uncle's "ancient war club & axe that give him power to compose epic songs, 'true songs.' . . . In trance or in sleep the songs come to him, taught him by his supernatural mentors (ancestors). He takes no personal credit for his compositions, does not even distinguish between those which he has composed himself & those old ones which his mother's brother must surely have taught him." (Cf. commentary on "Isaac Tens," etc., pp. 423–28; also Wm. Blake: "The authors are in Eternity," etc.)

The Fijian poems are chanted by the individual composer, some-times with the help of a chorus. "The rhythms implicit in the language are qualified by a musical style which can freely redupli-cate syllables to change the stress in words. For instance, the word *cere* may become *ceyececeyere* to suit the rhythm of the chant." But though "the lines tend to be of equal length . . . no deliberate patterning of rhythm appears." Rhyme is very insistent, so that the lines of Songs I & II, e.g., end consistently in U-A. Gesture, or what Quain calls "posture language," accompanies the songs.

There's also an interesting narrative device imbedded in the language itself, which Quain indicates by shifting to first person & past tense from the "normal" third person present. ["Fijian verbs in known dialects are (in fact) timeless."] He writes of this:

> Frequently in formal songs action is recounted in the first per-son to distinguish it from direct discourse. I have indicated this change of person by italics. The person referred to is always the most recently mentioned. . . . A particle (*wa*) which occurs frequently but not always, in these sections, has been interpreted by missionary students to indicate imper-fect tense. . . . At the Place-of-Pandanus it is not used in ordinary speech. In the songs it occurs always in the first line of direct narrative & nowhere else. To distinguish those passages which are direct narrative from those which are not, I have consistently translated the former as past tense throughout, although grammatical excuses for doing so are slight.

In short there's something going on that he can't put his finger on but knows to be there—like those devices described by Whorf & others in which the structure of a language determines the ways its users sense reality. However far from the linguistic solution Quain's intuition may be, the use of contrasting voices makes for meaningful movement in the English.

Compare the note on "Inatoipippiler" (p. 480, above) & the modern analogues mentioned in that commentary.

Addenda. Quain's translations are among the best examples the editor knows of an anthropologist with a very workmanlike sense of the possibilities of open verse in English. He died in 1939 at the age of twenty-seven, & the work—filed away in a kind of specialists' no-man's-land—is now long-out-of-print & all-but-for-gotten.

The Soaring-Dart, p. 350

Ibid., pp. 106–9.

This is the only one of the fifteen "epic songs" in Quain's book not composed by Daubitu Velema. That it's of a quite different order is indicated by Quain's note:

> This song, a *tau-sara* for male group dancing outdoors, was printed in May, 1892, in the *Mata,* a newspaper printed at Suva, in the missionary dialect of Fijian. (Yavala), the son of its composer, still lives at The-Place-of-the-Pandanus and has the supernatural right to teach it and its accompanying dance. (Because there was no time for him to) collaborate in the translation of its archaic language . . . the result as it appears here is inaccurate, (and) I have not dared to augment this inaccuracy with notes and explanation.

But the reader can, as elsewhere, jump in & enjoy its movements & shifts for their own sake. Quain does point out—as a hint of how-it-goes—that the protagonist in the first part of the second stanza is the woman, Yadi; that with the words "I enter inside," Roko Seruvati takes over the singing until the end of the stanza.

Animal Story X, p. 354

Ibid., p. 223.

Roko—highest native official of a province, under British regime.

Molau & basina—kinds of firewood; each has special function in Fijian fire-tending.

Quain further describes it as a "dance-song called *Village of the Animals* (which), though it makes but little sense . . . is filled with fine intralineal rhymes & bounding rhythms." Okay, but its making-but-little-sense didn't stop him from translating it, & having it now one feels an actual clarity about it: not necessarily in *what* it means (as some single equivalency) but in the positioning of the meaningful segments within it. It is very much what Rasmussen wrote of Iglulik Eskimo techniques:

The eskimo poet does not mind if here & there some item be omitted in the chain of his associations; as long as he is sure of being understood, he is careful to avoid all weakening.

Addenda. (1) For more on this last point, see, e.g., the commentary on Malinowski's translation of "The Gumagabu Song" (p. 505, above).

(2) Compare the poem's movement to the following, among many modern analogues:

Wallace Stevens

PLOUGHING ON SUNDAY

The white cock's tail
Tosses in the wind.
The turkey-cock's tail
Glitters in the sun.

Water in the fields.
The wind pours down.
The feathers flare
And bluster in the wind.

Remus, blow your horn!
I'm ploughing on Sunday,
Ploughing North America.
Blow your horn!

Tum-ti-tum,
Ti-tum-tum-tum!
The turkey-cock's tail
Spreads to the sun.

The white cock's tail
Streams to the moon.
Water in the fields.
The wind pours down.

520   TECHNICIANS OF THE SACRED

Appendix A, p. 359

(1) Paul Radin, *The Road of Life & Death* (Bollingen Series V, Pantheon Books, New York, 1945), p. 6.

(2) Bronislaw Malinowski, *Argonauts of the Western Pacific* (paper edition; E. P. Dutton & Co., New York, 1961), pp. 408–9.

(3) Knud Rasmussen, *The Netsilik Eskimos* (Copenhagen, 1931), p. 321. (Orpingalik said also: "How many songs I have I cannot tell you. I keep no count of such things. There are so many occasions in one's life when a joy or a sorrow is felt in such a way that the desire comes to sing; & so I only know that I have many songs. All my being is song, & I sing as I draw breath.")

(4) W. H. I. Bleek & Lucy C. Lloyd, *Specimens of Bushman Folklore* (1911), pp. 303–5. (‖kábbo was the narrator of "Girl of the Early Race Who Made the Stars," above, p. 34.)

(5) English version by Denise Levertov in *O Taste & See,* New Directions, 1964.

(6) As printed in Margot Astrov, *The Winged Serpent* (The John Day Company, New York, 1946), p. 85.

(7) The Book of Daniel X:7–10.

POST-FACE

WOULD-THAT-THEY-ALL-KNEW-THESE-SONGS is what
I think of you.

It seems as if we were beginning to walk. It seems as if we were
going as far as the earth is good.

JEROME ROTHENBERG was born in New York City in 1931 and graduated from the City College of New York. He received his Master of Arts degree from the University of Michigan before being sent to Mainz, Germany, with the United States Army. Since returning to the United States he has published nine volumes of his poetry as well as several translations which include *New Young German Poets,* Hochhuth's *The Deputy,* Enzensberger's *Poems for People Who Don't Read Poems* and *Gomringer by Rothenberg.* The founder of Hawk's Well Press in the early 1960s, he is presently co-editor of *some/thing* and ethnopoetics adviser to the *Stony Brook Poetry Journal.* Since 1968 he has been carrying on a series of experimental translations of American Indian poetry under a grant from the Wenner-Gren Foundation.